The United States Secret Service

WALTER S. BOWEN
AND
HARRY EDWARD NEAL

The United States Secret Service

With a Foreword by U. E. Baughman
Chief, U.S. Secret Service

CHILTON COMPANY — BOOK DIVISION
Publishers
Philadelphia   New York

Foreword

This book is a factual story of the U.S. Secret Service, a division of the Treasury Department. It gives the true origin of this law-enforcement agency of the Federal Government and dispels many fictions which have grown through the years. It recounts how the Secret Service, from its very beginning, became the nemesis of the counterfeiter. It then tells the exciting story of agents of the Secret Service, which for a long period was the only general Federal investigative agency, being loaned to other Government departments to investigate whisky rings, lotteries, extensive land frauds, espionage during the Spanish-American War and World War I, the Teapot Dome oil scandals, and other crimes. The book also relates heretofore untold experiences of Secret Service men in protecting Presidents of the United States and visiting dignitaries.

Walter S. Bowen and Harry Edward Neal, co-authors of the book, were both career Secret Service men. Their combined service represents almost 55 years. Walter Bowen served in a senior staff position, retiring from the Service in 1948. Harry Neal came up through the ranks from clerk-stenographer to Special Agent, Executive Aide to the Chief, and finally to Assistant Chief, which position he occupied at the time he elected to retire in 1957. With such background and experience, these men were eminently qualified to write a chronicle of the Secret Service.

Writing a history of the Secret Service from its beginning in 1865 was undertaken by Mr. Bowen and Mr. Neal with full knowledge of the many frustrations which would be encountered in researching and compiling the story of the early years of the Service. In the period following the Civil War and up to the beginning of this century, stenographers' notebooks and typewriters were not in common use. Correspondence, reports, and other records were written with pen and ink and in cryptic brevity. The value of complete records for historical purposes was apparently not foreseen at that time, but this did not deter Bowen and Neal, who spared no effort in their search for the real story of the Secret Service through its entire history, which spans a period of more than 90 years.

After researching such records as were available in the Secret Service, the National Archives, and the Library of Congress, they corresponded with and interviewed relatives of former Chiefs and other Secret Service officials, carefully reviewing their personal papers. In this way, with a dedication to their work born of personal devotion to the Service, they painstakingly gathered information which has made this book the most complete and authentic history of the Secret Service ever published.

From about 1906 to the present, records became progressively more complete, and for this period the task became one of selection more than combing for material. In these later years there was a wealth of material describing feats of skill and daring; more, in fact, than could fit between the covers of any one book.

In reading about the experiences of the men of the Service, in some of which I participated, my thoughts were that through the years the basic problems of law enforcement remain essentially unchanged. Scientific devices have increased the effectiveness of the investigator, but they have also increased the capabilities of the modern criminal. In years past, as today, we have been beset with personnel shortages and insufficient funds to reach our full potential in suppressing crime. Yet, overshadowing this thought is the satisfying realization that the achievements of the Secret Service have been accomplished despite such handicaps.

I am sure that those interested in history, students of criminology, and those who simply find pleasure and relaxation in good detective stories will find in this book much of what they are seeking.

U. E. BAUGHMAN
Chief, U.S. Secret Service

Preface

Many Americans have a misconception about the U.S. Secret Service—what it is and what it does. This book attempts to tell the story of the Secret Service from its beginning in 1865 to the present day.

There are scores of interesting criminal cases that have not been included for lack of space, just as there are a great many Secret Service agents—active, retired, or dead—who were involved at one time or another in highly dramatic situations, but whose stories must wait another day, another volume, to be told properly.

We have chosen to set out the undistorted facts in cases which best illustrate the variety of work the Secret Service has been called on to perform in its first century and also to show that its agents are men of courage, honesty, and intelligence, a credit to the Government of the United States and a threat to those who seek to hurt law-abiding Americans in any part of our land.

The years we spent in the Secret Service are now but memories, some pleasant, some sad, some exciting, others uneventful. We both feel that we have contributed something, however little, to the growth and betterment of our country, and we hope that this account may help to inspire young men now in the Service to carry on its fine traditions and to maintain its enviable reputation in the law-enforcement world. We hope, too, that it will show the average reader that all those who fight crime are engaged in a night-and-day battle for his protection and benefit.

We would be derelict indeed if we did not express our hearty thanks to our good friends, Chief U. E. Baughman, for giving us access to closed files and Secret Service archives, and Chief Inspector Michael W. Torina for his enthusiastic and valuable assistance throughout the project.

Since this book is the only one of which we know that tries to tell the whole story of the Secret Service without taking "literary license" with the facts, it is our feeling that it may represent a genuine tribute to those who preceded us and to those who will follow. Old-timers who read this book, and with whom we spent so many years in the Service, will understand better than most what we are trying to say. We hope they will agree that our mission has been accomplished creditably.

WALTER S. BOWEN
Historian, U.S. Secret Service (Retired)

HARRY EDWARD NEAL
Assistant Chief, U.S. Secret Service (Retired)

Contents

☆

The United States
Secret Service

☆

◦ 1 ◦

Der Führer's Biggest Fraud

In 1939 Delbruckstrasse was a quiet residential street in the Charlottenburg quarter of Berlin. The mansion at No. 6 was actually a dignified branch office of the Reichsdruckerei, the German equivalent of the U.S. Bureau of Engraving and Printing, but it resembled many large homes in the neighborhood—until Adolf Hitler loosed his legions to conquer the world. Then the house at No. 6 Delbruckstrasse shed its aura of tranquillity. Government officials paraded in and out of its austere entrance at all hours of the day and night, mingling with somber-faced officers wearing the black shirts of the Schutzstaffel (SS). In this once-quiet house important members of the Third Reich concocted paper plans for a paper weapon that conceivably would wreak more havoc than any gun, army, or explosive.

They would produce millions of counterfeit notes—enough to disrupt and scuttle the economic systems of their enemies. The resulting panic would be worth a score of victories on the battlefield.

The plot was simple, but transforming fancy into fact presented certain problems that were more complex. The counterfeit money must be perfect enough to defy detection, even by experts, and any intelligent person could understand that a counterfeit was merely a copy of an original and that no copy could be exactly like the original in every microscopic respect. Perfection was of paramount importance. Clearly, the success of this bold scheme must depend on the skills of experts in many fields—photography, etching, engraving, papermaking, watermark manufacture, printing, and others.

Responsibility for this paper sabotage was placed on the gold-braided shoulders of two minions of Dictator Hitler—Reichsführer Heinrich Himmler, Chief of the infamous Gestapo, and his deputy, Ernst Kaltenbrunner.

Himmler himself had none of the required talents for this unusual assignment. His closest association with counterfeiting was the toothbrush mustache he trimmed to look as much like Hitler's as possible. Nevertheless he assembled a representative of the Reichsdruckerei and four specialists in the graphic arts and told them to make some counterfeit 1-pound notes of the Bank of England.

To the credit of the men it should be said that they may have considered this task distasteful, for they were reputable folk and not criminals at heart. At any rate, they failed to produce imitations that could fool anybody.

"The paper is not good," they said. "It is not at all like the genuine English banknote paper, and it does not take the printing well."

Herr Himmler set another team to work on the production of better banknote paper. The government's technical research laboratories analyzed the genuine paper and created various experimental formulas in attempts to duplicate it, watermark and all. The manufacturing experiments were carried out in the Mahnemuhle Paper Mill at Dassel, where six long-time employees were assigned to this task exclusively and threatened with death if they so much as whispered one word to any other person about the nature of their work.

The threats were delivered in person by Sturmbannführer Bernhard Kruger, who was destined to play a starring role in the drama of fakery that was just beginning. Kruger was in his forties, short (about 5 feet 6 inches) but well proportioned, with dark hair parted on the left side, dark eyes, a wide, sensuous mouth, and a square chin that gave his jaw a grim carved-stone appearance. Herr Kruger was chosen by Ernst Kaltenbrunner to supervise the secret activities of the counterfeiting department, designated officially as AMT-F-4, but referred to in correspondence by the code word "Bernhard," a dubious tribute to the new commandant and his first name.

Many trials and failures at the Mahnemuhle Mill produced samples of banknote paper of increasing quality, and in 1942 the experts assured Herr Kruger and Herr Himmler that their experiments would soon result in a perfect product.

Himmler then used the one great asset he possessed to advance the conspiracy. The asset was power, and he had plenty of it. In his concentration camps were thousands of men, women, and children—mostly Jews—whose hopes and fears and loves and prayers died with them daily in the gas chambers, or on the electrified barbed-wire camp enclosures, or in filthy, crowded shacks where they succumbed to starvation or disease.

Surely among these hordes of despairing prisoners there were some who had once made their livelihoods as engravers, or photographers, or by other skillful use of their fingers; and just as surely, those who were sufficiently adept would welcome an opportunity to prolong their lives by engaging in a project which would contribute notably to the glory of the Third Reich. Welcome it or not, they would do it or die.

With characteristic German thoroughness the Nazis maintained records giving the histories of their captives, occupations and all. A list was made of those men with the talents needed, but before the list was used an appeal went out in the name of Der Führer to several camps in the Grosse Reich for volunteers who were engravers, designers, photographers, artists, or printers. All volunteers, however, must be of Jewish blood. The nature of the work was not revealed.

A few men in each camp believed the announcement that they would be given good food and special treatment if they volunteered for this mysterious assignment, but others harbored ugly memories of beatings and bruises, of gnawing hunger, and of corpses of friends and relatives who had been subjected to "experiments" of many kinds. Remembering these things, they had no wish to volunteer, so the orders went out to the camp commanders: "Send us Levy, and Gottlieb, and Bernstein . . ." Thus was much of the manpower recruited for the counterfeiting plant.

The plant was set up in a special section of the Sachsenhausen Concentration Camp at Oranienburg, not far from Berlin, and the first 7 prisoners, called "haftlinges," arrived there on August 23, 1942. Suspicion and fear surged through them as they were led to a building isolated from the rest of the camp and surrounded by three separate fences of electrified barbed wire.

Inside the building their fears began to subside. Unlike other camp structures, the interior was clean, there were cots and tables and chairs, and a modern, well-equipped print shop, with camera equipment and a photographic darkroom.

Commandant Kruger "welcomed" the new arrivals and told them bluntly what they were expected to do.

"You are privileged people," he said. "You have been chosen for a job that is of vital importance to the Third Reich. The Third Reich needs money, and we are going to make it!" The prisoners stared at each other, and Kruger laughed. "You are surprised, eh? I thought you would be. But you are lucky—very lucky. You will eat well. You will listen to music on the radio while you work. You can smoke sometimes—yes, we give you real tobacco! And down there," he added, pointing, "you can play ping-pong for exercise. As you see, we promised you would live well, and we keep our promises. Nein?"

One of the haftlinges spoke. "You said something about making money. What does this mean, please?"

Kruger laughed again. "It means making money. You will make English money, Danish money, Swedish money, Hungarian, Mongolian—maybe even some Jewish money." His happy expression gave way to a scowl.

"You will be counterfeiters—the best in the whole world, for this money must be perfect. It must be so good that it will deceive people who are familiar with genuine money, because much of it will be used in neutral countries to buy weapons and supplies for our victorious armies."

As they stood silently, he shook a pointing finger at their surprised faces. "If you fail," he went on, "then Germany may lose the war. If Germany loses the war, we will all die. Yes, you and I will die. You do not want to die, and I don't want to die, so we must help one another to stay alive. We are friends." He smiled benevolently. "When we have won the war, Der Führer plans to send all of you to a wonderful settlement in the country, where you will be reunited with your families and will live in peace and happiness. Der Führer will be most generous with his appreciation."

The haftlinges were confined to their isolated compound. Their food was brought into an outer room by a prisoner from another part of the camp. At no time did he ever see a single person in the room. He simply left the food and later went back to get the empty dishes.

There was much conjecture in the camp about what was going on in the mysterious section, but no one outside really knew. The haftlinges were warned that they would be killed immediately if they were found communicating in any way with outsiders. They were guarded by picked SS men who were also cautioned never to speak about anything whatever concerning Project Bernhard. One night two of the guards got drunk and were overheard to mention the secret goings-on. Next day both were court-martialed and sentenced to 15 years in prison. Any guard who was not constantly alert was promptly replaced and sent to the bloody Russian front.

By the end of 1942 there were about 30 haftlinges at work on the counterfeiting project. One of these, a Russian named Sukenik, had frequent coughing spells which led the Nazis to suspect that he might be suffering from tuberculosis. When a medical examination confirmed this suspicion, SS Guard Heinz Beckmann shot Sukenik to death to prevent the spread of infection to the other workmen.

The papermaking group did not succeed in making a perfect imitation of the British banknote paper until 1943, but once they discovered the right process they produced watermarked paper that was the equal of the genuine in every respect. When Himmler and his cohorts approved the product, the first shipment of about a quarter of a million sheets, each large enough for the printed impressions of four English £5 notes, was sent to Sachsenhausen in July. Thereafter, the plant received 50,000 sheets monthly until the end of 1944.

Other types of paper were used for notes of other countries, and various specialists outside the camp produced the plates from which the other counterfeits were printed. The British bills, however, constituted the greatest output, and the plates for these were engraved by a diminutive, shrewd Russian Jew named Sali (Solly) Smolianoff.

Smolianoff, then 50 years old, was the only professional counterfeiter in the compound, and he was no stranger to counterfeiting. Since 1928 he had spent most of his life in jail for manufacturing spurious currencies of various nations, including Great Britain, and it was following the completion of one such sentence in 1942 that he was merely transferred from the prison he left to the Sachsenhausen camp, to make the plates for the British notes.

Smolianoff was more happy than sad. "Imagine!" he exclaimed, looking at his SS guards. "Making counterfeit money with police protection!"

When a series of trials finally resulted in perfect plates, production went into high gear. From the presses the counterfeits were dried, baled, and made smooth by "ironing" under terrific pressure. The notes were stacked and the edges rubbed with files to resemble the genuine rough edges, after which they underwent a novel sorting operation.

The most deceptive notes—that is, those in which no printing flaws could be detected—were classed as First Grade, and it was these which were used to buy military supplies in neutral countries.

Notes with only one or two slight detectable errors due to faulty printing were stored in bins as Second Grade—deceptive enough to be used to pay off Nazi spies on missions in foreign countries.

Third Grade notes had inferior watermarks and more than two or three printing flaws, but they were so minor that the currency was considered passable, and the Third Grade went to pay agents in Nazi-occupied countries and also to buy more war matériel in such countries.

The Fourth Grade product could be detected more readily than the other three, *provided* the notes were examined by experienced money handlers, but it was unlikely that the average British citizen could identify them as counterfeits. Therefore, the Fourth Grade was earmarked to be flown over England and dropped from the air to float down like huge snowflakes in the hope that the British population would retrieve them and launch a spending spree that would plunge the Bank of England—and the nation—into bankruptcy.

That left one more classification—the Fifth Grade. These notes the haftlinges called *auschuss,* the German equivalent of "junk." In time the ink could be removed from these by chemical means and the paper could be reduced to pulp so that it could be remade for another try. Meantime, the notes would be held available for possible emergencies.

A complete record was kept of the quantities of notes and of the serial numbers used, after which the sorted packages were handed to special SS men who carried them into the mansion at No. 6 Delbruckstrasse in

Berlin, the once-dignified building now surrounded by barbed wire and patrolled by armed sentries.

The haftlinges at Sachsenhausen worked in two shifts of 12 hours each. Their fakery included not only foreign currency, but also counterfeit credentials for spies, forged identity cards of British and French flying officers, phony paybooks of the American Army, and hundreds of rubber stamps like those used in validating official documents of all kinds.

The emphasis, however, was clearly on the British banknotes, which rolled off the presses by the hundreds of thousands. Then, in 1944, Commandant Kruger assembled Smolianoff and the other haftlinges, now numbering 140, and made a startling announcement.

"We will now stop making the English pounds," he told them. The men glanced at each other, many with the look of fear, as though to say, "Here it comes. Our job is done, and we are to be taken to the gas chambers."

"Do not worry," Kruger said. "I did not say we were through working. On the contrary, we have a new job." Standing erect, with his hands on his hips and smiling broadly, he went on, "Now we will make the American money!"

A babble of voices filled the room. "Listen to me!" Kruger shouted, though not angrily. "If you do this new job as well as the other and get through with it, it will be good for you. I know you are all in fear of death, but if you do your work right I promise that nothing will happen to you while I am chief of this camp. Behind this barbed wire you are no more Jews. You are my fellow workers, and here we work together in the fight for the new Europe. The victory will be ours. Now go and work, and do everything you can so that I will not have to fall on my nose before Himmler. If you disappoint me, or if you do not finish the job, then you will go and die together with me. All my hope is based on you. We will make first the fifty- and hundred-dollar bills, and when they are done we will make the five hundreds, so there will always be enough work for you—don't worry about that."

Once again Smolianoff was chosen to make the counterfeit plates for the U.S. money. Smolianoff's part of the story was revealed after the war, when A. E. Whitaker of the U.S. Secret Service (now Special Agent in Charge of the New York District) found Smolianoff in Rome, Italy, and heard it from his own lips.

"During an American air attack," Smolianoff recalled, "three of us were sitting in the phototyping room when the lights went out. We took advantage of the darkness to talk, and we agreed to sabotage the whole work. We decided that each of us would complain about the work of the others in order to gain time, because we hoped for liberation soon by the approaching Allied troops. That's what we did, and sometimes the

SS guards had to interfere and separate us because we fought each other so hard—but they couldn't dismiss us because all the work depended on us."

The strategy worked for several months. "Then we heard that the Russians had taken Kuestrin, only sixty kilometers from our camp," Smolianoff went on. "There was no more time for long experiments. Finally the eldest of our hundred-and-forty-man group came and told us we must stop our fighting and produce at least one sample, or we would all be liquidated. Two days later we made what we thought was a fair copy of the back of a hundred-dollar bill, and this was reported to Chief Kruger in Berlin."

Some 2 hours later Kruger arrived at the camp in his car and rushed into the plant. "Where is it?" he asked. "Let me see what you have."

Continuing his recollection Smolianoff said: "We spread over a table fourteen genuine American hundred-dollar bills that we had used as patterns, and our one sample counterfeit. Only the backs were showing. Kruger stood a long time—oh, a very long time—before the table, studying each of the bills. All you could hear was soft breathing as we waited. Finally he put his finger on the one he chose as the counterfeit—and to our great surprise he picked one of the good ones! We were very glad, of course, but the most happy was Kruger. He grabbed the sample and immediately rushed off in his car to show it to Himmler in Berlin. The same night everyone was happy because we heard that Himmler approved the work, appreciated our efforts, and gave the order to continue."

The Allies were advancing rapidly and the haftlinges were urged to work harder and faster, but the making of currency plates is delicate and tedious work. "After a week of working overtime," Smolianoff said, "my eyes were all red and swollen, and my companions were worried that I might not be able to continue. Then, suddenly, there was a big surprise. Kruger arrived unexpectedly, called everybody together, and read us an order from Himmler to evacuate Sachsenhausen. We worked day and night to pack the whole camp, machinery and all, into sixteen railway cars at the railroad station, and in March 1945 we were all taken to the concentration camp at Mauthausen."

The prisoners and the machinery stayed at the Mauthausen camp for about a month, but no work was done there, and at the end of March the men and equipment were transported to Redl-Zipf, Austria, where it was planned that they would continue their counterfeiting operation inside a mountain!

The mountain had two tunnels which had been constructed long before the war by a nearby brewery, and which were originally intended and used for storage purposes. The Nazis, however, had taken over the tunnels, enlarged the underground space, and had set up the factories which made parts for the V-2 rockets that were blasting Britain.

The printing machinery was set up under the mountain, but so swift was the advance of the American forces that the counterfeiting operation could not be resumed.

The haftlinges were given a rush job to erect a small brick enclosure with a concrete roof and two chimneys. The building was a little taller than an average man, and about 10 feet long and 6 feet wide. When it was completed, a fire was built inside it and the prisoners were ordered to begin dumping into the enclosure the counterfeit currency which had not been distributed.

Thousands and thousands of notes were thrown into the flames under the supervision of the SS guards, who made sure that the destruction was complete. (When Allied investigators later inspected this scene they found only ashes which had been stirred until they made a fine powder.)

The Americans were coming closer, and there was not enough time to burn the huge stock of notes, or to destroy the machinery. The Nazis did not want the enemy to discover any evidences of counterfeiting, so early in May 1945 they assembled trucks to cart the remaining crates of notes and the machinery away from the mountain, to be sunk in Austrian lakes and rivers.

The trucks were loaded, and each was commanded by an SS officer who was responsible for disposition of the load. One 10-ton truck, hauling a 5-ton trailer, was filled with boxes of the false currency and taken to Toplitzsee, where there was a lake some 300 feet deep. Other trucks had already dumped machinery into this water. The big truck and trailer could not get close to the lake because of the size and weight of the vehicle, so in the middle of the night the SS guards pounded on the doors of nearby farmhouses and forced the farmers to harness their wagons and to help transfer the contraband from the truck to the smaller vehicles. The wagons were then driven to the lakeshore, where the SS guards and the farmers unloaded the boxes and dumped them into the water.

All the boxes except one were heavy enough to sink to the bottom. The one that did not sink broke open as it floated, and in a short time the lake was bright with thousands of counterfeit British notes. The villagers were warned that the bills were counterfeit, but they collected what they could and dried the pieces for use as paper, because paper was so scarce that it was valuable in itself.

Other truck convoys hauled notes to the River Enns, a swift-water stream. The boxes were thrown into the river, carried by the current to the rapids, and broken open on the jagged rocks, spewing thousands of the bills into the river. Downstream the people who lived nearby did not know the bills were bad, and when they saw thousands of British notes swirling past their homes they considered that a miracle had been wrought. They fished out the notes, hung them on clotheslines to dry, and later spent many of them without difficulty in various European countries.

After the notes were burned and the trucks dispatched, the haftlinges were told to throw away their personal possessions because they were all to be killed in the gas chambers. Commandant Kruger, who had promised them peace and happiness, was in parts unknown.

When the time came for the prisoners to be taken to the gas chambers, no SS guards appeared. In fact, there were no guards to be seen anywhere in the camp! To escape the advancing Americans all the SS men had fled, and the prisoners were free. Some moved from their filthy quarters into the officers' barracks. Others walked away, glad to be out of bondage, yet having no clear destination.

On May 4, 1945 a young Austrian named Robert Mathis, a German soldier, was in Ebensee, Austria, with a truck unit. An SS officer named Hantsch told Mathis that a convoy had broken down and ordered Mathis to transport an important cargo to the lake in his trucks.

"Remember this," Hantsch told him. "Under no circumstances must any part of it fall into the hands of the Americans."

Mathis insisted on knowing what was in the cargo, and Hantsch finally told him that it was counterfeit British money. Mathis started out with the load, but never intended to destroy it. Instead, he hid his truck and stayed under cover himself until May 8, when the Americans took over the area. Mathis then located an American colonel at Gmundon and told him about the counterfeit cash. The colonel promptly impounded the whole load.

In Germany at that time was Capt. (now Lt. Col.) George J. McNally, acting as Special Adviser, Financial Intelligence Branch, Finance Division of the U.S. Army. McNally had spent several years in the U.S. Secret Service, chasing counterfeiters and forgers, and because of this experience had been given a military furlough from the Service for a special Army assignment to investigate currency frauds or counterfeiting in Europe. McNally received word about the truckload of English notes and promptly notified Scotland Yard in London. The Yard rushed Chief Inspector Rudkin to the area, and he and McNally teamed up to piece together the story of the fantastic counterfeiting plot as it has here been told. (More than 40 of the haftlinges who worked on Project Bernhard were tracked down and questioned by the investigators after the war.)

The boxes in Mathis' truck were filled with fake British £5, £10, £20, and £50 notes representing (in dollars) about $100 million dollars.

This, of course, was but a small fraction of the total production. There was no way to tell how many notes were actually made in the plant, though a fair estimate would seem to be more than half a billion dollars. There are no records to show how many notes were used to pay off Nazi agents, although it was established that one spy named Eliaza Bazna (code name "Cicero") received 300,000 British pounds (about a million dollars) for cracking the safe of the British Ambassador in Ankara and copying important military documents which he delivered to the Nazis. All the notes paid to Cicero were counterfeit.

Because so many of the First Grade notes were circulated and defied detection, the English paid off on all notes which were not obviously counterfeit, and subsequently the British Government changed the design of its currency. Only the Bank of England can estimate the extent of the silent sabotage caused by Hitler's counterfeiting plant.

The evidence proves, however, that counterfeiting is no piddling crime, but is a serious crime against the people, an offense close to treason, and one which, unrestricted, is capable of destroying a whole nation. If an all-out world war comes again, never doubt that the presses will roll in more countries than one. Even now, perhaps, in some dark corner of the globe, a stockpile of counterfeit money may be stored up, along with H-bombs and other instruments of destruction.

Counterfeit money as a weapon of war is not new, though the Nazi operation was undoubtedly the biggest of its kind. Napoleon Bonaparte once established a counterfeiting plant in Paris to turn out fake Russian money which he used to buy supplies for his Russian invasion.

During the American Revolution the British dumped tons of phony Continental currency into the American economy, destroying all public faith in that money.

Public confidence in a national currency is essential to the economic welfare of any country. During the American Civil War it was estimated that one third of all money in circulation was counterfeit. Paper money then was issued by private banks and the counterfeiters enjoyed unprecedented prosperity because there was no standard of excellence, no uniformity of design, and people were not familiar with the many types of workmanship represented by so many notes.

In 1863 the Federal Government authorized the first national currency, popularly known as "greenbacks." With considerable relish the counterfeiters discontinued their operations with the private banknotes and turned to the new Government issue.

Until 1865 the counterfeiters were opposed only by local police forces and occasionally by investigators in the War Department, but there was no Federal law-enforcement agency assigned to the suppression of counterfeiting.

When the Government realized that the counterfeiters were flooding the nation with imitations of the new Federal money, it was evident that drastic action must be taken to combat the crime wave, or public confidence in the greenbacks would be completely destroyed and the nation would face a serious crisis.

Thus, on July 5, 1865, Secretary of the Treasury Hugh McCulloch administered the oath of office to William P. Wood as the first Chief of the U.S. Secret Service, newly created to crack down on the manufacturers of homemade money.

∘ 2 ∘

Wood Could and Did

William P. Wood, swashbuckler, spy, a man without fear, without a complete stock of scruples, and sometimes without good judgment, had shot and slashed his way through the Mexican War as the head of a column of guerrilla marauders who christened him with a nickname that stuck to the war's end—The Daredevil Leader of Company C.

Contrary to the fashion of his day, Wood wore no mustache, no beard. (Of the 13 men who headed the Secret Service from 1865 to 1960, only 4 have been clean-shaven.) He was tall, stocky, with a Dick Tracyish granite face and piercing eyes, a mop of dark brown hair parted on the left, and he had a deep, furry voice.

During the Civil War Wood's personal friend, Edwin M. Stanton, Secretary of War in Abraham Lincoln's Cabinet, hired Wood to uncover thieving contractors seeking to defraud the Government, and to detect and arrest other criminals preying upon Uncle Sam's urgent wartime needs. Stanton and Wood had first met in 1854 when Stanton, a practicing attorney, represented a client who was being sued by Cyrus H. McCormick, inventor of the reaper. The whole case rested on the shape of a divider blade on a reaper that had originally been bought from McCormick and had been in use for 15 years. If the divider was straight, McCormick would lose the suit. If it was curved, he would win. The reaper was brought into court. The divider was straight, and McCormick lost.

The divider was straight because it had been straightened by William P. Wood! In 1897 Wood, approaching the end of his life, made a death-bed affidavit swearing that he had been ordered by Peter Watson, one of the lawyers opposing McCormick, to change the shape of the blade. Working secretly and at night, Wood straightened the curved divider and covered evidences of his tampering with dirt and vinegar.

Wood claimed that lawyer Stanton had no knowledge of this skulduggery. The fact remains, however, that Stanton, after he became Secretary of War, was apparently instrumental in having Wood placed on the Government payroll in various capacities.

When rumors reached Lincoln that Union prisoners were starving in Confederate prisons, Stanton sent Wood to investigate. Wood made frequent trips through the Southern lines, sometimes posing as a Confederate agent, sometimes disguised as a Confederate soldier. On a few occasions he let himself be taken prisoner, later making successful escapes. He learned that shipments of food intended for Union captives had been intercepted and used by hungry Confederates, and that the reports of starvation were true.

On one occasion Wood organized some forty of his friends into a company of volunteer scouts, claiming that this was the first armed Federal posse to invade Southern territory. With this force he engaged in a harassing expedition by crossing the Potomac at night in rowboats loaded with guns and ammunition which they fired to make the rebel pickets "think a whole regiment of Yanks was coming."

Wood was appointed by Secretary Stanton to be keeper of the Old Capitol Prison, where offenders of many kinds were confined. It was here that Wood initiated an intelligence system that cobwebbed all sorts of valuable information in a way that was downright unlawful. Wood assigned undercover agents to pose as Southern sympathizers who could smuggle mail from Richmond to Washington. The letters were brought to him at the prison, where he skillfully opened, read, copied and resealed them for transmission to their destinations. The information they contained was funneled to Stanton's office and served as invaluable leads for the conduct of the war. Prospective movements of Southern forces were revealed in this way, including plans for Lee's northern advances which ended in the Battle of Gettysburg.

Once, Wood reported later, Stanton summoned him to his office. "Wood," the Secretary said indignantly, "is it true that you're running a Confederate mail service from Richmond to Washington?"

"Yes, sir, it is," Wood answered.

"By whose authority?"

"My own. My object is to post you on the latest news from Richmond."

"How long has this been going on?"

"As long as I've been furnishing you with information."

Stanton told Wood that the practice should stop immediately, but Wood, a persuasive talker, convinced the Secretary that all was fair in love and war, including the reading of other people's letters. The mail interception continued, though without formal authority.

Formal authority was of little concern to Wood. One night he decided to take 150 Confederate prisoners out of the Old Capitol Prison to be exchanged for Union prisoners at Richmond and Salisbury. With a small guard Wood took the prisoners aboard a steamer in Washington and sailed down the Potomac.

When the vessel was halted by Army officers because Wood could not produce proper military clearance, he pretended that he would turn back. Instead, he armed the prisoners, disarmed the soldiers, and proceeded to Richmond, where he arranged with the Military Governor for exchanges at Libby Prison, then went to Salisbury on a similar errand. At both places Wood distributed quantities of Confederate money to the Union prisoners.

Secretary Stanton received a telegram from Gen. John A. Dix complaining about Wood and saying that he refused to follow orders. General Dix had won considerable fame for a telegram he sent in 1861 to the commander of an American revenue cutter in New Orleans: "If anyone attempts to haul down the American flag, shoot him on the spot." In a sarcastic reply to Dix's complaint about Wood, Stanton wired: "If he doesn't obey orders, shoot him on the spot." Wood continued to operate as a rugged individualist throughout the war, thanks largely to his relationship with Secretary Stanton.

The war diverted considerable attention from civil law enforcement, and counterfeiting was one of the crimes that prospered. With the creation of the new national currency, Secretary Stanton was asked in 1864 to lend Wood to the Treasury Department to clamp down on the producers of homemade money.

In his own later words Wood said: "At that time it was currently reported that about half the money in circulation was counterfeit. I was permitted to use my own methods and I determined to capture the engravers and principals active in the counterfeiting business. It was also my purpose to convince such characters that it would be no longer healthy for them to ply their vocation without being handled roughly, a fact they soon discovered."

Wood's raids were swift and unexpected. "In eight months," he said, "I rounded up counterfeiters in nearly every state east of the Alleghenies. I made no pretenses that my arrests were sanctioned by civil authority. Because my raids were made without military escort and I did not ask the assistance of State officers, I surprised the professional counterfeiter. I was threatened with every species of demolition, but took my chances at capture or being captured in these lively undertakings."

At the end of 1864 there were 34 counterfeiters serving time in the Old Capitol Prison. These represented but a small fraction of the total population (1,990) of the prison, and Wood's responsibilities as warden prevented him from giving full time to the fight against counterfeiting.

This was the picture when Abraham Lincoln began his second term on March 4, 1865. When his Secretary of the Treasury, Hugh McCulloch, attended a Cabinet meeting at the White House on April 14, 1865, McCulloch called attention to the growing counterfeiting menace. The Government, he said, had paid rewards for information leading to the arrest and conviction of counterfeiters, but this method had failed to trap the important offenders. Private detectives had been employed to put the criminals out of business, but had been unable to find them.

"In my opinion," McCulloch said, "everything possible has been done that could be done under the plans pursued, but as you see, it is not enough."

The President, his shoulders stooped, his gaunt face creased from the strains and cares of war-weary years, looked at McCulloch. "You say that present efforts are too weak. Do you know of a better way?"

"I think so," the Secretary answered. "I believe there should be a continuous organized effort, aggressive rather than merely defensive, and that the work should be undertaken by a permanent force managed by a directing head."

The other Cabinet members agreed that this was a sound approach, and from the President came the clear approval: "Work it out your own way, Hugh. I believe you have the right idea."

Mr. McCulloch reported later that those were the last words President Lincoln ever spoke to him. At 10 o'clock that night the President was shot by John Wilkes Booth.

The wave of sorrow and indignation that spread across the nation after Lincoln's murder interrupted most of the normal business of government, but in June plans were nearing completion for the creation of the new agency. One question remained: Who should be its head?

The answer was not difficult. William P. Wood had already made effective inroads against counterfeiters. He had proved that he was a competent and courageous investigator. His most recent activity was in helping to piece together the story of the plot to assassinate President Lincoln, by his interrogation of all the principals. It was unanimously agreed that Wood was the man for the job.

He was sworn in as Chief of the U.S. Secret Service on July 5, 1865, in the office of Edward P. Jordan, Solicitor of the Treasury.

Solicitor Jordan made a few brief remarks about the purposes of the new agency. "The main object," he said, "is to restore public confidence in the money of this country. Our policies and rules can take shape as your work progresses."

Wood's force numbered about 30 men. Some of these were former private detectives who had worked on counterfeiting cases. Others were trusted friends or associates of Wood who had worked under his direction during the war.

As a guide a list of six "general orders" was issued. Some are still in effect, though in more elaborate form. Here are the original rules:

1. Each man must recognize that his service belongs to the government through 24 hours of every day.
2. All must agree to assignment to the locations chosen by the Chief and respond to whatever mobility of movement the work might require.
3. All must exercise such careful saving of money spent for travel, subsistence, and payments for information as can be self-evidently justified.
4. Continuing employment in the Service will depend upon demonstrated fitness, ability as investigators, and honesty and fidelity in all transactions.
5. The title of regular employees will be Operative, Secret Service. Temporary employees will be Assistant Operatives or Informants. (Note: The title today is "Special Agent, U.S. Secret Service.")
6. All employment will be at a daily pay rate; accounts submitted monthly. Each operative will be expected to keep on hand enough personal reserve funds to carry on Service business between paydays.

A national headquarters was established in Washington and 11 cities were chosen for the location of field offices. The operatives' credentials were handwritten letters of appointment. Badges were not yet provided. A formal circular was sent out by the Treasury to U.S. marshals and other peace officers announcing the formation of the Secret Service and describing its purposes. The Secret Service was in business.

The men chosen to set up the field offices left for their destinations. In some cases there was only one man to a district; in others, two or even three. They were pioneers, bringing a new kind of law enforcement to the frontiers. They had to be courageous, shrewd, bold, and decisive. Often an operative would have to travel for days to get from one boundary of his district to another. There were no automobiles, no telephones, no paved highways—but there were counterfeiters and more counterfeiters. Some criminals had given up bank robbing, smuggling, forgery, or other unlawful enterprises and turned to counterfeiting, hiring engravers, printers, or other talents as required, because counterfeiting seemed more profitable and less risky than other criminal specialties.

Although this was the horse-and-buggy era, many of the big-time operators made profits that today would put them in the solid-gold-Cadillac class. A good example was Lewis M. Roberts, alias John B. Altic, alias Henry Harrison, alias "Mysterious Bob," a lone wolf who said little, sold much, and traveled a great deal, mostly on the back of a mule.

Roberts set up a regular trade route through Pennsylvania, Ohio, and Indiana, making trips on which he visited some 700 regular customers who bought his counterfeit money. On the first day of each month he picked up his bulk supply from a countrywoman who met him on the road between Philadelphia and Lancaster, Pennsylvania. His first delivery was in Harrisburg, then up the Susquehanna into the coal-mining regions, to Pittsburgh, and on into Ohio and Indiana.

Each month he sold about $50,000 in counterfeit money, for an average of $600,000 a year—a sizable figure even in today's underworld market.

Roberts was at the peak of his career when the Secret Service was created, and he had been operating for some 5 years when he was finally caught in 1867.

He was caught primarily through a competitor known as "The Flying Dutchman," who traveled more swiftly than Roberts, had a flashier approach, and undercut Roberts' prices. The Secret Service, however, was even faster than The Flying Dutchman and grabbed him as he was making a delivery in Pennsylvania. Spitefully, he informed on Roberts, his rival, and the Secret Service captured Roberts so swiftly that both men were prosecuted at the same time. To seek leniency, they implicated about 30 other offenders who were also taken into custody. Leniency, however, is a matter of degree. Roberts and his rival were sentenced to serve 20 years in prison and to pay fines of $10,000 each.

In 1866, when the Secret Service was about a year old, more than 200 counterfeiters had been captured by the operatives with the help of marshals and local police departments. United States attorneys prosecuted vigorously, and Federal judges meted out severe sentences. Counterfeiting was becoming more risky than armed robbery.

On July 1, 1866 the Government imposed a 10 per cent tax on all currency issued by state banks. The tax had the effect of forcing most of the state banks to liquidate or to become national banks. State banknotes dwindled to the vanishing point, and gradually the Government greenbacks and national banknotes became the country's circulating medium. Some counterfeiters who had enjoyed a field day by imitating state banknotes now found themselves with printing plates that were of no further use. Many engravers who might have made new plates for the Federal currency were serving prison sentences, thanks to the Secret Service. Counterfeiting began to decline, and by 1867 both Secretary McCulloch and Solicitor Jordan were congratulating each other and Chief Wood when an alarming discovery was made in the Treasury Department's Redemption Division.

· 3 ·

The Busy Mr. Brockway

Answering an urgent summons to appear in Secretary McCulloch's office, Chief Wood there met the Secretary, the Assistant Secretary, the Treasurer of the United States, the Solicitor of the Treasury, and the Director of the Printing Bureau (now known as the Bureau of Engraving and Printing).

On the Secretary's desk were several $1,000 Treasury bonds. He picked up two of these and handed them to Wood.

"Notice anything unusual about those?" he asked.

Wood's sharp eyes scanned the bonds closely. "They both have the same serial number," he replied.

"Exactly. Now these men all tell me that this could happen only through accident or some mechanical error in the Printing Bureau—or maybe because of some dishonest employee there. I want you to find out which."

Wood took a small magnifying glass from his coat pocket and walked to the big window, where he examined the two bonds. After a minute or two of ominous quiet, Wood returned to the Secretary's desk and dropped one of the bonds on it. "That bond was made by the Printing Bureau," he said. He handed the other to the Secretary. "This one wasn't."

The seated men jumped to their feet and crowded around the desk. "You don't know what you're talking about!" the Director of the Printing Bureau exclaimed.

"Are you saying this bond is counterfeit?" the Secretary asked.

"I am, sir," Wood answered. "It's almost perfect, but it's not genuine."

"This is absolutely preposterous!" the Solicitor put in. "Why, the Treasury has already redeemed about eighty thousand dollars' worth of these bonds with duplicate numbers. Certainly our Printing Bureau knows the difference between the genuine and the counterfeit!"

The Director of the Printing Bureau reached for the bond in the Secretary's hand. "May I, Mr. Secretary?"

McCulloch handed him the bond, which he examined closely. "With all due respect to Mr. Wood," he declared, "I say this is not a counterfeit."

Placing the bonds side by side under his magnifying glass, Wood pointed out flaws in the one he claimed to be spurious, and with considerable reluctance the Director of the Printing Bureau finally admitted that there was some basis for Wood's opinion. Secretary McCulloch was satisfied beyond any doubt that the bonds were not genuine.

Realizing that there might be millions of dollars' worth of the worthless bonds in existence, McCulloch ordered Wood to make an all-out effort to find the makers. In addition, however, he hired a Philadelphia bank detective named Schlemm to conduct an independent investigation to track down the counterfeiter and the bond plates, and offered a reward of $20,000 for the delivery of the plates.

Chief Wood, on learning of this offer, asked the Secretary whether or not he, Wood, might be eligible to receive this reward if he turned up the all-important printing plates. McCulloch assured Wood that the $20,000 would be paid to him if he succeeded.

Wood was secretly sure that the counterfeit bonds had been made by a notorious counterfeiter named William E. Brockway. Wood knew Brockway and his work quite well; in fact, some sources indicate that they were friends, although their friendship seems to have been based on Brockway's value as a sometime informant to Wood. In any event, Wood went looking for Brockway.

The law had looked for Brockway, off and on, for quite a few years and had occasionally caught up with him. The criminal career of this tall, gaunt character who became known as "The King of the Counterfeiters" began when he was about 15 years old, bound out as an apprentice in a printing shop in New Haven, Connecticut. Born William E. Spencer, the boy had been adopted by a family named Brockway after his mother died before he was a year old.

The printing shop was rented and run by 67-year-old Ezra Becker. Man, shop, and business showed evidences of wear and tear, but Becker's work was still of such quality that one of his regular customers was the New Haven City Bank, which had its paper money printed there from plates and on currency paper furnished by the bank. Ezra Becker was generally rated as "honest, but slow pay," and after some 22 years in business his trade began to slump, mostly because rivals were installing new processes and turning out better work in faster time at lower prices. Also, Becker's sight was failing.

Brockway became a highly capable printing craftsman, and within a few years, to meet his competition, Becker decided that young Brockway should go to school and study the new electroplating processes being used in modern shops. Such a course was given at Yale University, and it is probable that Brockway studied there. At any rate, he learned about lithography and how to make electrotypes.

In electrotyping, a wax or a leaden mold is made of the impression desired to be duplicated. Then, in an electroplating process, an electric current deposits metal, such as copper or steel, on the mold, thus producing a thin metal plate which is later backed by the addition of more metal to provide strength.

Brockway returned to the shop with his newly acquired knowledge and also with some new ideas about using it. Boldly he approached his boss with a scheme to produce counterfeit money that would be virtually guaranteed to defy detection. Old man Becker was at first reluctant to consider any such knavery, but his declining business, fading sight, and his need for cash finally made him a willing apprentice to his young tempter.

When the New Haven City Bank next placed an order for a supply of $5 notes, the bank president and the cashier brought the plates and the currency paper to Becker's shop, where they would supervise the money-making job to its completion, just as they had done for years. The press was operated by young Brockway under the vigilant eyes of the bankers.

Playing his assigned role, Becker picked up a sheet of the currency paper, examined it closely, and said: "You gentlemen ought to complain to the mill about the quality of this paper. It isn't as good as it used to be."

"What's the matter with it?" the president asked.

"Come over to the window a minute and I'll show you," Becker said.

Both the president and the cashier followed him to the window, where he held the paper up to the light. "You see those white spaces that look as though the paper is oily? Those are weak places in the sheet. They won't stand up long under use."

The president shook his head. "It looks all right to me—but I'll make a note of it. Thank you, Mr. Becker." They returned to the press, where Brockway was still turning out the $5 notes.

In the few moments that their attention had been diverted, the youth had pulled a thin sheet of lead from underneath his apron, placed it on the genuine $5 plates, and let pressure be applied just as though it were a sheet of the currency paper. Quickly he yanked away the lead, now bearing an impression of the original plate, and restored it to its under-apron hiding place before the bankers came back from the window.

In the nights that followed, Brockway produced a copper electrotype from the lead plate, thus obtaining an engraved impression of the $5 bill which was exactly like that on the plate so zealously guarded by the bank.

This early attempt by Brockway to hit the counterfeiting jackpot took place long before the Secret Service was established, and available records are not clear about his use of the paper used to print the counterfeit $5 notes. There is some indication that he or his partner managed to steal a quantity of the genuine paper, though it is more likely that they merely used a grade of available stock which was as close to the genuine as they could get.

Whatever the quality of paper, they did produce somewhere between $10,000 and $100,000 in counterfeit fives, on many of which Brockway cleverly forged the handwritten signatures of the bank officers. The notes were passed in stores and banks without difficulty until one day, months later, when a bank teller noticed some peculiarity about one of the signatures. A comparison indicated that the names had been forged, and in the resulting investigation the bank discovered that scores of notes received from customers were also suspect. The bankers could find no flaw in the printed design, but were satisfied that the notes could not have been produced from the genuine plates. The bank had little choice but to continue to honor all notes, though it also reported the mystery to the police department and requested an investigation.

A routine police inquiry at Becker's print shop was not immediately productive. Becker bore an excellent reputation and apparently the investigators did not suspect that he was a party to the crime. The investigation, however, frightened the old man so much that he decided to "retire," and before leaving town he offered to sell or rent his shop to Brockway. Brockway, believing that discretion was better than jail, took his plates and some equipment, and fled.

The police soon took these disappearances as evidence of guilt and offered rewards for the capture of the fugitives. Becker's fate is not recorded, but there is evidence that Brockway was arrested once or twice and bribed his way to freedom. According to one report, Brockway went to New York and, in the best dime-novel tradition, disguised himself in a false red beard, an assumed limp, and a pair of dark glasses, but an acquaintance recognized him and tipped off the police to claim the reward. Through the marvel of mysterious and swift communication known as the grapevine, Brockway discovered the danger and ducked for cover into the woods behind Bergen Hill, New Jersey, where he holed up for 5 days without food before he was taken into custody.

He was convicted and sentenced to serve 6 years in Sing Sing Prison.

It appears that Brockway served less than a year and was released in 1852 on a plea by his wife, the former Margaret Welsh, whom he had married shortly before his conviction. Together they went to live in Philadelphia as "Col. and Mrs. William E. Spencer."

Profiting by his experience, including advice received from his erstwhile prison associates, Brockway set himself up as a middleman between engravers and printers who produced counterfeit money and the buyers and passers who were anxious to obtain it. For a commission, or a share of the counterfeits, he brought buyer and maker together, taking no part in the actual counterfeiting operations. His Philadelphia home became a show place, complete with servants, and he was a respected and prosperous member of the community.

Secret Service records describe Brockway thus: "Slim build; features long and spare; very long neck; sharp nose; faint anchor tattooed on back of left wrist three inches long and a half inch wide." A rogues' gallery photograph shows him to bear a skinny likeness to actor George "Gabby" Hayes of Western movie fame.

In 1862 Brockway formed a partnership with another phony money merchant, one James Brace Doyle. This pair pooled their funds and invested in oil wells, coal mines, and other legitimate business ventures, all of which provided them with a veneer of respectability which was a perfect cover for spending counterfeit money made by their hirelings.

Their hirelings included some of the finest engravers in the country, many of whom had worked for private banknote companies and had been offered higher pay by Brockway and Doyle. One of these skilled banknote engravers was Charles H. Smith, of the National Bank Note Company of New York. Smith held his legitimate job, but also worked in his spare time producing counterfeit plates for Brockway.

In 1865, when the Civil War had heavily drained the nation's financial assets, the Government issued special $50, $100, and $1,000 bonds, or notes, which were commonly known as "seven thirties" because they paid interest of 7.30 per cent. It was the $1,000 denomination of this bond issue that Brockway decided to imitate, using counterfeit plates produced by Smith. These were the counterfeits labeled as such by Chief Wood, who knew Brockway of old, and the superb quality and printing led Wood in Brockway's direction.

Through his business connections Brockway successfully disposed of an unrecorded number of the bonds. In good faith, the New York investment firm of Jay Cooke & Company had actually redeemed $85,000 worth of the $1,000 bonds in the Treasury Department; that is, the Government had accepted the bonds and had paid out $85,000 to Cooke for 85 bonds that were actually worthless! This was probably the only time in history that the Treasury was victimized by imitations of its own securities.

Wood's search for Brockway began at Sing Sing Prison, but Brockway had been released long before, and it took the Chief 12 days to follow the trail to William E. Spencer in Philadelphia. When he made cautious inquiries of Spencer's neighbors he discovered that they considered "the colonel" to be a respected retired gentleman whom they were proud to claim as an acquaintance. Wood also learned that Col. and Mrs. Spencer were in a New York hotel for a few days, preparatory to making a trip to Europe.

Wood located the Spencers in New York, and with a police officer went to their hotel room at 4 o'clock one morning. Brockway insisted that his name was Spencer and that he knew no one named Brockway. Wood ordered them to get dressed, dismissed the policeman, and then demanded that Brockway and his wife accompany Wood. After leaving the hotel, Wood took the pair across the Hudson to Taylor's Hotel in Jersey City.

"What does this mean?" Brockway demanded. "This is an outrage, sir, an incredible outrage! I'll have you prosecuted for kidnaping! I tell you that I am not this Brockway you're after, nor do I know anything about him. I am Colonel William E. Spencer and this I can prove by dozens of reputable and upright citizens of Philadelphia."

Wood and one of his agents kept Brockway at the hotel for 5 days, ignoring his protests and threats. Wood said later: "I kept him on tenterhooks day and night. Our interviews were continuous and spicy—and by evidence I put before him he finally admitted that he was Brockway, the former New Haven counterfeiter. Then he changed his tactics and appealed to me to allow him to buy his liberty. He said he could pay a higher amount than any reward I might receive from the Government. I told him I had never accepted bribes and had no notion to begin now; that he must surrender to me the copper electroplates that printed these bonds, and the sooner he produced them the sooner he would be told what his next step was to be."

Brockway was allowed to send for an attorney, ex-Judge Stewart, of New York. "Later," said Chief Wood, "on the lawyer's advice, the plates from which the bonds were printed were brought to me in the presence of Assistant Solicitor Risley, summoned by wire from Washington."

Although the plates had been engraved by Charles H. Smith for Brockway, there was no solid proof that such was the fact, and Smith was not arrested.

In consideration of the surrender of the plates by Brockway and for giving information to the Government, Brockway was placed on probation.

Chief Wood was paid $5,000 as part of the promised $20,000 reward. Secretary McCulloch said Wood would get the balance of $15,000 when the Government had recovered its $85,000 from the firm of Jay Cooke. Wood resigned as Chief of the Secret Service in 1869, devoting his time to efforts to strengthen the civil suit brought by the Government against Cooke. The Cooke defense was that the bonds were genuine. The case depended mainly on Wood's testimony and was won by the Treasury, which collected the $85,000.

Secretary McCulloch now refused to pay Wood the $15,000, claiming that there were no appropriated funds available for that purpose. Through friends in Congress, Wood contrived to have a special bill introduced and passed, authorizing a special appropriation of $25,000 to the Secret Service. However, the Treasury then brought up technicalities, questions, and vague objections, all aimed at denying Wood's claim. Even though the claim was later supported by a new administration and even by President Rutherford B. Hayes himself, Wood never collected another dime of the promised reward money.

Brockway apparently went to live in peaceful, modest retirement, but in the spring of 1878 there appeared in circulation an issue of a $100 National Bank note that some experts pronounced counterfeit, others genuine. When this disagreement was publicized in newspapers the notes stopped circulating, but only for a short time, for the counterfeiters improved their plates and made detection of the bills even more difficult than at first.

The notes appeared in Maine, California, Texas, in the South and the Midwest. By the time the notes were identified as spurious the trail was cold. The Secret Service, however, knew that a counterfeiter's handiwork is as distinctive as handwriting, and a careful analysis of the deceptive counterfeits convinced the experts that the notes were being produced by Brockway and his engraver, Charlie Smith.

In 1880 A. L. Drummond, head of the New York District of the Secret Service, located Brockway living in Canarsie, New York. Agents kept his house under surveillance, and one day saw a strange man enter the building and emerge carrying a package. The man later proved to be Brockway's former shadowy partner, James B. Doyle.

Doyle was kept under observation and was seen to board a train for Chicago. Two Secret Service men became his fellow passengers. In Chicago the Secret Service arrested Doyle and searched his luggage, finding more than $200,000 worth of $1,000 Government bonds. Doyle, a respected businessman, waxed indignant and insisted the bonds were genuine. A reputable banker in Chicago examined the bonds and agreed with Doyle that they were the real thing. The bonds actually were genuine, but were of smaller denominations and had been altered, or "raised," to represent $1,000 bonds.

The next day Drummond arranged for two Brooklyn detectives to pick up Brockway, while Drummond and a Brooklyn police officer went to the home of Charles H. Smith, who lived next door to the Superintendent of Police. Smith was at home with his wife and 18-year-old daughter.

Drummond identified himself and said, "Smith, you're under arrest for counterfeiting."

Smith's wife gasped. An instant later she exclaimed: "This is ridiculous! It's—it's blackmail, that's what it is!"

"That's enough, mother," Smith said. "Don't say any more."

Drummond recited the charges against the engraver, describing the offenses he had committed with and for Brockway. Smith admitted knowing Brockway, but insisted that he had never made any plates for him. Drummond, he said, was completely mistaken. Smith was an innocent man.

"Listen to me, Smith," Drummond told him. "You're an old man. For twenty-six years you've lived in this house next door to the Superintendent of Police. You've made a lot of friends in the neighborhood and I've talked with many of them. The one thing they're emphatic about is that you won't lie. Now you tell me where the plates are that you made for Brockway."

Smith, obviously disturbed, was silent for several moments. Then tears came to his eyes and he said, "He's got them."

Smith made a full written confession implicating Brockway.

Detectives Scanlon and Blackwood arrested Brockway, who assured them that they had made a terrible mistake. No, he had never heard of Smith or Doyle. He was Colonel Spencer, and to accuse him of counterfeiting was a colossal absurdity.

There was no real evidence against Brockway except Smith's confession. What the Secret Service wanted was Brockway's plates. Brockway's attorney called on Drummond, whom he knew well, to ask what sort of case the Government had against his client.

"If Brockway can bribe twelve jurors, he might get free," Drummond told him. "If he can bribe only eleven, there will be a disagreement because our case is so strong that the twelfth man will hold out forever for a conviction."

The lawyer nodded slowly. "If my client should tell everything, what kind of recommendation would you be willing to make?"

"If he pleads guilty and turns up his plates, I think the Government would settle for a ten-year sentence."

The lawyer quickly argued that this was too much for an old man, and asked if Drummond would talk with Brockway. Drummond agreed, and they met the following day.

Brockway had lost his indignant front as Colonel Spencer. He was

"Long Bill" Brockway, beaten and discouraged, seeking whatever leniency he could get.

"What is it you want?" he asked.

Drummond produced a list of plates for counterfeit bills and bonds. "I want all these plates, together with any others you may have stowed away."

Brockway nodded. "All right. They're buried in lead caskets in the woods near Richmond Hill."

The next morning Drummond, Brockway, Brockway's attorney, the U.S. Attorney, and two deputy sheriffs walked into the shade of a chestnut tree in Richmond Hill, where one of the men began to dig with a pick. Only a few inches under the surface they found the containers, made of 6-inch lead pipe flattened and soldered at the ends. They held 22 sets of steel and copper plates for $100, $500, and $1,000 bills and bonds. Buried with them were glass jars containing $350,000 in counterfeit $100 notes.

James Brace Doyle was convicted in Chicago and sent to prison for 12 years. Smith was released because his confession had been the means of forcing Brockway to surrender the plates. Brockway received a suspended sentence—but he failed to learn his lesson.

In 1883 Brockway made counterfeit bonds of the Morris and Essex Street Railway Company and was sentenced to Sing Sing Prison for 5 years.

In 1896 he turned again to the manufacture of homemade $1,000 U.S. bonds. This time the government showed no mercy, and on his conviction he was imprisoned for 10 years.

Brockway was 82 years old when he was paroled in 1904. He finally went to live in a rooming house in New Haven, Connecticut, where his counterfeiting career began. He outlived many of the Secret Service men who were his nemesis, and the accomplices who had helped him to compete with the Government's money factory.

On December 1, 1920 William Brockway was found dead in bed, the victim of gas escaping from a jet in which the flame had accidentally been snuffed out. The reign of The King of the Counterfeiters was ended.

Others, however, were aspiring to the throne.

○ 4 ○

The Ghouls

While "King" Brockway held sway in counterfeiting circles in the East, another monarch of money-making flooded the Midwest with phony bills of several denominations. His name was Ben Boyd, he was a skilled engraver, and he headed a gang of thieves and note passers who had no talent for craftsmanship, but whose warped imaginations conceived a ghoulish plot that could astound the entire world.

The plot: To steal the remains of Abraham Lincoln from the Lincoln tomb in Springfield, Illinois, and to hold it for a strange kind of ransom.

Ben Boyd was arrested by the Secret Service early in 1876 in Indiana, was convicted of manufacturing counterfeit money, and sent to Joliet Penitentiary for 10 years. Several passers were also arrested, but Boyd's closest partners, Jack Hughes and Terence Mullen, remained at liberty for lack of evidence to warrant their arrest. Although they still had a supply of counterfeits on hand, Boyd's imprisonment cut off their source and ruined their chances of printing more from new plates, and since they were neither capable nor desirous of becoming engravers or turning to honest labor, they connived to set Ben free so that they might resume business as usual.

Terence Mullen owned a small dirty saloon called "The Hub" at 294 West Madison Street, Chicago—a run-down grogshop frequented by cutthroats, robbers, swindlers from the river boats, and other underworld scum. Many burglaries, killings, and other crimes had been planned in the beery atmosphere of The Hub, but the law had never been able to implicate Mullen in any of them with proof that would stand up in court.

Mullen himself, questioned frequently by police, simply patted the checkered vest across his fat belly, or gently stroked his tired black mustache, and decried the charge that any of his customers were guilty of criminal acts.

In October 1876, since Boyd's notes continued to appear in circulation, Secret Service Agent Patrick D. Tyrrell, of Chicago, was convinced that Mullen and his crony, Jack Hughes, were either passing the bills or selling them to others. Hughes, an all-around crook, had a bushy light brown beard and a perennial scowl—an ugly exterior with a personality to match.

Agent Tyrrell was known to Mullen and Hughes, so Tyrrell employed a trusted undercover informant, Louis C. Swigles, to frequent The Hub in an effort to connect Boyd's former cronies with the circulation of the bills. Swigles won the confidence of Mullen and Hughes, and although he failed to pick up information about their counterfeiting activities he suddenly found himself involved in a much more startling venture.

Swigles' first report of this incredible conspiracy was made to Agent Tyrrell on October 27, 1876. "They figure they've got to get Ben Boyd out of Joliet," Swigles said. He squirmed in his chair and went on, "Now, Mr. Tyrrell, I know this sounds crazy, but here's what they're going to do. They plan to break into the Lincoln tomb, steal President Lincoln's body, and hide it in the Indiana sand hills. Then—"

"Wait a minute, wait a minute!" Tyrrell said incredulously. "Did you say they're going to steal Abraham Lincoln's body from the tomb and—"

"And hide it—that's right. And then they'll try to make a bargain with the government. They will return the body if and when Ben Boyd is released from jail."

Tyrrell stood up and looked down at Swigles. "You said it sounded crazy. You were right. And you know what? I think you're either drunk or nuts yourself!"

Swigles held out both arms. "Honest, Mr. Tyrrell—it's the truth! And I'm telling you they're going through with it. It's all set."

Shaking his head slowly, Tyrrell sat down, obviously skeptical. "All right, all right. Let's hear the rest of it, then."

"Well, they already have a jimmy, a crowbar, and a saw to break into the tomb. At the cemetery they'll have a team big enough to carry away the coffin. They'll haul it to the sand dunes in Indiana and bury it, and then get word to Ben Boyd so's he can make the proposition about his release." He grinned, adding, "I'm to hire the team and driver."

"Good boy!" Tyrrell exclaimed. Thoughtfully he asked, "The Indiana sand dunes, you say?"

"That's right. Mullen says the winds will shift the sand so that there will be no trace of the wagon tracks and no signs to show where the casket is buried."

Since the investigation of a conspiracy of this kind was not customarily performed by the Secret Service, Tyrrell telegraphed the facts to Chief James J. Brooks, who instructed him to tell the entire story to

Mr. Robert Lincoln, the late President's surviving son, then residing in Chicago.

Tyrrell saw Robert Lincoln on October 28. Mr. Lincoln said he would appreciate it if the Secret Service would do whatever it could to thwart the plot. When this conversation was reported to Chief Brooks, he authorized Tyrrell to take all possible action to prevent the theft and to arrest the grave robbers.

On November 3 Swigles reported a new development. "We had another meeting in my room last night," he said, "and Mullen has the idea that they can use the body to get a lot more than Ben Boyd. He says the Government will not only release Boyd, but also will gladly pay a ransom of two hundred thousand dollars for returning the body." With a faint smile he added, "Mullen also thinks this will get them a lot of respect from the American people."

"Respect? Hmpf!" Tyrrell shook his head. Then, "All right—just when do they expect to pull this job? Do you know that yet?"

"Not yet. I'll give you the word as soon as I can."

The word came on the morning of November 6. Swigles was tense as he told Tyrrell that the robbery was scheduled for the following night, November 7. "Mullen picked the time," Swigles explained, "because it's election night and everybody will be in town. There'll be a lot of celebrating and excitement—and besides, he said they wanted to do it before the weather got colder and froze the ground. They'll take the nine o'clock train out of Chicago tonight for Springfield."

Agent Tyrrell told Swigles to stay close to Mullen and Hughes. Tyrrell then called on Mayor C. W. Dean, who had been Lincoln's friend, and on Elmer Washburn, a former Chief of the Secret Service, who lived in Chicago. After unfolding the story to them, Tyrrell invited both men to accompany him to Robert Lincoln's office to report the latest activity.

There Tyrrell pointed out that since he was the only Secret Service agent available at the time, he would need more help.

"You can count on me," Washburn said.

Robert Lincoln had a suggestion. "Since my father was friendly with Allan Pinkerton," he said, "I'm sure Mr. Pinkerton would be glad to give whatever assistance he can."

Tyrrell and Washburn called on Allan Pinkerton, who promptly assigned two of his best detectives, John C. McGinn and George Hay, to work under Tyrrell's orders. In addition, Tyrrell enlisted the services of Detective John McDonald, who had assisted in the arrest of Ben Boyd; and Robert Lincoln sent another man, John English, to help if he could.

That night Tyrrell, Washburn, Robert Lincoln, McDonald, English,

McGinn, and Hay were among the people at the railroad station, their eyes intent on the passengers boarding the train for Springfield. The conductor, a lantern in one hand, dredged up his heavy gold watch as he glanced up and down the platform preparatory to shouting "All aboard!" Tyrrell tried not to show that he was edgy and nervous, but Hughes and Mullen had failed to appear, and in another minute or so the train would leave without them. Had the plans been changed? Had Swigles been trying to get in touch with Tyrrell?

As the conductor raised the lantern to signal the engineer to pull out, Tyrrell saw Hughes, Mullen, and Swigles rush out of the depot to the train. Tyrrell, McGinn, Hay, McDonald, and English hurried to the last car and climbed aboard, waving to Elmer Washburn, who was to accompany Mr. Lincoln home and meet Tyrrell in Springfield the next day. Slowly the train chugged away. The first act in a unique drama had begun.

The train arrived in Springfield at 6 o'clock the next morning, and Tyrrell and the Pinkerton men registered under assumed names at the St. Nicholas Hotel. At half-past eight Swigles met Tyrrell there.

"We're staying at the St. Charles," Swigles reported. "Mullen's registered as T. Durnan and Hughes as James Smith. They were asleep when I left. They wanted to be called at ten-thirty. And here's the latest— they will tear a section out of a page of a foreign-language newspaper and rip it in two. One piece will be left in the tomb and the other will be given to Ben Boyd so that he can use it later to prove that he can produce Lincoln's body."

"All right," Tyrrell said. "You try to meet me here about four o'clock so we can go over our plans."

At 9 o'clock that morning Tyrrell kept an appointment to meet John T. Stuart, President of the Lincoln Monument Association, in whose office the late President had once read law. Together they went to Oak Ridge Cemetery, 2 miles away, where the Lincoln monument had been completed only 2 years before. Dark clouds scudded low and ominously across a leaden sky as the chill breeze sighed through the bare trees in the wooded graveyard—a dismal day for an evil task.

Tyrrell trudged through the dry leaves, carefully scrutinizing the shrubbery and trees surrounding the tomb, and examining the padlock on the entrance to the catacomb. The custodian of the tomb, J. C. Powers, opened the door so that Tyrrell could inspect the interior of the tomb itself—a rectangular structure with a labyrinth of passages leading 175 feet from a circular memorial hall at one end to the catacomb and sarcophagus at the other, where lay the mortal remains of Abraham Lincoln. There was another outer door at the catacomb entrance.

After his inspection Tyrrell gave instructions to Custodian Powers.

"I believe," he said, "that sometime this afternoon two men will visit the tomb and ask a lot of questions. Don't act suspicious and don't do anything out of the ordinary. Just tell them whatever they want to know." He gave Powers complete descriptions of Hughes, Mullen, and Swigles.

McGinn and Hay, the Pinkerton agents, were assigned to keep Hughes and Mullen under surveillance.

About 3 o'clock Hughes and Swigles appeared at the tomb, paid their admission fee, and signed fictitious names in the visitors' register. Hughes asked Mr. Powers all sorts of questions about the catacomb, its protection (there was none except for a heavy padlock), the weight of the sarcophagus and casket, and other matters pertinent to the proposed robbery. As instructed, Mr. Powers answered every question as completely as he could. Terence Mullen, it was learned later, had not accompanied Hughes and Swigles to the cemetery because he stayed in town to round up the rest of the tools needed to break into the tomb and force open the marble sarcophagus.

At 4:45 P.M. Swigles met Tyrrell and told about the visit to the tomb. "It's like this," Swigles said. "I'm to help Hughes and Mullen get the casket out of the sarcophagus. Then I'm to go for the wagon, which is supposed to be on the road outside the cemetery." He smiled. "You know and I know that there isn't any wagon. But if *they* find it out they'll bust my skull. You be sure and get 'em!"

"Don't worry," Tyrrell said. "When you go for the wagon, come to the entrance to Memorial Hall. I'll be there just inside the door." He paused. "We'd better use a password, just in case. Come to the door and say 'Washburn.' Then I can be sure it's you."

At 5 o'clock that afternoon Elmer Washburn arrived and went to Tyrrell's hotel room, where Tyrrell had assembled McGinn, Hay, McDonald, English, and Swigles.

"Does everyone have a gun?" Tyrrell asked.

The men nodded, or pulled back their coats to expose their weapons. George Hay, grinning, drew out a huge Colt which he displayed proudly. "I wouldn't be without her," he said.

Mr. Washburn took the gun and examined it with interest. "That's the old percussion-cap model," he said. "I haven't seen one of those in some time." He held it straight out, aiming at a picture on the wall. "They were all right in their day," he went on, "but you couldn't trust them. Sometimes the cap would pop off without firing the cartridge." He handed the weapon to Hay. "You'd better get one of the new models, George. They're much more dependable."

Hay laughed. "This old gal hasn't failed me yet," he said.

Tyrrell outlined the plan of action, Swigles answered various questions for the group, and at 6 o'clock Swigles left to meet Hughes and Mullen, while Tyrrell and the others started for the cemetery in a carriage hired by Washburn. They arrived at 6:40 P.M. It was dark, cold, and foreboding.

Tyrrell showed the men the location of the sarcophagus, then assigned them to their posts inside Memorial Hall. When he received the word from Swigles, Tyrrell would lead the men out of Memorial Hall, along the side of the tomb to the catacomb entrance at the other end. There they would pounce on Hughes and Mullen in the very act of moving the coffin.

In the pitch blackness of the chilled tomb the silent, motionless watchers took their appointed places, huddled against the penetrating cold. Seven o'clock. Seven-thirty. Eight. Eight-thirty. Tyrrell was growing concerned and impatient. Had they called off the job? Even as he wondered, he heard the faint sound of crunching footsteps on the gravel walk outside the entrance to Memorial Hall. Then someone climbed the stairs to the doorway. Tyrrell became tense, alert.

He heard whispered voices through the grillwork in the door. Then the rays of a bull's-eye lantern bored through the darkness, a finger of yellow light probing the inside of the hall from one wall to another, as Tyrrell crouched against the door. A low voice (later proven to be Hughes') said gruffly, "All right." The lantern disappeared, and the tell-tale footsteps faded as the prowlers went away. Despite the cold, Tyrrell realized that there were beads of sweat on his forehead.

At 9 o'clock Tyrrell again heard someone approaching. Through the grillwork a voice whispered, "Washburn!"

Tyrrell rose and saw Swigles.

"I told 'em I wanted to make sure the team was on hand," Swigles said. "Mullen and Hughes are sawing the padlock off the catacomb door. They may have it open by now."

"All right," Tyrrell answered. "You'd better get back there."

Stillness closed in again, but at about 9:20 Swigles returned. "They got in," he said. "They pried off the marble cover of the sarcophagus, and when I left they had moved the casket out a foot or more. They said it was heavier than they figured, so they sent me to get the driver of the team to help carry it."

"This is it," Tyrrell said. "You stay here, out of the way." Tyrrell summoned the other men from their hiding places and told them that the crucial moment had arrived. He began to untie his shoes.

"What the devil are you doing?" Washburn asked.

"Taking off my boots," Tyrrell answered. "I'm going along the gravel walk, but in my stocking feet I won't make noise. You and the others walk on the grass. Have your guns ready, but don't use them unless it's necessary." He left his boots on the floor. "Let's go."

They advanced cautiously to the side of the building and through the blackness toward the catacomb, some 150 feet away. When they had gone perhaps a hundred feet the silence was shattered by a *crack!* like an exploding firecracker behind Tyrrell. Tyrrell stopped and whirled around, his gun ready. "What's that?" he asked in a husky voice.

The shadowy form of George Hay came out from behind a bush. "I'm sorry, Mr. Tyrrell," he said in a loud whisper. "The percussion cap on my gun snapped."

"Damn!" Tyrrell exclaimed. "Come on!" He ran down the walk, followed by the others. The door to the catacomb was closed, but Tyrrell could see that the lock had been sawed off. He opened the door carefully, standing to one side. "You in there!" he yelled. "Come out with your hands up. If you've got guns, throw 'em out here. One wrong move and you're dead men."

There was no reply, no sound of movement. Tyrrell stepped quickly through the doorway and flattened himself against the inside wall. He stood stock still, listening, listening hard. He heard absolutely nothing. He struck a match, holding it at arm's length from his body. In its puny, flickering light he could see that the room was empty except for the sarcophagus. He called to his men to come in.

In his later report to Chief Brooks, Tyrrell wrote: "The marks of their devilish work were plainly visible. They had sawed the lock off the door and had removed two marble slabs that formed the top of the sarcophagus, then moved the coffin about fifteen inches endways toward the door."

"Search the grounds!" he commanded. "They were probably frightened away by the noise, but they can't have gone far."

The men rushed from the tomb, but George Hay stopped at the door. "I'm really sorry, Mr. Tyrrell," he said.

Tyrrell nodded. "So am I. But what's done is done."

On the floor near the sarcophagus Tyrrell found an ax, a chisel, wire nippers, a piece of a saw blade, and the broken lock. McGinn came in with a hammer and the bull's-eye lantern that he had found on the grounds nearby. Tyrrell collected all these articles for use as evidence.

With Elmer Washburn, Tyrrell returned to Memorial Hall to get his boots. His official report then describes the most dramatic incident of the night.

"I put my boots on," he wrote, "and started for the high ground, thinking that Mullen and Hughes might have gone there to await Swigles with the team. I advanced up the stairs near Memorial Hall,

Mr. Washburn following. As I walked the terrace I saw the form of a man near a column. I fired my revolver at him. He retreated behind the column, firing one shot at me as he retreated.

"Thinking he intended to escape to the other side of the terrace, I started to meet him, fired at him again, and he returned the fire by two shots. I then went to the head of the stairs where Mr. Washburn was standing, and called to the men: 'Come up here! the devils are up here!'

"Some of the men soon appeared. I called again for them to surround the terrace. Then the man I was firing at asked, 'Tyrrell, is that you?'

"I made no reply, but called again for the men to surround the terrace. Then a man came from behind the column and said: 'Tyrrell, for God's sake—is that you?' Then, for the first time, I discovered that I had fired at Pinkerton's men, and they fired at me. What a mistake! McGinn and Hay came up. They had returned from where I sent them sooner than I thought they would."

A search of the cemetery was fruitless. The men assembled in Memorial Hall for a conference. They agreed that Mullen and Hughes would probably leave for Chicago on the first possible train—probably at midnight. After sending McGinn, English, and Washburn to try to find Mullen or Hughes in or around Springfield, Tyrrell, Hay, and McDonald hurried to catch the midnight Chicago & Alton train, meeting Swigles at the station.

Swigles reported that he had not seen the fugitives, but agreed to aid in locating them.

Tyrrell and the others combed the train from end to end, satisfying themselves that Mullen and Hughes were not aboard.

On November 9, with Mayor Dean, Tyrrell reported developments to Robert Lincoln. "I'm glad you stopped them," Mr. Lincoln said, "though I'm sorry they even got their hands on my father's casket. I only hope you'll find and arrest them."

Tyrrell's visits to the usual haunts of Mullen and Hughes convinced him that they were in hiding. On November 17 Louis Swigles told the Secret Service man that Jack Hughes had been hiding at his father's farm at Buckley, about a hundred miles from Chicago, but that Hughes had just returned to the city.

With Elmer Washburn, McGinn, and Detective Simmons of the Chicago Police Department, Tyrrell followed Swigles to a rendezvous with Hughes, but it was decided to postpone Hughes's arrest to see if he would meet Mullen, when both could be taken into custody at once.

Not until 10:30 that night did Hughes finally go to The Hub Saloon. Through the dirty window the pursuers saw him meet Mullen at the far end of the bar. Tyrrell gave instructions to Simmons and McGinn. "Go into the saloon and order drinks. Place yourselves so that you'll cut off any retreat through the back door. Washburn and I will be right along."

When Simmons and McGinn took up their posts, Tyrrell and Washburn strode into The Hub. Hughes, recognizing Tyrrell, made a break for the back entrance. Simmons grabbed him. At the same moment McGinn seized Mullen. Tyrrell yanked out his handcuffs and handcuffed Mullen and Hughes together.

On November 18 the prisoners were transported to Springfield to be prosecuted. A special grand jury was convened and voted two indictments against Mullen and Hughes—one for conspiring to steal the remains of Abraham Lincoln from the tomb, the other for attempting to steal a casket belonging to the Lincoln Monument Association. At that time there was no law specifically prohibiting the robbing of graves. After weeks of legal delays and maneuvers by the defense lawyers, Mullen and Hughes were tried May 30, 1877, in the Circuit Court of Sangamon County, Illinois. On May 31 the jury returned a verdict of guilty, and Judge Lane, presiding, sentenced each man to serve 1 year in jail—mild punishment considering the nature of their crime.

The story has an ironic twist. On November 8, the morning after the dramatic episode at Oak Ridge Cemetery, the newspapers were crammed with political stories about the election of Rutherford B. Hayes, a Republican, to the Presidency the night before. It was a close election, later resolved by an 8 to 7 vote of a special Electoral Commission. President Lincoln had been a Republican. Local Democrats quickly labeled the affair at the tomb an insidious frame-up by the Republican Party to win sympathy for itself and to gain new friends to fight its cause. The Republican newspapers gave some space to the story, but it was practically lost among the flood of political reporting and comment. Thus one of the most sensational news stories of the century was given little attention in the public prints.

Perhaps Abe Lincoln would have preferred it that way.

○ 5 ○

The Black Hand

In the early part of the 20th century the U.S. Secret Service stalked a gang of murderers, extortioners, and counterfeiters, packed them off to jail, and smashed the best-organized Mafia brotherhood in the country at that time.

The Mafia had its origins in Sicily at the beginning of the 19th century. A weak and corrupt Italian Government and Napoleon's invasion of Italy in 1796 plunged Sicily into chaos. Outlaw bands pillaged and plundered, and the wealthy owners of great estates, seeking protection for their lands and crops, hired tough, unscrupulous men to provide this protection by whatever means were necessary.

At first the numbers of "protectors" were small, but their ruthless methods served to terrorize the peasants and the tradesmen in towns and villages adjoining the estates, and gradually the terrorists discovered that by joining forces they could dictate to their employers and establish absolute reign over local businesses, which they did. They recruited more members at the expense of the landowners, and forced the latter to raise rents and prices of crops, then to pay a fat percentage of the income to the new "brotherhood."

As might be expected, various factions soon began to fight among themselves. One group, ignoring the co-operative aspects of the organization, would rob a town, seize money or valuables from storekeepers under threat of death, rape wives and daughters in the village, and retreat to their headquarters.

Competitors with the same idea, or perhaps members who felt that all loot should be shared, sought violent revenge. Fights were common among the factions, and the man who ventured too far in the dark might be found with a dozen stiletto holes in his neck and one or two through his heart.

This was the Mafia. These men were the *mafiosi*.

The Mafia flourished in Sicily during the next half century, as did murder, robbery, extortion, and other crimes. Mafia notes demanding money were signed with a symbol that came to mean "Pay or die!"—an impression in black of a human hand. The merchant who was the unlucky recipient of a Black Hand letter rarely hesitated about satisfying its demands.

So powerful did the Mafia become that in 1860 the Italian Government launched an attack designed to crush the brotherhood in Sicily, but the local authorities in the Sicilian provinces lacked any enthusiasm for the drive. After all, many of the police officials had brothers or sons or fathers or uncles or friends who were active *mafiosi*—and even some of the officials themselves were members in good standing! Consequently the government's campaign was less than a complete success, although it did result in some arrests and motivated some of the Black Handers to flee to other countries, including the United States.

It didn't take long for the Mafia to set up shop in the United States in organized fashion. New York City, with its big population of Italians, most of whom were law-abiding people employed by others or operating businesses of their own, provided an ideal headquarters—and desirable prey—for the American branch of the society. Its activities were directed mainly by two men: Giuseppe Morello and Ignazio Lupo, alias Lupo the Wolf.

Morello was a granite-jawed Sicilian with black hair and a thick, droopy mustache. He was easily identified by a deformed right arm and a right hand without fingers, a defect he carried from birth. Lupo was moonfaced, heavy, and clean-shaven. Together they made their headquarters in a dingy building at Elizabeth and Prince Streets, where Lupo ran a saloon and Morello operated a restaurant in the rear, a dark hole smelling of garlic and sour wine.

Their unlawful activities differed little from those of their forebears, though their opportunities for blackmail were greater. Fire insurance, for example, provided cash windfalls in the United States that were nonexistent in the Sicilian villages. Lupo and Morello, or their pawns, would force small shopkeepers to buy fire insurance on their properties —or, if they already had such insurance, to increase the amounts. Once the insurance was in effect the *mafiosi* would set fire to the stores and collect a major portion of the insurance settlements.

In one case Lupo and Morello sent a Black Hand letter to an Italian who owned a stable and several work horses of an excellent strain. The horses were much in demand and were rented out daily to contractors and others. The Black Hand letter demanded payment of $500, threatening the loss of one or more animals on failure to comply. The horse owner refused to pay.

Within a week after his defiance, a wagon with two of his horses stood outside a store on New York's lower East Side. Nearby, a short stocky man with a long black mustache leaned against a post eating an apple. A boy about 10 years old came down the street whistling, and as he reached the post the man stopped him.

"You happy, hey, boy?" the man asked, grinning. He reached into his right-hand coat pocket and took out an apple. "You like to eat an apple?"

The boy smiled as he accepted the fruit. "Thanks, mister," he said, biting into it.

Now the stranger drew another apple from his left-hand pocket and with a jackknife he cut it in half. "You see those horses there, boy?" He pointed across the street. "They like the apple, too. Here—you take these pieces. You feed them to the horses, eh?"

The boy nodded eagerly, ran across the street with the apple halves, and fed one to each horse. A few minutes later the driver emerged from the store, climbed aboard the wagon and drove away—but before the horses had clopped four blocks they collapsed and died in the street, poisoned by the gift of Mafia fruit.

The Secret Service had no official interest in Morello and Lupo until 1900, when scores of small shopkeepers on New York's East Side were victimized by passers of counterfeit $5 bills. Secret Service agents, with police help, arrested a few of the passers and sifted leads and facts which pointed to Morello as the brains of the counterfeiting ring.

Under the direction of Agent in Charge William J. Flynn (later to become Chief of the Secret Service), New York agents finally raided Morello's store and arrested Morello and some of his hirelings. The U.S. Attorney decided that the evidence against them would not warrant their prosecution, and they were released.

In 1902 another flood of counterfeit $5 bills appeared, and once again Morello was under investigation. An analysis of the paper and inks led the Secret Service to believe that the bills had been manufactured in Italy and smuggled into the United States. Passers were arrested and linked with known associates of Lupo and Morello, though there was no direct tie with these principals.

Searching for the trick used to smuggle the counterfeits into this country, the Secret Service turned for advice and help to another Treasury agency, the Bureau of Customs. Together, laying out the known facts, they uncovered what might be the answer.

Morello imported olive oil from Italy. Under the tariff laws, olive oil could be brought in by the barrel considerably cheaper than by gallon cans. It was therefore common practice for importers to receive the oil in barrels and also to receive Italian shipments of empty cans into which the oil would be poured for eventual retail sale after its arrival.

Armed with can openers, a squad of Secret Service agents descended on Morello's establishment, ripped open his supposedly empty cans, and shook out several thousand dollars' worth of bogus $5 bills.

Again Morello and several accomplices were locked up. This time a jury convicted the accomplices, but decided that the evidence was not strong enough to link Morello himself to the contraband. He was free once more.

Agent in Charge Flynn decided on new tactics. He assigned an Italian agent, Peter A. Rubano, to frequent Morello's neighborhood in an effort to infiltrate the organization. The undercover man was aware that any slip on his part would undoubtedly make him a corpse, and he was cautioned to proceed with care. Rubano centered his attention on Lupo the Wolf, and gradually became one of Lupo's confidants—*except* in the counterfeiting racket.

Flynn himself decided to make observations in the vicinity of the Lupo-Morello hangout, and on the night of April 12, 1903, he saw Morello and other known *mafiosi* in a meat market, talking with a man who was a stranger to Flynn. After some conversation the stranger walked away with Morello and Domenico Pecoraro, a Morello lieutenant. Flynn did not follow them, but remained to see who else frequented the saloon.

The next morning the body of a man was found jammed into a barrel in front of the New York Mallet Works at Avenue D and Eleventh Street. The victim was in his forties, well built, with a swarthy complexion and pierced ears for the wearing of earrings—a common Sicilian custom. His throat had been cut from ear to ear, and a double-edged knife had been plunged completely through his neck several times. This was the familiar mark of the Mafia. There were no papers on the body, and the police were unable to establish the identity of the dead man.

Flynn read about the murder in the newspapers, and although this crime was not within Secret Service jurisdiction, he was interested because it had all the markings of a Mafia execution—and Lupo and Morello were of the Mafia. Flynn went to the city morgue to look at the victim. It was the stranger he had seen with Morello in the meat market the night before.

Flynn went immediately to the New York Police Department to report his discovery. Police detectives and Secret Service agents promptly arrested Morello, Lupo, and nine other members of their gang—all Sicilians, all armed with revolvers and knives, and all carrying permits for the weapons! Each man was compelled to look at the murder victim in the morgue. Each shrugged and insisted that he had never seen the man before. Detective Joseph Petrosino, of the police Italian Squad, was assigned to establish the identity of the victim.

As soon as Petrosino began to ask questions in the Italian quarter, he received an anonymous letter declaring that the killing was an act of revenge and cautioning him to be careful lest he be killed. "I cannot tell you my name," the writer said, "because the Black Hand would kill me too."

Petrosino showed the letter to Flynn. "I have a suggestion," Flynn said. "It might or might not be good."

"I'll try anything," Petrosino answered. "I'm not getting anywhere as it is."

"Go up to Sing Sing," Flynn told him. "Some of Morello's boys are serving time there for counterfeiting. Show 'em a picture of the dead man. You just might run into somebody who won't like this particular killing."

At Sing Sing, Detective Petrosino had little success until he showed the photograph to Giuseppe DiPriema, who grabbed the picture from the officer's hand.

"That's my brother-in-law!" DiPriema yelled. "Who did this? Who killed him?"

"That's what I'm trying to find out. What's his name?"

"Marueno Benedetto." Grimly he stared at the detective, then began to curse and shake his fists, swearing that he would have revenge on the killer.

"Who might have done this?" Petrosino asked.

DiPriema shrugged. "Who knows? I am here in jail. I cannot know what is going on outside."

In further questioning, Petrosino learned that Benedetto, the victim, had owned an unusual and heavy gold watch and chain. It had not been found on the body. Back in New York, examining personal effects of the prisoners, Petrosino found a pawn ticket belonging to one Luciano Perrino, known as "Petto the Ox." The ticket proved to have been issued for a watch such as described by DiPriema. It was pawned for one dollar by Petto on the day the body in the barrel was found.

Petto the Ox was indicted for first-degree murder. Immediately the Mafia bore down on storekeepers, laborers, housewives, and others to contribute funds for Petto's defense. Enough was collected to hire a clever attorney. The lawyer proved that Petto could have come into possession of the watch in any of a dozen ways, and asked that his client be released on his own recognizance. With some reluctance the Court agreed and Petto was set free.

Although Petto's companions were in New York City, the Ox moved to Pittston, Pennsylvania, and Agent Flynn believed that the move was made because Petto feared death at the hands of Benedetto's avenger. One night Petto heard a shrill whistle outside his little house. He doused the lights, grabbed a revolver, and cautiously went to the front porch, squinting into the darkness. He heard a movement directly ahead and fired once. Instantly 5 flashes answered from the yard, and 5 bullets tore through Petto's body. When he was found a few hours later, a dagger was in his heart.

Petto's killer was never found.

Some time later Detective Joseph Petrosino was sent to Palermo, Italy, on a special mission for his Commissioner of Police. Part of the mission was to investigate the background of Lupo and Morello, for both had been convicted of crimes *in absentia*—crimes that apparently motivated their migration to the United States before the convictions were returned. While walking on the streets of Palermo, Petrosino was shot and killed "by a person or persons unknown." This officer was no longer to be hated and feared by Lupo, Morello, and their cutthroats.

The Secret Service, convinced that Lupo and Morello were responsible for most of the counterfeiting in the East, moved relentlessly to trap them so effectively that they could not again squirm out of a conviction and prison sentence—but this was no simple task.

Morello invested considerable money in barber shops, shoe repair shops, and restaurants. Lupo bought a number of grocery stores and became one of the major importers of olive oil and lemons in the United States. Both men were believed to be worth more than $200,000 within a few years.

In 1909 a deluge of counterfeit bills swept over New York, Philadelphia, Boston, Cincinnati, Baltimore, and other cities. The bills were all of the same manufacture and all were being passed by Italians. Passers were arrested in droves, but none would talk, saying only that they had no wish to die. The fate of Lupo, Morello, and their trusted accomplices was to be sealed by a young, meek, and educated Italian named Antonio Comito, known, ironically enough, as "The Sheep."

Comito, a native of Catanzaro, Calabria, in southern Italy, came to New York in 1907. A printer by trade, he was also a schoolteacher and had spent some time in educational work for the Italian consul in Rio de Janeiro. In New York he landed a job on an Italian newspaper, but business was poor and he was frequently out of work.

Later Comito recalled: "I was in love with a young Italian girl, Caterina, who lived with me and who was my best friend throughout all the trials which came. We divided our money equally when times were hard, and sometimes Caterina made much more than I did. On November 5, 1908 I was at a meeting of the Sons of Italy, and I chatted with various

members. One, Don Pasquale by name, clasped my hand and said,
'Professor, will you take a walk with me? I have something to say that
will interest you.'"

Pasquale said he believed he could find Comito a job as a printer. The
youth was both eager and grateful, and the next day Pasquale introduced him to Don Antonio Cecala, explaining that Cecala owned a
printing shop in Philadelphia. Comito did not know that Cecala had
once served a prison term for counterfeiting.

Cecala said: "I need a man I can trust to handle my printing business
when I am away. Now—do you think you can handle work like this?"
He showed him several order blanks, letterheads, and handbills.

Comito was delighted. "Why, this is the kind of work I do best," he
said. "I have specialized in this kind of printing."

Cecala told Comito that they were about to buy new photographic
and printing equipment and wanted Comito to select it. With Cecala,
Comito picked out cameras, plates, and a secondhand press. Cecala then
introduced Comito to Salvatore (Don Turi) Cina, a huge man whom
Cecala identified as his godfather.

Said Comito later: "Cina took my hand in his great paw and shook
it so that the bones crackled, and I could have groaned with the pain of
it. He was a terrible man. That I knew at the first sight of him."

Cecala had more good news for Comito. "I will pay the rent you owe
here, and you can take your Caterina with you to Philadelphia. We will
pack your furniture and pay your expenses."

Caterina was overjoyed with Comito's good fortune, for their money
was almost gone. Cecala sent men to pack Comito's furniture for shipping. Comito noticed a shipping tag marked, "S. Cina, Highland, N.Y."

Comito went to Cecala. "I thought we were going to Philadelphia,"
he said. "The furniture is marked for Highland, New York."

Cecala laughed. "You do not yet know much about this country.
Highland is close by Philadelphia. Besides, that is where the boat stops."

"Boat? What boat?"

"We go by boat instead of train, because it is cheaper. It will be a
pleasant trip, Tony. You will enjoy it, you and Caterina."

They boarded the river boat in New York that evening—Comito the
Sheep, Caterina, Cecala, and several of the latter's friends. Once under
way, Cecala went to Comito and Caterina. "I am embarrassed," he said,
"but I do not have enough money to pay for all these people to go to
Philadelphia. I can get more money later, but I need some now. Do you
two have any?"

Comito displayed a handful of coins. "This is all I have."

Caterina lifted her skirt and took a $5 bill from her stocking. "I have
only five dollars," she said.

"That will help," Cecala answered, taking all the money. Now, he knew, Comito and Caterina were entirely dependent on him.

At Highland, New York, the group was met by a wagon and driver who took them to an isolated farmhouse. At Cecala's direction the press, the equipment, and the furniture were unloaded and taken into the old house.

"What place is this?" Comito asked. "I thought we were going to your printing establishment."

"We are here," Cecala said. "This is it."

When the press was set up for operation, Cecala brought Comito a package and opened it. Comito saw zinc plates for the face and back of U.S. and Canadian $5 bills, and looked at Cecala in amazement. Cecala grinned. "This is your real job," he said. "To print with these."

"That is counterfeiting!" Comito explained. "I cannot do such a thing."

Cecala now lost all pretense of friendship as he glared at the timid young printer. Grabbing him firmly by the front of his shirt, Cecala said in an ominous tone, "You will do as I say, or you and Caterina will die."

Comito, pale and trembling, nodded, and Cecala released him.

"But I know nothing about printing money," Comito protested. "I am not sure I can do it."

"You will learn," Cecala said. "We will leave you here with Caterina. Enjoy yourself for a couple of days. Then get to work. Understand? And do not be foolish enough to try to leave. Wherever you go we will find you and kill you both."

So Comito and Caterina stayed, and to stay alive The Sheep printed the counterfeit money. It was not a particularly good job, because the green ink was not the shade of that used in the genuine. Cecala took Comito to New York and introduced him to a tall man with a dark mustache and who wore a brown shawl that concealed a shriveled right arm. The man was Giuseppe Morello.

"How is it you cannot make a better color of the green ink?" Morello wanted to know.

"Because this is a new business for me," The Sheep answered. "I am doing the best I can."

"Then we will get someone else to mix the inks—but you will stay with us to do the printing. If you so much as whisper our secret to the trees, you will die! If you are arrested, you must not tell about me or you will die. But if you are in trouble, we will help you with everything we have."

While in New York, Comito and Cecala visited an Italian restaurant where one of the customers happened to be Pete Rubano, the undercover Secret Service agent assigned by Flynn to "rope" Lupo some time before. He had already unearthed evidence and information that had resulted in several arrests of distributors and passers of counterfeit notes, but he was not yet close enough to Lupo and Morello to learn the location of the plant. On this particular night, however, a companion with Pete pointed out Cecala and Comito and said: "There is Cecala with The Sheep. He must be taking a vacation."

"Vacation from what?"

The man glanced around furtively. "Have you not heard? The Sheep is the one who prints the *moneta falsa*. He doesn't want the job, but he cannot help himself. After all, he is The Sheep."

"Where is it he works?" Rubano asked.

"Who knows?" His companion gave him a knowing smile. "I think it is healthier not to know, eh?"

Rubano relayed this information to his office as soon as he had the chance, but Cecala and Comito returned to the farmhouse in Highland before they could be shadowed. Soon they were joined by one Don Peppe, sent by Morello to mix the green inks, and by three others who could help or could act as guards and lookouts. They were Vincenzo Giglio, Giuseppe Callichio, and Giuseppe Palermo. Don Turi Cina spent some time at the house to make sure that everything was running smoothly.

One night there was a pounding on the front door. Comito the Sheep, frightened, was sure it was the police. The others, however, were apparently expecting an important visitor, for they opened the door and admitted Ignazio Lupo, The Wolf, who brought with him rifles, revolvers, and a thousand rounds of ammunition for use if needed.

The guns were not needed, for Comito completed the printing of nearly $50,000 in counterfeit bills, and was permitted to return to New York with Caterina. His return was discovered and reported by Agent Rubano, and Flynn and his men quietly visited Comito's small apartment late one night to arrest him. Both Comito and Caterina were there, and both were taken to Secret Service headquarters.

Flynn had a long talk with Comito, during which The Sheep cried, then told the entire story of the counterfeiting venture, including the meetings with Lupo and Morello. Flynn asked Comito if he would make a statement in writing. "I will write it all down myself," he replied— and he proceeded to make a full confession, written in his own hand, involving all his confederates. This time Flynn figured that he had an airtight case.

He sent one of the agents who had been shadowing Morello to learn definitely in what apartment the *mafioso* lived in the Italian quarter in downtown New York. The agent was the late Thomas J. Callaghan, who later and for years headed the Chicago District of the Secret Service.

Young Callaghan, weeks before, had set up a shoe-shine stand near Morello's home and had worked as a bootblack in the neighborhood to make observations without arousing suspicion.

Before he died (in 1957) Tom Callaghan reminisced about his assignment to locate Morello's apartment. "I figured that the only way to do it," he recalled, "was to go in and look around, but it was a dangerous rookery in which to be trailing a killer. It was a four-story building with long hallways, closed stairways, and bare walls. When I finally saw Morello coming down the street about midnight, I noticed that he had his two brothers, Vincenzo and Ciro, and another man with him. I ducked into the house and sneaked up to the second floor. It was pitch dark because the janitor had turned out all the lights at ten o'clock."

Morello and his companions entered the house and started up the stairs. "I tiptoed to the fourth floor," Callaghan recalled, "and then I thought, *What'll I do if they keep going to the top?* Sure enough, they didn't stop at the third, but kept coming up. I figured I was a squashed bug no matter what I did. Then, suddenly—I don't know why—I decided to walk nonchalantly down the stairs. I met them between the third and fourth floors, my heart thumping like a pile driver. When they heard me, and when we came face to face, what do you suppose Morello said? 'Scusa, please.' They stepped aside and I kept going. I'll never know how I got down, but once out in the street a sudden sense of the ludicrous struck me and I actually started to laugh."

Early the next morning Flynn and his agents descended on the homes of Lupo and Morello, taking the pair into custody along with Callichio, Palermo, Cecala, Cina, Giglio, and Nicolo Sylvestre, another conspirator. They were all sullen, all silent, all sneeringly confident that they would never be convicted. At Highland the plant had been dismantled, and the agents found no contraband.

When the prisoners were brought to the Secret Service offices, Flynn took Morello into his private office and sent for Agent Callaghan. "Ever see this young lad before?" Flynn asked.

Morello squinted, then shook his head. "Never."

"Well," Flynn went on, "he's been on your trail every day for about a year. Do you remember meeting anyone when you were going upstairs to your apartment last night?"

Morello stared at the ceiling. "Yeh—a boy. A little boy."

Said Flynn. "This is the little boy."

The *mafioso* stared at Callaghan with cold, angry eyes. "If I know this last night, I cutta you throat."

In searching the prisoners and their homes, Flynn discovered a notebook belonging to Giuseppe Palermo which contained one of the most unusual finds in police history. In Palermo's handwriting, in Sicilian, were the codified rules of the Black Hand. Nine in number, and some here condensed, they are:

1. Whoever reveals to a non-member any operations of his companions, or offends or quarrels with a fellow-member, or refuses to comply with an order, or who leaves town for more than one day without notice, shall be fined $20 and cannot "come to his place." But the companions who judge him must be all of one accord, pro or con. . . .

2. He who swears falsely . . . who draws a weapon without his companion draws another of the same dimension, always with the point uncovered, if it is a knife, or who fights a duel with a companion of the Society without the permission of the Society, shall be undressed (summarily deprived of his rights).

3. The companion who knows of the fault of another and does not inform the Society at large is liable to the same penalty.

4. He that does not attend at the precise hour of the meeting of the blackmailers of the day, to do his duty without any orders, shall be punished. If he explains his lateness in a manner satisfactory to the Society he will be pardoned and may take his place. Otherwise he may not participate at the next division.

5. A recruit who produces gain to the Society is entitled to one-fifth of it as his own share.

6. The Society cannot act without the consent of all the companions. Even the opposition of one mouth is enough to overrule the opinions of all the others, always provided the person objecting gives a reasonable explanation of his views.

7. No companion who becomes a member of the Society may in any way alter its rules.

8. Every meeting of the Society must be announced to those on duty on the day of the meeting at least 24 hours before it takes place, except in cases of emergency.

9. The date and place of meetings is absolutely in the hands of the head of the Society, and none may oppose him.

A tenth law, unwritten but perhaps most important of all, was the rule of *omerta*, which required that no *mafioso* furnish information to the authorities, or seek their help, or give assistance of any kind in the detection of crimes against members or their families. Under this code vengeance was to be wreaked by the individual *mafioso* on any person, persons, or families considered guilty of wrongs against or defiance of the Mafia member.

Flynn kept Comito and Caterina in protective custody until the case was called for trial. The Federal Court was packed with spectators, mostly cold-eyed men whose scowls centered on the Government's star witness, Comito the Sheep.

Comito folded and unfolded his hands, looking at the counsel table or the floor or the ceiling, aware of the multitude of vengeful eyes watching him, and striving to avoid meeting the gaze of any of them. He was plainly frightened.

When The Sheep was called to testify, he centered his attention on the U.S. Attorney and the defense counsel as they questioned him, but at one fearful moment he looked at the spectators, and in that moment one of the men near the front of the courtroom signaled the Sign of Death. He clenched his fist, crooked the index finger and gripped the bent finger between his teeth, then pulled the finger away and ran the fingertip around his collar. Comito turned cotton-white and slumped in his chair, his head bowed.

"I thought he would collapse," Flynn said later, "but he was tougher than I gave him credit for."

Comito the Sheep displayed the courage of the lion, for he went through with his testimony, which resulted in the conviction of all 8 defendants on February 19, 1910.

Callichio was the first to be sentenced. His punishment: 17 years and $600 fine. Callichio cried out, waved his arms frantically, mumbled loud protests, and burst into tears as he was led away by deputy marshals.

Palermo drew 18 years and a $1,000 fine, and Sylvestre, Cecala, Cina, and Giglio received 15 years each and fines of $1,000.

Giuseppe Morello, facing the bench, was asked if he had anything to say before sentence was pronounced. In a whining voice, with tears in his eyes, Morello the killer, blackmailer, counterfeiter, and chief of the dreaded Mafia, held up his shriveled right arm with its deformed hand.

"You see how I am crippled," he said. "This arm I have had from the day I was born. I have a family—a big family. They need me. If the judge will suspend my sentence, I promise to take my wife and children and go back to Italy."

Judge Ray, who had received Black Hand letters threatening to kill him if he did not show leniency to Morello and the others, showed instead his contempt for the threats by imposing a sentence of 25 years on Morello. The once-powerful *mafioso* stared openmouthed at the judge, then suddenly wavered and collapsed in a dead faint. He was promptly carried from the courtroom. (Morello served 18 years and was paroled. About 10 days after his release he was shot and killed as he waited for a haircut in a barber shop. His killers were never identified.)

Ignazio Lupo, apparently seeking to show that he was made of sterner stuff, strode boldly to the center of the courtroom when he was called for sentencing. His attorney began an eloquent plea for leniency, describing his client's penchant for honesty, his love for his fellow man, his generosity to all people. The plea may or may not have impressed the judge, but it certainly had an effect on Lupo, for he suddenly bowed his head, covered his face with his hands, and wept long and loudly.

His tears did not water down his sentence: 30 years and a $500 fine. Lupo the Wolf had been trapped and beaten by Comito the Sheep.

The Black Hand had extorted thousands of dollars from scared countrymen, yet the tribute collected by the blackmailers was trivial compared to the multimillion-dollar treasure laid up by a group of more genteel swindlers in what began as a legal lottery in the United States —a legitimate gambling syndicate that turned crooked and presented the Secret Service with one of its most challenging assignments. . . .

o 6 o

The Chance Takers

The inventor of "an electric lottery machine, 100 per-cent foolproof, to be controlled by the Government and operated through the banks," recently tried to sell it to the Treasury Department. His contraption, he claimed, "would require no tickets, no tags, no salesmen, and would pay off 50 per cent to Uncle Sam and 50 per cent to the player." He didn't make the sale. His letter, however, is but one of hundreds from other thoughtful Americans who firmly believe that a government-controlled lottery is the panacea for many of our national economic ills.

Few of these letters appear to be from crackpots. They are from intelligent and shrewd financiers, from attorneys, industrialists, Army officers, stockbrokers, engineers, and plain no-letterhead citizens. One New England factory owner who estimated that some 3 billion dollars a year were wasted in gambling suggested a national lottery in which 30 per cent of the receipts would be applied to the reduction of the national debt, 30 per cent to medical research, 30 per cent to prizes in all the states, 5 per cent to charity, and the remaining 5 per cent to defray the cost of lottery operation. "Because the clergy does such a swell job running raffles to pay off church debts," he wrote, "we should place the management of the lottery in their hands."

Soviet Russia, in its war with Germany, conducted a lottery to finance military operations. Tickets were issued without extra cost to every citizen who bought a war bond, and prizes were as high as 100,000 rubles (about $25,000).

There have been countless arguments for and against a national lottery in the United States. Those in favor say that many foreign countries have prospered from lotteries for years. Gambling, they insist, is part of man's nature, and they point to the fact that pari-mutuel windows at American race tracks, the Irish Sweepstakes, and other foreign lotteries drain millions of dollars from American pocketbooks.

The lottery proponents, on the other hand, point to history, showing that Faneuil Hall in Boston, after the fire of 1761, was rebuilt with lottery profits and that the Continental Congress raised funds by lotteries. Some buildings at Harvard and Yale, they claim, were lottery-financed. Other arguments: There could be a close tax check on lottery winners; millions of Americans gamble on the stock market, at the card tables and the roulette wheels; lottery players would not be compelled to buy tickets, and those who didn't like the idea needn't participate.

In rebuttal the opponents argue that a national lottery would disrupt thousands of American homes by encouraging gambling on the part of those who could not afford it; that it would destroy the morale of all the people, promote crimes such as the counterfeiting of lottery tickets, increase juvenile delinquency, and wipe out social progress made by church and welfare agencies. While the pros claim that the government's receipts would be greater by reason of the fact that big prize winners would be heavily taxed, the cons say this means that winnings would be only paper profits, since Uncle Sam would deduct most of the winnings for taxes.

As a horrible example, the lottery opponents point to the Louisiana Lottery, which started off with a bang about 1862 and finally had to be suppressed because its operators turned crooked and gypped ticket buyers out of millions of dollars.

The Louisiana Lottery began about 1862 in the State of Louisiana. By 1868 the State legislature granted a license to the lottery operators for a yearly fee of $40,000—a paltry sum considering that the receipts climbed to an average of $2,000,000 a month when the lottery was at its peak.

The venture flourished for years, but by 1890 there were rumblings and complaints that the lottery was crooked. A prominent design engineer named Samuel Homer Woodbridge opened a campaign to enact legislation that would outlaw the lottery. "Immense individual wealth among the lottery promoters had been amassed," Woodbridge declared. "Banks had been generously patronized and grown fat; churches felt the fever of easily gotten gain; the press fell an easy victim to the purpose of the lottery; the courts became pliant to its pulse; the ballot was polluted by its disguised and specious bribery; legislators were elected by its money; and legislation was, in all things pertaining to or affecting the lottery, controlled by its dictation. The sovereignty of the State was prostituted to gamblers."

A minority of Louisiana citizens opposed the lottery, but they were weak against the popular feeling and the rich and powerful lottery interests which were spread across the nation. To gain strength the opponents chose Gen. George G. Johnston, late of the Confederate Army, to go North to enlist moral and financial support to fight the gamblers. Through Western cities General Johnston traveled to New York and to Boston, where literature was prepared and distributed in a nation-wide antilottery campaign.

The original charter of the lottery company was about to expire, and a new, perpetual charter was sought. Thanks to General Johnston's efforts the Louisiana forces opposing the lottery marshaled a 44,000 majority and ordered the lottery operators to halt activity. The only way they could continue was to leave the United States and do business in a foreign country.

The wealthy gamblers tried and failed to locate in the Sandwich Islands (Hawaii) and in Mexico. Then, by holding out rosy promises of great wealth to the government of the Republic of Honduras in Central America they won a concession for a term of years and set up their headquarters in the city of Puerto Cortez, operating under two names —the Honduras Lottery Company and the Louisiana Lottery Company.

Honduras, hot and fever-ridden, was uninviting as a place of residence for the operators and the employees of the lottery company. Most of the revenue continued to come from people in the United States through local agents, and if the lottery was to prosper it must locate its real operating center in the States. Secretly the headquarters was established in Wilmington, Delaware. New York City became the chief distribution point for tickets, although the drawings supposedly took place in Puerto Cortez. Prizes were paid through a New Orleans bank.

About this time the State of Florida, ostensibly seeking drastic legislation to prohibit lottery operations there, enacted a law which contained a sleeper—a clause that permitted a company located in Florida to print lottery matter and do other clerical business connected with a lottery. No actual lottery was permitted, no drawing of tickets nor turning of the gambler's wheel; only printing, receiving, distributing, and disbursing might be done on Florida soil. Tickets cost from 25 cents to $3 each. Huge buildings were erected at Port Tampa and the "Graham Printing Company" did an immense business.

Now Congress stepped in and enacted laws forbidding the distribution of lottery material by mail.

The Honduras Lottery Company bought and operated the steamer *Breakwater*, fully equipped for illegal printing and for drawing the winning numbers at sea. The *Breakwater* made frequent voyages between Puerto Cortez and Port Tampa. Lottery literature, tickets, and money, excluded from the mails, were transported by express all over the country. Newspapers advertising the lottery were also excluded from the mails, but unmailable editions flooded the towns in which the papers were published, expurgated issues being specially printed for mailing.

Theater managers were paid to advertise the lottery on their programs. Cartons of lottery pamphlets were delivered to storekeepers for distribution to their customers.

Samuel Woodbridge, centering his activity in Boston, appealed to newspaper editors, statesmen, clergymen, college presidents, and prominent businessmen to help stifle the lottery. A petition signed with scores of impressive names was sent to President Grover Cleveland and to both Houses of Congress. Senator George F. Hoar of Massachusetts presented a bill to the Senate on February 15, 1894, which was passed and signed by the President on March 4, 1895. The bill prohibited interstate shipments of lottery tickets.

To evade the interstate law the gamblers established a distribution center in Washington, D.C., since the District of Columbia was not regarded as a state within the letter of the law. Also, to avoid use of express lines in shipping tickets interstate, the promoters employed trusted messengers who loaded steamer trunks with the lottery tickets and carried the trunks as personal baggage, traveling from Boston to San Francisco and points en route.

By such maneuvering and manipulation the lottery continued to operate. In 1902 the Federal Government, badgered by complaints from hundreds of indignant citizens, set out to smash the racket. The Secret Service was assigned to do the job, and Chief John Wilkie selected 23 agents to work with the Department of Justice in putting the lottery out of business for good.

For many months the Secret Service men probed, observed, and questioned, accumulating facts and evidence which could be used for a successful prosecution. Several small-time ticket distributors were arrested. In March 1905 the steamship *Hiram*, bound from Puerto Cortez to Mobile, Alabama, was stopped in Mobile Bay by Customs inspectors who searched the baggage of 3 employees of the Honduras Lottery Company. In the baggage were found tickets of prior drawings as well as the winning numbers of tickets for the current month. This damaging evidence was turned over to the U.S. Attorney in Mobile.

Leads developed by the Secret Service pointed to the fact that lottery tickets supposedly printed in Honduras were actually printed in Wilmington, Delaware. A careful investigation there was climaxed by a raid on the big printing establishment of John M. Rogers, a prominent citizen of Wilmington, where agents seized thousands of lottery tickets and supplies. In the search of the plant Agent Matthew J. Griffin found a loose board in the floor, which he ripped up, revealing bundles of papers linking the plant to the original Louisiana Lottery Company and dating back as far as 1862.

From correspondence and other writings found in Wilmington, agents swooped down on four addresses in Chicago, where lottery executives maintained suites of lavishly furnished offices. Here the agents seized warehouse stocks of tickets, administrative files, records of returns from lottery agents—and the plates from which tickets were printed. David H. Smith,* alias D. H. Marsh, was arrested as the Chicago head of the scheme. Smith, 70 years old and feeble, lived luxuriously at the Great Northern Hotel in Chicago, had been in active charge of the establishment since 1885, was a representative of the big operators, and had accumulated vast wealth from the gambling enterprise. In the year preceding his arrest his losses due to speculations were estimated at 2 million dollars.

Agents learned that one Herman Burns, a man of wealth, was a principal distributing agent for the Honduras Lottery in Mobile, Alabama, and that he supervised operations of others in the Far West. Agent Irving C. Sauter placed Burns under surveillance in Mobile in an effort to identify his accomplices, and when Burns prepared to leave for California, Sauter alerted the Secret Service office in Los Angeles and followed his quarry to that city, where Sauter was joined by Agents George W. Hazen and John F. Cronin.

The agents followed Burns to a palatial residence in Dolgeville, California, which was his West Coast home. Also living in Dolgeville were two brothers, John and Frank Anderson. The agents observed meetings between Burns and the Andersons and made guarded inquiries which established that these three were directly concerned with the operations of the lottery company. John Anderson, in fact, was popularly known as "Mr. Fixit" and acted as attorney for the company. All three were subsequently taken into custody.

Meantime, in Mobile, Agent Harry T. Donaghy maintained a midnight vigil at a printing plant where it was believed lottery tickets were being printed for distribution to other cities. At 1 o'clock on the morning of February 22, 1907, Donaghy watched a gang of men emerge from the plant carrying large heavy boxes which they carted to the Southern Express Company. Donaghy notified his superiors and was told to stay with the boxes. Other agents were assigned to raid the printing plant.

The boxes were put aboard a train bound for Atlanta and Agent Donaghy rode on the same train. When the train reached Atlanta the boxes were unloaded and were promptly confiscated by Agent Donaghy, who found them filled with lottery tickets.

In Mobile agents raided the printing plant, arrested the operators, and seized thousands of printed lists of lottery numbers. They also proved that representatives of the express company were aware that the

* Names of the conspirators mentioned in this chapter are fictitious, since the available records concerning the final dispositions of their cases are incomplete.

boxes they shipped contained lottery tickets, so the express company employees were arrested as part of the plot. As a result the owners of the company rushed to offer their services in tracing previous shipments, and from their records the Secret Service was able to trace tickets and drawing lists to virtually every major city in the United States.

The Secret Service seemed to be everywhere, and for the first time in many years the lottery opponents had reason to believe the lottery would end. From evidence at hand the agents could assemble a reasonably good picture of the lottery operation. After drawings were supposedly made in Honduras, the promoters would not release winning numbers to ticket buyers for a week or more, claiming that they had to wait until their steamer could carry the list of winners from Honduras to New Orleans.

This delay provided an excellent opportunity for the promoters to select, as big winners, ticket numbers which had not been sold, which would mean that the only big payoffs (as high as $300,000) would go into the pockets of the promoters themselves. As a result of this practice many old-time lottery players turned to the policy game, with headquarters in New York City, where drawings were held twice daily with no delay in the announcement of winners.

Many people doubted that the Secret Service could stop the lottery operation, since it was well-known that the lottery was backed by men of great wealth and influence. The Secret Service, however, plodded ahead stubbornly, confident that it could make the lottery business both dangerous and unprofitable.

In Mobile the agents succeeded in obtaining indictments against 24 conspirators, 5 of whom were estimated to be worth 100 million dollars. One of those indicted was the son of the man who had been instrumental in obtaining the 25-year charter for the original Louisiana Lottery Company and who served as its first president until his death.

From records maintained by David H. Smith, the 70-year-old Chicago millionaire, the Secret Service identified and arrested 30 other men who had operated the lottery in the name of the Old Reliable Guaranty and Trust Company of Chicago. Smith and the others pleaded guilty to conspiring to violate the interstate commerce laws by transporting lottery tickets, and heavy fines were imposed on all 31.

Simultaneously with the Chicago arrests, agents in other cities nabbed more of the regional promoters. The lottery agent in St. Louis, Missouri, was taken into custody with a load of tickets and other paraphernalia.

Other victims of the dragnet were lottery agents at Fort Wayne and Indianapolis, Indiana, and at McKeesport, Pennsylvania. Five men were arrested, indicted and fined in Cincinnati, Ohio, and Covington, Kentucky.

Agents seized quantities of lottery tickets, bulletins, and other incriminating evidence and arrested several conspirators at Paterson, New Jersey; New Haven, Connecticut; New York and Brooklyn, New York; Butte, Montana, and Boston, Massachusetts.

By 1908 the Louisiana Lottery, alias the Honduras Lottery, was out of business, thanks to the persistence and efficiency of the U.S. Secret Service. But there was no letup in the need for Secret Service agents, for there were other types of crooks whose peculiar talents required the attention of clever investigators. Consider, for example, some of the thieves who tried to rob the U.S. Mint and the Bureau of Engraving and Printing—the Government factories that produce the nation's coins and paper money. . . .

Robbing the Money Factories

The fabulous treasures of silver coin, gold ingots, and newly printed paper money that lie in the vaults of the U.S. Mints at San Francisco, Denver, and Philadelphia, and in the Bureau of Engraving and Printing in Washington, have probably tempted many thieves; yet few have tried to lay crooked fingers on this wealth of the nation. And the few who have tried have not completely succeeded, thanks partly to security safeguards and partly to the efficiency of Secret Service agents.

One of the earliest of such cases in Secret Service records began in 1889 when Agent (later Chief) A. L. Drummond was aboard a train on a vacation, heading from Washington to Maine. At the railroad station in New York he received a telegram from Chief John S. Bell in Washington. The message was cryptic: "Go see Director Preston, Philadelphia Mint, at once. Highly important."

Drummond had a flair for solving mysterious cases. They were a challenge, a means of pitting the shrewd against the clever, the hunter against the prey, the puzzle solver against the puzzle maker. Perhaps something had happened at the Mint which would make up for the interruption to his vacation. Drummond boarded the next train for Philadelphia.

He was not disappointed. At the Mint he sat with Director Preston and Superintendent Bosbyshell in Preston's office.

"We're missing about a hundred and thirty thousand dollars in gold," Preston said. "I don't have to tell you that we're pretty damned upset about it, and we're hoping you'll be able to recover it for us."

"Do you have any leads?" Drummond asked. "Any idea at all who might have taken it?"

"None," Preston replied. "That's seven hundred pounds of gold, and there's not a single clue. The vault doors hadn't been tampered with. The combination of the inside grilled door was intact, and everything was just as it should be, except that fifty gold bars had disappeared!"

"When did you discover the loss?"

"Yesterday. Superintendent Bosbyshell was with me when we went into Vault Six and learned of the shortage. To make sure there was no mistake we weighed the contents of the vault, and we were shy fifty bars. I wired Chief Bell in Washington—and you know the rest."

Drummond nodded thoughtfully. "How many men know the combination of the vault?"

"Only three. Bosbyshell, Cochran, who is our official weigher, and I. But even if Cochran or I could have opened the main vault door, there was still the inner iron grilled door. That's always sealed and locked, and the combination is known to only two other men—Jamieson and Strubel. Whenever gold bars are to be put in or taken out, one man of each team must be on hand—one to open the main door, one to open the inner grill."

"It sounds pretty thief-proof," Drummond commented. "But what's the possibility of collusion between Cochran, for example, and either of the two who hold the combination to the grill?"

"Oh, come now, Mr. Drummond," Preston said. "All these men are above suspicion, and—"

"But they're the only ones who could open the doors," Drummond interrupted, "and the fifty gold bars *have* been removed." He paused a moment, then: "You mentioned that the inside grilled door was sealed and locked. Was the seal intact when you discovered the loss?"

"That's another thing," Preston answered. "The grilled door was locked and properly sealed with the official stamp—and the stamp is put on only in the presence of both men who know the combination. If there was any inside conspiracy, it would have to include at least three people —Jamieson, Strubel, and Cochran, Bosbyshell or myself. But I must remind you, Mr. Drummond, that we're talking about seven hundred pounds of gold. That's a load that a man can't simply put under his shirt and carry out. Besides, there's a guard at every door and nobody is allowed to take out any kind of a package unless the guard examines and passes it."

"Thank you, Mr. Preston," Drummond said. "Now let's not spread the news that I'm here to investigate this shortage. I want to scout around a while, if you don't mind."

"Of course, of course. We're in your hands. We'll do whatever we can to help. From what you already know, do you have any ideas?"

Drummond shook his head. "Not yet. But I've learned that nine times out of ten the crook who tries hard to hide every possible clue will overlook some little thing that gives him away. I want to find that little thing if I can." He stood up. "May I have a look at the vault?"

"Sure thing. But I should tell you that we took the grilled door off its hinges to carry out the vault contents for audit. That's how we discovered the shortage. The door hasn't been replaced yet."

In the basement Drummond was introduced to Cochran, the weigher, as "a visitor who'd like to see our vaults."

As they approached Vault 6 Drummond said, "I wonder if I might have a look inside this one?"

"You certainly may," Preston said. "Go ahead, Cochran—open it."

Cochran twirled the dial, right, left, right and left, then stopped and pulled on the handle to open the door. It didn't budge. Again he worked the combination. Still it failed to open. "It doesn't seem to work," Cochran said.

"Let me try," Superintendent Bosbyshell said, stepping to the door. Under his manipulation the heavy door swung back noiselessly and smoothly.

Inside, Drummond looked closely at the bars of the grilled door from top to floor, then asked that the door be replaced on its hinges. Cochran set it up level with the floor, merely holding it in place. "Is that the way it always hangs?" Drummond asked.

"No, sir," Cochran said, "but it's very heavy and I thought you just wanted a general idea about how it looked."

"I'd like to see it on the hinges, if you don't mind. Here—I'll give you a hand," he said, taking off his coat. "Better take off your coat, too," he added, smiling. "This is going to take some muscle."

Cochran glanced inquiringly at the superintendent, who nodded. Cochran removed his coat and helped Drummond place the door on its hinges. Drummond stood slightly behind Cochran, his eyes on the man's back and waist.

"Thanks very much," Drummond said.

Cochran left the vault, and Director Preston scratched his head. "What was that all about?" he asked.

As Drummond donned his coat he pointed at the bottom of the grilled door. "Did you notice those scratches on the bars, about four feet from the floor?"

Preston shook his head. "What about them? That door has been there a long time. Probably all the doors in the other vaults have the same kind of scratches."

"I hope not," Drummond said, "because if they do, you've probably had shortages there, too."

The Director chuckled. "You're way off, Mr. Drummond. We've weighed the gold in all the other vaults and it's intact. This was the only shortage."

"Fine! Then we won't have to worry about the others. Now, may I use the telephone in your office?"

On the way upstairs Preston wanted to know more about Drummond's suspicions. "Let's wait until I prove things out," the agent said. He telephoned the Philadelphia office of the Secret Service and asked that 3 agents be assigned to him immediately. After telephoning he obtained a list of the home addresses of Preston's assistants. In a little while the 3 agents met Drummond at the Mint and he left with them, telling Preston he would return in 2 or 3 hours.

Drummond and the agents returned about two-thirty. "Ask Cochran to come up," he said, "and bring in Mr. Bosbyshell, too."

Bosbyshell was the first to arrive, and Drummond told him to stand at the far side of the office. Two of the agents were stationed on either side of the doorway. Then Cochran came in and closed the door.

Drummond wasted no time. "Cochran," he said sternly, "I want to know what you did with the fifty gold bars you took from Vault Six."

Director Preston looked incredulously at Drummond and at Cochran. "What are you talking about?" Cochran asked, his face flushed. "Are you trying to say—"

"I'm saying that you stole that gold," Drummond interrupted. "The sooner you return it, the more leniency you can expect."

"Mr. Preston!" Cochran exclaimed. "This is ridiculous! I—why, you know that I couldn't possibly carry seven hundred pounds of gold out of the building, even if I had the chance."

"You had the chance, all right," Drummond put in, "and I know how you got the gold out. You took a piece of bent wire and dislodged the bars from the top of the pile next to the door, then slipped each bar underneath the door. You didn't have to go inside the grill at all. And I know how you smuggled the bars out of the building." He pointed at the 3 Secret Service men. "These are Secret Service agents," he went on. "This afternoon it took the four of us less than an hour to find the tailor who made the secret pocket in the front of your pants—and this morning I needed only one look to see that your suspenders were specially made to be much stronger than usual. You wore an exceptionally long coat to cover any suspicious bulge in your false pocket, and no guard would stop you at the door unless you were actually carrying a package he could see. You took the bars out one at a time—and you might still be stealing them if the shortage hadn't been noticed yesterday. What about it, Cochran? Want to tell us the whole story and save yourself a lot more trouble?"

Cochran stood silently, staring at the faces of the men in the room. Suddenly he lowered his head and began to sob. No other confession was necessary. Later he led Drummond to an old unused sewer pipe leading from the basement of his home, where the gold was hidden.

"I still don't understand how you figured it out," Preston told Drummond.

"Just common sense," the agent said. "The scratches were a pretty clear indication of the way the bars had been taken out. I suspected Cochran when he seemed unable to open the vault door, and I think a guilty conscience made him nervous. When he didn't want to put the door on the hinges, I figured there was a reason—he didn't want me to see that there was space enough underneath to pull a gold bar through. I saw that he had those peculiar suspenders and that his trousers were unusually wide at the waistband. The bars had to be smuggled out under someone's clothing. I put all the facts together and—luckily—came up with the right answer."

Drummond shook hands with Preston and sent a telegram to Chief Bell: "MINT CASE SOLVED. REPORT FOLLOWS. GOING ON VACATION."

Another robbery, this one at the San Francisco Mint, resulted in the arrests of the culprits but a loss of the stolen money.

On July 3, 1901 the Mint officers discovered that two sacks of double-eagles ($20 gold coins), worth $30,000, were missing from the main vault. Superintendent Frank Leach, hoping that the shortage would prove to be only an administrative error, delayed for 6 days before he notified George W. Hazen, Agent in Charge of the San Francisco Secret Service office.

In this case Agents Thomas B. Foster and William J. Burns were able to establish that the time lock on the vault had been tampered with to permit the unauthorized opening of the vault by Chief Clerk Walter N. Dimmick, who was arrested, tried, convicted, and sentenced to prison for 5 years.

Perhaps the most sensational theft from the nation's money factories occurred in December 1953, when James Landis, 29, an employee of the Bureau of Engraving and Printing in Washington, carried $128,000 in newly printed $20 bills out of the building, and concealed another $32,000 in the Bureau itself to be taken out on another trip.

Landis' job at the Bureau was to operate a currency-wrapping machine. The new $20 Federal Reserve notes, in bundles of 4,000 bills, held together tightly by flexible steel bands, were sent to his section to be neatly machine-wrapped in heavy brown paper. To each bundle, or "brick," was affixed a label describing the contents, including the serial numbers of the bills. Once wrapped and labeled, the bricks were piled on skids, or wooden platforms, to be carted into the vaults and stored until requisitioned by the Federal Reserve Banks.

Landis plotted long and carefully for his bold thievery. During the weeks before the actual robbery he removed metal bands, paper straps, and small boards (used for stiffening the packages) from waste material at the Bureau and concealed them under his clothing, taking them to his home.

At home he cut a large quantity of plain bond paper into pieces the size of genuine bills, using the blank paper and stolen waste to make up two dummy packages exactly like those in which the $20 bills were wrapped at the Bureau. The plan was simple. He would substitute the dummies for two real packages of $20 notes, worth $160,000. The dummy packages would be stored in the vault, perhaps for weeks, along with many other packages, and when they were finally discovered it would be virtually impossible to identify the thief among the many people who would have had access to the contents. The discovery would undoubtedly not be made until the packages were opened at the Federal Reserve Bank, which would mean that bank employees might also be under suspicion.

On December 30, 1953, at 6 o'clock in the morning, Landis telephoned a friend, Charles H. Nelson, asking him to buy a metal box. He also asked Nelson to invite another friend, Roger C. Patterson, to Nelson's home that night, where Landis would meet them both.

Landis wrapped the two fake bundles together and took the package to the Bureau when he reported for work later that morning. In his pockets were two ordinary paper bags. Under Bureau regulations, employees were not permitted to carry packages to their work areas and were required to check all parcels in a room provided for that purpose in the main building.

Landis carried the wrapped package past the guard at the door and deliberately headed for the parcel booth, ostensibly to check his package. The guard watched him as he approached the checking booth, but turned away to keep an eye on other employees arriving for work. Quickly Landis hurried away from the parcel room, carrying his package to the third floor, where he promptly concealed it under a burlap sack suspended within a large trash can in Locker Room No. 327. He then went to his own locker room, D-101, on the first floor, changed into his work clothes, and reported for duty at his regular hour, 7:30 A.M.

Twenty minutes later he lifted two wrapped bricks, each containing $80,000 in new $20 bills, from a skid parked several feet from the entrance to Vault D-19. He took the bricks to his wrapping machine and bundled them in a 4x5-foot sheet of brown kraft paper, then carried this package to the fifth floor of "A" Wing, which was a section of the Bureau used for dead storage.

There he unwrapped the package, removed the labels bearing the package number and serial numbers, and put the labels in his pocket.

Next he cut the steel bands from the bricks and placed the packages of $20 bills in the two paper bags which he had brought from home. He put $128,000 in one bag and $32,000 in the other, and hid both bags under a pile of material in the dead storage area. He then returned to his post on the currency-wrapping machine on the first floor and stayed there until 10:50 A.M., when he was given a customary 20-minute coffee break.

Landis went to Locker Room 327, soaked the labels off the brown paper with hot water, and dried them on the hot radiator. He took the labels to the trash can where the dummy bricks were concealed, removed the fake packages, and took them into a toilet stall. There he pasted the genuine labels on the ends of the dummy bricks, using glue which he had brought from the wrapping room. With a rubber stamp, purchased especially for the theft, he stamped the labels "HA 12-31-53," to indicate that a Bureau employee with the initials "HA" had machine-wrapped these packages on December 31, 1953.

After covering the two dummy bricks with heavy brown paper, Landis carried them to the first floor and placed them on the storage skid among other packages containing $20 bills, wrapped exactly as the dummies were.

At 3:10 P.M. Landis finished work, changed clothes in his locker room, and went to the dead storage area on the fifth floor where his fortune was hidden. He stuffed a pair of dirty trousers, taken from his locker, on top of the $128,000 in one paper bag, leaving the other bag with the $32,000 under the storage material. Now, with the bag holding the cash and the pants, he went to the first floor prepared to walk out of the building.

At the door the guard pointed at the bag. Calmly, yet breathlessly, Landis opened the bag, pulled the dirty trousers part way out and grinned at the guard, who motioned him to proceed, making way for the scores of other employees quitting for the day. Thus Landis walked out of the Bureau of Engraving and Printing with $128,000 in new $20 bills in a wrinkled brown paper bag.

He went direct to the home of his friend, Charles Nelson, where Nelson and Patterson awaited him as planned. In the bedroom Nelson showed him the green metal box he had bought at Landis' request. Landis took the trousers out of his paper bag, turned the sack upside down over the bed, and laughed as his friends stood goggle-eyed at the cascade of money that tumbled out.

"Where'd you-all get that money?" Nelson asked in awe.

"Man!" Patterson exclaimed, grabbing a package of the notes. "Is it real, man? Is it good?"

"It's plenty good," Landis answered. "Brand new. Just made."

"How'd you do it?" Nelson asked.

"Never you mind," Landis said. "I did it. But now you guys gotta help me. We have to change this for other money."

"How you mean, boy? What we gotta do?"

"Spend it, that's what. Buy stuff in stores and get change." Landis divided 200 of the notes among the trio and told his companions to buy inexpensive merchandise, bringing the change back to Nelson's home, where it would be put in the metal box as a collective pot.

This was one of the most welcome tasks that Nelson and Patterson had ever performed, and they undertook it with gusto. Nelson's first purchase was a half pint of Seagram's VO whisky. Then he hailed a taxicab and rode to the vicinity of Fifteenth and H Streets in Northeast Washington, where he embarked on a huge spending spree, buying more liquor, toilet goods, candy, neckties, shirts, playing cards and poker chips, and other articles.

Nelson finally returned home, his arms filled with packages, his pockets bulging with bills and coins. There he found Landis, Patterson, and a girl, Edith Chase, who knew all three. The proceeds from the spending spree were placed in the metal box, and the men and girl then celebrated by drinking much of the liquor that had been bought with the $20 bills.

When Landis, Patterson, and the Chase girl finally left Nelson's, Landis and Patterson went to a used-car dealer in Hyattsville, Maryland, where Landis bought a 1946 Chevrolet for $375.

The next day, December 31, Nelson and Patterson spent several of the bills until Nelson had more than $100 in small denominations. They went then to another used-car lot, where Nelson bought a 1950 Packard, paying $150 down and owing a balance of $687.

That night they all met again at Nelson's home and put their proceeds in the pot.

The next day (New Year's Day) Landis met another friend, William Giles, who was also a friend of the Chase girl. "Boy," Landis said, "I got enough money to take care of my friends and me for the rest of our lives! Come on. We're going out."

In Nelson's Packard car Landis drove to Brentwood, a Washington suburb, and sent Giles into various liquor stores to buy whisky with the $20 bills.

On January 2 Landis and his mother bought a 1953 Oldsmobile sedan costing $3,200. Landis made a down payment of $1,224.46, including about 100 one-dollar bills and a number of $5, $10, and $20 bills.

Throughout January 2 and 3 Landis and his companions continued to spend the $20 notes. On January 4 Landis reported for work at the Bureau at his regular time, 7:30 A.M. Everything was normal until about

8 o'clock, when another employee, Sewell A. Davis, a stockman, was assigned to transfer bricks of currency from a skid in Vault D-19 to another location.

Davis' method was to pick up one package in each hand simultaneously. As he grabbed two of the bricks he paused for a moment, then "hefted" them carefully, raising and lowering each hand slowly. He glanced at a co-worker, Paul Coakley. "One of these bricks feels light," Davis said. "Does it feel light to you?"

Coakley held the bricks. "Yes, it does," he agreed.

Davis tore open the kraft paper wrapping and was startled to see only blank white paper. Coakley delivered the fake brick to the supervisor of the section and returned to the vault, where still another worker, Frederick A. Minor, had just discovered Landis' second dummy. This was also turned over to the supervisor and the facts were promptly reported to the then Director of the Bureau, Alvin W. Hall. Mr. Hall immediately called Chief U. E. Baughman of the Secret Service.

Agents from the Washington Field Office were dispatched to the Bureau and began to question various employees who would have had access to the money bricks. It was decided to use the polygraph, or lie detector, to interrogate those who did not object to this device, since the machine is used only in questioning those who voluntarily permit it. At quitting time on January 4 the investigators had not yet interrogated James Landis, and he left with others at the customary hour, meeting Giles, who was to drive him home.

The car radio was loud, and Landis turned down the volume. "They found out about the money," Landis said. "We gotta do something and do it fast!"

"How'd they find out?" Giles asked.

"The dummy packages were light." Landis kept pounding one fist into the palm of one hand.

"What we gonna do?"

"We gonna hide the money, that's what."

Before they reached Landis' home they heard a news flash on the radio announcing the theft of $160,000 from the Bureau of Engraving and Printing.

At the Landis apartment they put the remainder of the $20 bills and the other money in a large wooden box, and Landis, Giles, and Landis' wife, Mamie, put the box in the car and drove across the Potomac to Virginia.

"Where we going?" Giles asked.

"To see my wife's father," Landis said. "He'll hide the money for us. Nobody'll ever find it then."

In Fairfax County they stopped at a hardware store and bought a steel strongbox for $7.50 and a 50-cent padlock. At about 9:30 P.M. they arrived at the home of Landis' father-in-law, William I. Grant, who was employed on a private estate near Middleburg.

After some family conversation Landis and Giles went with Mr. Grant into a bedroom, where Landis told Grant about the theft of the $20 bills.

"You shouldn't have done that," Grant said. "You know it wasn't right. You might know they'd catch up with you. You was foolish, boy, plain foolish."

"I ain't so foolish, Pop," Landis said. "I got the money, ain't I?"

"Where is it?"

"Out in the car. And we gonna leave it with you. You gonna hide it for us."

"Oh, no. You don't mix me up in this. Not me!"

"Not for three thousand bucks?"

Grant looked surprised. "Three thousand bucks?"

"That's what you get for hidin' the dough." Landis grinned. "Okay, Pop?"

While Grant hesitated thoughtfully, Landis and Giles brought in the box with the money, and the new strongbox. Landis counted out $3,000 in $5 and $10 bills which he gave to Grant, then the money was all placed in the strongbox which was locked.

"You hide it some place good," Landis said.

Landis, Giles, and Mamie returned to Washington that night.

William Grant must have spent a sleepless and worried night thinking about his daughter and her wayward husband, for he finally sought counsel from his brother-in-law and also from his family physician; and at 5:20 the next morning he telephoned an acquaintance, Trooper S. S. Secrist of the Virginia State Police at Middleburg, asking Secrist to come to his home.

Trooper Secrist learned the whole story from Grant, who turned over the empty wooden box and the strongbox filled with $88,100 in new $20 bills and $4,671.13 in other money.

Secrist took Grant to the Centreville State Police substation and telephoned the Secret Service. Inspector (now Deputy Chief) Russell Daniel and James M. Beary, Special Agent in Charge of the Washington Field Office, sped to the substation, received the boxes, and listened to Grant tell his story.

Rushing back to Washington, the agents promptly arrested Landis at the Bureau of Engraving and Printing. Confronted with the evidence, Landis admitted the theft and led the agents to the place where he had secreted the $32,000 which he had intended to remove from the Bureau at a later date.

In a search of the Landis apartment agents found $1,390 in the pockets of an American Legion uniform coat hanging in a closet, representing some of the proceeds from the spending of the $20 bills.

In rapid succession other agents arrested Edith Chase, Giles, Roger Patterson, and Charles Nelson, all of whom admitted their complicity.

Landis and the other four were arraigned and held for prosecution, but the story was not yet ended. More than 3 months after the arrests Charles Nelson was picked up with a friend, William F. Johnson, on a police charge. Johnson told police that some of the stolen $20 bills might still be hidden in Nelson's home. Detective Earl Huber of Prince George County called the Secret Service and met Agents Daniel O'Driscoll and James Griffith, with whom he then searched Nelson's home.

Hidden in the rafters near some heating pipes, close to the front door, they found a brown paper bag containing packs of the $20 bills, all discolored and stuck together. In bureau drawers in Nelson's bedroom they found other notes in the same condition. In all they seized 266 bills, amounting to $5,320.

Nelson confessed that he had heard a radio flash about Landis' arrest and became panic-stricken. He carried the $20 bills in a paper bag to a swamp in the Maryland suburbs and threw the bag into the deep grass and standing water. It was soon after this that he was first arrested. When he was released on bail he returned to the swamp, recovered the money, and brought it to an abandoned pigsty on a farm owned by his grandfather, where he spread the bills out to dry. He took the bills home on April 12 and his arrest with Johnson followed on April 15.

Some people learn slowly, even from experience. Nelson was arrested again on April 28 for spending more of the stolen $20 bills!

On May 3, 1954 all defendants pleaded guilty in Federal court. Landis was sentenced to serve 3 to 9 years and to pay a $10,000 fine.

Nelson and Giles each drew 2 to 8 years, Nelson to pay a $3,000 fine, Giles $2,000.

Patterson got 20 months to 5 years.

Edith Chase was given a suspended sentence of 1 to 3 years.

William F. Johnson, who was arrested with Nelson in April, pleaded guilty June 9, 1954 to spending one of the $20 bills, knowing it to have been stolen, and was sentenced to serve 180 days and pay a $500 fine.

The Secret Service sent descriptions of the $20 bills to all banks and stores in the Washington area, asking to be notified when any of the notes were detected. As a result the Service received $17,160 from these sources. The money recovered from Grant, the $32,000 hidden at the Bureau, and the sum found in the coat pocket in Landis' closet totaled $127,840. As of December 15, 1954, $15,000 in the new $20 bills was still unaccounted for. They may have been destroyed or may have been hidden by one or more of the group.

The amount of money involved in the robberies of the money factories was insignificant compared to the values represented in an entirely different kind of investigation made by the Secret Service near the turn of this century—values which could not be expressed in dollars and cents, because they involved the lives of scores of unfortunate people thrown into virtual slavery by ruthless and greedy landowners whose tyrannical methods disgraced the United States as a land of liberty. . . .

∘ 8 ∘

Freeing the Peons

A young man is arrested for walking on the grass in a small town. He is unable to pay a fine of 10 dollars. He is taken to a convict camp, thrown into a dark room with 20 other men, a room without ventilation or sanitary facilities, and stinking of human offal. He gets a crust of moldy bread and a tin cup of water. In the morning he is put to work in the sun-baked fields, and when he pauses to wipe the sweat from his face and to say a few words to a fellow worker, one of the armed guards approaches with a shotgun and a whip and lashes the backs of both men until the blood streams to their waists.

It can't happen here? It has happened here!

This or some similar form of peonage was practiced in virtually every State in the Union at the turn of this century.

One dictionary defines *peonage* this way: "The practice of holding persons to work off debts."

The Thirteenth and Fourteenth Amendments to the U.S. Constitution prohibit slavery and "involuntary servitude," and prohibit any State from depriving "any person of life, liberty, or property, without due process of law. . . ."

In his annual report for the year 1904, Secret Service Chief John Wilkie included this brief cryptic statement: "In certain districts of the country there were numerous violations of the Federal laws against peonage, and at the request of the Department of Justice the matter was investigated and several violators were tried and convicted." No other details were given.

The Secret Service archives do not reveal many details of peonage cases, nor could more information be obtained from the archives of the Department of Justice. In the Secret Service files, however, was found an account of a typical peonage case, and although the defendants were subsequently acquitted, the dramatic conditions revealed by the investigation were representative of peonage practices in other places.

The names of individuals in this case are fictitious. The facts are true.

Drew R. Miller of Illinois, 19 years old, lived with a sister in St. Joseph, Missouri, where Drew worked for the railroad. One day he received a letter from a friend in Brownsville, Texas, who was a civil engineer, saying that he could get Drew a better job. The boy started for Brownsville, but by the time he reached Fort Worth he had only a couple of dollars left, and because of his former railroad employment he was able to ride free in the cab of an engine as far as Somerville, a division point. At Somerville the locomotive fireman said he would introduce Drew to the fireman on an outgoing train that would take him on to Brownsville. Since it would be an hour or so before the other train would arrive, Drew walked into the town of Somerville to get something to eat if he could find an open restaurant. It was 2 o'clock in the morning.

A small restaurant was open, and Drew walked in, but before he could order any food a burly man came up to him and said, "Well, young fellow, what are you doing here?"

"I just want to get something to eat."

"You got money to pay for it?"

"I got about two dollars. Why? Who are you, anyway?"

"I'm the law around here, that's who. How'd you get here?"

"On the train."

"Ridin' the rods, huh?"

"No. I rode in the engine cab. I used to work on the railroad."

The big man smiled and nodded. "You come along with me, boy."

"Where to?"

"You'll see. Come along, you hear?"

The man took Drew to a small shack, pushed him into a dark, filthy room, and locked the door. The boy pleaded with him to get the engineer and fireman from the locomotive to prove his story, but the big man merely laughed and walked away.

At 11 o'clock in the morning another man opened the door, put down a bucket of water and two sausages, and locked it again. Drew saw no one else until evening, when the man who arrested him came in with another man. The arresting officer was Walter S. Horton. His companion was introduced as John W. Beech, Justice of the Peace.

Beech asked Drew a few questions—his name, home address, occupation. "You've been arrested for stealing a ride on a train," Beech said. "You're fined twelve dollars. You got twelve dollars, boy?"

"I only got two."

"Then give me the two and you owe ten dollars. You'll have to work it off. Sixty days."

"You can't do this!" Drew said. "I haven't done anything wrong. I got a free ride in the engine and I can prove it. I want a trial."

The men grinned. "You done had your trial," Judge Beech said.

At 5 o'clock the following morning Drew was put in a wagon with another prisoner, a Negro woman, and driven to a plantation 15 miles away. There he was stripped of his good suit of clothes, his heavy underwear, and a nearly new pair of shoes, and was given a pair of thin white cotton pants and a cotton blouse. In place of his Size 7 shoes he was made to wear a pair of Size 11 rough brogans. He was given no underwear, no socks.

When he put on the big shoes he discovered that the insoles were rimmed with protruding rough wooden pegs, intended to hold the soles secure. Strips of thick leather covered the inside backs of the shoes, and within a few days these strips had scraped away the skin above the boy's heels, exposing the raw tendons. He was denied any medical attention.

Drew was put to work in the fields with other prisoners—8 or 10 white boys, a number of Negro men and Negro women. The first evening, dead tired and blistered, he was taken to the prisoners' quarters.

"The building was of frame, about fifty feet long," he said later. "The windows and door were barred. Running down the center were two tiers of bunks, fourteen in all. In this room slept forty to fifty men. In a corner of the room was the place where the prisoners deposited their excrement. It was simply an open hole in the ground and was a place of indescribable filth and stench. In another corner was a faucet where we washed. No soap was allowed."

Supper was generally the same every day—sowbelly, often putrid, and corn bread filled with cornhusks and bugs. Twice a week there were turnip greens boiled with rancid fat pork, and once in a while there were sweet potatoes.

"The coffee came in cakes so hard that a hammer had to be used to break them into bits before boiling." Drew recalled. "It wasn't really coffee. I had never seen anything like it before, and I don't know what it was."

All prisoners ate from tin plates, but were not allowed to have knives, forks, or spoons. The plates were always covered with dirty grease, because it could not be washed off with the cold water.

On his first night at supper one of the armed guards named McNair came up to Drew, carrying his "bat." The "bat" was a broad leather strap about 6 feet long, having one end loaded with lead, the other end cut in narrow strips.

"Where you from, boy?" McNair asked.

"Illinois," Drew said.

The guard sneered. "So you're one of them damyankee sons o' bitches,

are you? Well, I'll just show you what we think of your kind down here."
He lifted the bat and brought the heavy end down between the boy's
shoulder blades, sending him sprawling across the room.

"That was the first and the least of the blows I received," Drew remembered. "Whipping was common, and the guards often lashed the men
and women for their own amusement. I've seen the guards and the superintendent enter the 'hell room' where we slept and call up the men one
by one, whipping 'em with the bat until eight or ten had been beaten.
Some would get fifty to sixty strokes, and blood would flow. When the
superintendent got tired he'd turn the bat over to McNair and he'd lash
until he was tired. If a man didn't keep up with his work in the fields
he was taken out and hit with the bat."

When the guards decided a beating was in order, one guard made the
victim remove his shirt, pull down his trousers, and lie down. Then one
of the heaviest prisoners was made to sit on the man's head and another
on his feet. One guard covered the other prisoners with a revolver while
another did the beating, often lashing the victim into unconsciousness.

One white man who died from such a beating was buried in an un-
marked grave. No one knew his full name.

A Negro prisoner had one of his eyes gouged out by a guard.

"The fields where we worked," Drew reported, "were about five miles
from our quarters. The morning getting-up bell usually rang at three-
thirty and as soon as it was light enough for the guards to count us, we
were made to run to the fields. Men and women had to run the whole five
miles, with the guards on horseback. If anyone fell back from weakness
or exhaustion he was loaded in a wagon, taken back to the camp and
beaten. Young white boys who had never done any manual labor were
forced to keep up with big strong men who were used to digging ditches
or doing other heavy work, and if these kids fell behind they were whipped
unmercifully."

Drew himself received many beatings, with men sitting on his head
and feet, and when he eventually won his freedom and was examined by
physicians he learned that he had suffered injuries to his kidneys which
would remain with him for life.

His heavy brogans cut so deeply into the soles of his feet and his
tendons that he could barely stand, but his complaints only brought more
whippings. Working in his light cotton clothing in the cold February rain
brought on a severe cold that settled in his lungs and deprived him of
his voice.

Wracked with pain, sick, desperate, and helpless, Drew tried writing
letters to his relatives, but learned from other prisoners that the letters
were never mailed. One day he witnessed a scene that gave him new
hope. A prisoner named Everett Strong, a Canadian citizen, told the

superintendent that if he was not released promptly he would see that strong protests were lodged with the State Department by the British Government, and that the superintendent would suffer for holding him unlawfully. He was a British subject, Strong said, and he knew his rights.

Superintendent Bransom decided to release the Canadian, and Drew talked with him before he left the farm. He gave Strong the name and address of his sister, asking him to write to her when he got away.

Strong kept his promise, and Drew's sister wrote to the county judge asking about the amount of Drew's fine that was outstanding. The judge answered that the amount was 9 dollars. She sent the money in a registered letter addressed to her brother, but it was not delivered to him until 2 weeks later, when McNair came to Drew's bunk. The boy had been beaten again and was only half conscious.

"Here, you Yankee sonofabitch," McNair said. "Here's a letter for you. See if there's money in it."

Drew paid the full 9 dollars, though he had worked for 2 weeks after the judge had written to his sister. Originally sentenced to 60 days, 6 months had passed when he was shoved out of the building and walked in excruciating pain to the highway, half a mile away, where he fell to the roadside, too weak to take another step.

A man in a wagon carried him into town. A storekeeper, horrified at Drew's condition, took the boy to his home and summoned a doctor. After a month the youth was able to leave the house, but by that time the townspeople were incensed by his accounts of the inhumane treatment on the plantation. The citizens wrote to the governor, demanding an investigation. The governor sent a brief reply—he was referring the matter to the county judge.

Drew Miller returned to St. Joseph, Missouri, where he became virtually blind and paralyzed as a result of the beatings he had received. It was months before he recovered enough to move about. By then the U.S. Attorney in Kansas City had heard about Drew's experience and had submitted a report to Washington. As a result, two Secret Service agents, J. W. Vann and E. T. Clyatt (their real names) were assigned to conduct an investigation in Texas.

The agents inspected the camp where Drew had been held, questioned the plantation owners, the armed guards, and the prisoners. They discovered that Drew Miller was only one of many hundreds of men and women who had been arrested on slight provocation and thrown into peonage on this and other big Texas farms. From Miller himself they obtained the names of other prisoners who had worked with him on the farm and had later been released. The agents interviewed each of these people, who confirmed Miller's story and also furnished names of others who had been confined and mistreated on the farm.

Vann and Clyatt found that the industrial and agricultural growth of Texas had resulted in labor shortages in many areas. Where men and women, Negro and white, once descended on communities in droves seeking work, planters were now sending representatives into various towns to recruit labor. Conditions had reached the point where landowners were bidding against each other to get help to pick their cotton, for without pickers the cotton crop would be lost.

To ease the labor situation, Texas began to lease convicts to the farmers. Inmates of Huntsville and other penitentiaries were "sold" to owners of cotton and sugar plantations, to mine and factory operators. Careful watch was kept on railroad trains stopping at various points, and any hapless hobo who happened to be riding the rods was grabbed by local constables and whisked away to a convict camp for work in the fields or shops or mines. From their interviews and investigation, the agents estimated that from 1,500 to 2,000 men and women had been kidnaped and thrown into this form of slavery in Texas during the year preceding their inquiry.

The agents arrested Constable Horton, Justice Beech, Superintendent Bransom, and Guard McNair, all of whom were held in $5,000 bail pending the action of the grand jury. The grand jury indicted all four on charges of unlawful holding of persons in condition of peonage and conspiracy. The defendants pleaded not guilty. After a trial lasting about 2 weeks the jury returned a surprising verdict: Not Guilty.

The peonage brought to light in Texas was not restricted to that State. In the New York metropolitan area, scores of newly arrived Irish and Italian immigrants were promised pleasant living and high wages to work in the turpentine camps of Florida. Once in the camps their dreams became nightmares. They worked from dawn till dark, were beaten savagely if they loafed, lived in filthy hovels, were stricken with fever and given little or no medical care, and remained at the mercy of their captors until they escaped or were set free.

A railroad company, building a railroad from the Florida keys to Miami, recruited laborers in New York City. "You will live in a tropical paradise," the men were told. "Every morning you will have bananas and oranges and apples for breakfast. Food is cheap. Clothing is cheap. The weather is always sunny and warm and you will never have to wear overcoats."

When a large group had been recruited they were taken to a train at Jersey City and locked in the cars. Their meals consisted of stale bread and bologna. Arriving in Miami the men were herded off the train at dockside and aboard a boat which took them to the keys. Some who refused to leave the train were forced out by streams of water from fire hoses. Many had never heard about the Florida keys, did not know what they were, never realized that the work was to be done on tiny islands 40, 50, or more miles from the mainland.

Armed guards accompanied the men on the boat, and when one laborer attempted to leap over the side the guards threatened to shoot him or anyone else who tried to jump.

Some of the men were landed on islands which were little more than coral reefs. Others were marched ashore on islands covered with jungle growth and infested with snakes and insects. One man later reported that the cockroaches were larger than his hand.

The company sold the workers their shoes, some of which lasted only a few days before being cut to shreds on the sharp coral. The company also said the men owed for their transportation. All charges were to be "worked out," which meant that the men were captives for weeks or months.

Among the workers were boys in their teens, many of whom were beaten with pick handles when they complained about their treatment. A few men managed to escape on passing banana boats and carried letters from their companions to relatives at home. One youth wrote to his mother: "Dear Mamma—Help me home. I am kept here against my will and I can't get away. There is no road to walk on and I ain't got no money to get away from here, so help me away from here, Mamma, for God's sake send me money." His mother sent him money, but it was never delivered to him.

When the stories about conditions came to light, the 4 men in Brooklyn who operated the recruiting center for the railroad were arrested and prosecuted—but the jury was directed by the Court to return a verdict of Not Guilty.

Some of the most dramatic peonage cases developed in Alabama. In the early 1900's there were some 2,500 justices of the peace in Alabama who could impose fines or prison sentences (of one year or less) for such offenses as vagrancy, drunkenness, petty larcency, and other minor violations of law. In addition there were some 700 notaries public who acted as ex-officio justices of the peace, and more than 1,600 special constables.

Men and women were frequently arrested for petty offenses, were fined and sentenced to months at hard labor—and consequently vanished, for the justices of the peace were not required to make any report to any State or other official about such arrests or sentences.

In one peonage case a Negro convicted of larceny was sentenced to serve 12 months on a chain gang. The prisoner was delivered to a convict work camp by the county attorney, who received a hundred dollars in cash from the private contractor for whom the prisoner would work. A few months later the authorities discovered that the man had not committed the crime for which he was now doing hard labor. The judge and jury who had sent him away petitioned the governor to set him free, but the county attorney refused to sign the petition because he had divided his hundred dollars with other county officials and did not want to refund the money. The prisoner was eventually freed.

Not all the peonage took place in the South. It existed in most States, including those in New England. Thanks partly to the Secret Service and partly to the widespread publicity given to peonage cases in the South, the abuses declined noticeably in that area of the country. In 1910, however, the U.S. Immigration Commission, following an intensive inquiry, issued a report which included this statement:

"Since the evils of involuntary servitude have been largely stamped out in the Southern states, there has probably existed in Maine the most complete system of peonage in the entire country. In late years the natives who formerly supplied the labor for the logging concerns in that State have been compelled to import laborers, largely foreigners, from other States. Boston is the chief labor market for the Maine forests. The employment agents misrepresent conditions in the woods and frequently tell laborers that the camps will be but a few miles from some town where they can go for recreation and enjoyment. Arriving at the outskirts of civilization the laborers are driven in wagons a short distance into the forests and then have to walk sometimes 60 or 70 miles into the interior, the roads being impassable for vehicles. The men will then be kept in the heart of the forest for months throughout the winter, living in most rugged fashion with no recreation whatever. Many have rebelled against this treatment and have left their employers by the score."

The people who made peons of the poverty-stricken, the illiterates, the immigrants, were a disgrace to the freedom-loving people of the United States, but no more disgraceful, and perhaps less so, than many rich, shrewd, and influential citizens who sought to rob the Federal Government by stealing public lands and natural resources in the great and untamed West.

For effectively spiking these unprecedented land grabs and exposing people in high places, the U.S. Secret Service was to suffer one of the most severe and unfair blows in its entire history.

° 9 °

The Land Thieves

November 3, 1907 was a fateful day for four men who trudged into Dead Man's Gulch, about 4 miles from Hesperus, Colorado. One would never come out alive, and the other three were marked for death.

It was also a day that would add another act to a drama that was to strike a blow at the Secret Service from which it has never recovered.

The four men were Joseph A. Walker, in charge of the Denver District of the Secret Service; Agent Thomas J. Callaghan; an experienced prospector and miner named Tom Harper; and John E. Chapson, a civil engineer employed by the Department of the Interior.

They were there primarily because President Theodore Roosevelt had received reports that thousands, perhaps millions, of acres of government-owned land in the West were being stolen and misused. Coal and lumber companies were bribing war veterans and others to file claims for homesteads, which would require that the homesteaders build houses and cultivate the land. Instead, when the claimants received their ownership papers, the coal and timber interests paid them off, grabbed the land and denuded it of its big trees, or sunk shafts to dig coal. When these reports reached President Roosevelt, an ardent conservationist, he ordered a thorough investigation by the Secret Service.

The case near Hesperus, Colorado, was only one phase of this investigation, and it involved activities of the Porter Fuel Company, one of the largest coal-mining interests in that section of the country.

The company's main works were located near Hesperus, some 17 miles from Durango. During a recent prospecting trip, Tom Harper had noticed what seemed to be an air shaft on land which had been claimed as a homestead by William R. Mason, superintendent of the Porter Fuel Company's Hesperus Mine. Harper had reported his discovery to Agent in Charge Walker, and Walker had decided to learn why an air shaft should be sunk on homesteaded property.

Agent Walker, elderly and asthmatic, rode horseback while his companions walked the trail. The men reached Dead Man's Gulch and the shaft about 10:30 A.M. They peered down into the opening, then lowered a rope to the bottom and measured the depth. The shaft was perhaps 4 feet square and 65 feet deep, lined with heavy logs. The men decided to climb down and investigate further. Agent Walker, in deference to his years and his asthma, was appointed to remain topside as a lookout and to help pull the others up when their inspection was completed.

Before descending, Tom Harper lowered a lighted candle to the bottom of the shaft to make sure that the air was not foul. Satisfied, the men lifted a single log across the top of the opening and tied the rope to it, then Callaghan, Harper, and Chapson lowered themselves down the rope, hand over hand.

At the bottom, in the flickering flames of their candles, they saw an opening, or tunnel, about 3 feet high. On hands and knees the trio crawled into the dark hole. After proceeding for some 25 or 30 feet they suddenly found themselves "in the main workings of a large coal mine." The mine was now deserted, but it was rich in coal and it was evident that Superintendent Mason, the "homesteader," was not interested in raising vegetables as required by the terms of his claim. Plainly, the coal was being dug out of the Government land and taken to the Hesperus Mine, which adjoined Mason's homestead.

John Chapson, the engineer, took careful measurements of the size of the "room" of coal, and about a half hour later the three men crawled back through the small tunnel to the bottom of the shaft. Callaghan was the first through. In the candle flicker he was startled to see a tangle of rope on the shaft floor. He grabbed it as the others came out of the tunnel. "Hey, look!" he exclaimed. "Our rope's been cut!"

Quickly they all glanced upward. They could see only a few slivers of sunlight. The top of the shaft had been covered over.

"Hey, Joe!" Harper shouted. "Joe Walker!"

The others joined in. "Joe! Joe!" Their cries echoed as in a tomb, and brought no response from Agent Walker.

"Something's happened to him," Harper said. "We've got to get out of here."

"Sure," Callaghan said, "but how?"

Harper looked up at the shaft. "I think I could climb those log walls."

"I don't know," Chapson put in. "The logs are pretty round. They'll be slippery."

"We could draw straws to see who tries it," Callaghan suggested.

Harper grinned. "You ever climbed a shaft before, son?"

"No, but—"

"Have you, Chapson?"

"No."

"All right, then. This won't be the first time for me. And my chances of getting to the top are better than both of yours."

"There's something we ought to do before you go up," Chapson said.

"What's that?"

"Well, we can't be sure we're getting out of here. And if we do get out, we don't know what's waiting for us up there. I think we ought to write a report of what we found and what happened down here. If anything happens to us, maybe somebody will find it."

"Good idea," Callaghan said.

Using Callaghan's notebook and papers on which Chapson had noted measurements of the mine, Chapson wrote by candlelight their collective version of the drama and concealed the report beneath his undershirt. "I guess we're ready," he said. "Take this." He handed Harper a tapeline that he had used for measurements. "You can lower it from the top, and we'll tie the rope to it."

Harper, who was about 6 feet tall, weighing around 200 pounds, was boosted up by Callaghan and Chapson. Bracing his strong arm against one wall, his feet against the other, he began the climb. When he had gone about 15 feet he suddenly slipped and went crashing to the bottom. The others rushed to help him.

"I'm all right," he said.

"Let me try it," Callaghan said.

"Not yet. I'll make it. Give me another boost."

Again he started up the shaft. This time he climbed only 10 or 12 feet before he slipped and thudded to the ground. His face was scratched and bleeding.

"Look," Callaghan said. "I'm smaller and lighter than you are. Let me try."

Harper grinned. "Three times and out, kid," he said. "If I don't make it on this try, it's your turn."

Slowly, carefully, the big man pushed himself up the log walls inch by inch—20 feet, 30, 40. Callaghan and Chapson could hear him puffing and grunting, though they could not see him clearly in the dark shaft.

"I don't think I can make it, boys," Harper called from the darkness. "I don't think I can make another damned inch."

"Yes you can, Tom," Chapson answered. "You're almost there, fella. You're doing fine, just fine!"

A fall now might mean Harper's death.

"Keep it up," Callaghan called. He glanced at Chapson, and the look in their eyes needed no words to show their concern.

Once more they could hear Harper's heavy boots scraping the logs. His progress was slow, and the men watched tensely for half an hour or more before they suddenly saw daylight as Harper pushed aside some of the covering from the top of the shaft. They cheered as they saw him climb into the open. Within a few moments Harper lowered the tapeline. They tied it to the rope, which he then hauled up, and with the rope Callaghan and Chapson were brought out.

The top of the shaft had been covered over with logs, sticks, and heavy brush. Joe Walker's horse was tethered nearby.

"Where's Joe?" Callaghan asked.

"I don't know," Harper said. "Let's look around."

A few feet from the shaft opening, in the brush, they came upon the dead body of Joe Walker, his back and side riddled with bullet holes which Callaghan counted. "Seventeen holes in the back," he said. "A shotgun." Walker's revolver, still holstered, had not been fired.

Chapson suggested to Callaghan, "You'd better take his horse, ride into Durango, and notify the sheriff. We'll wait here."

On the way to Durango, Callaghan met two men in a buggy on the main road, about 5 miles from the shaft. When he saw that one of the men carried a shotgun, he ordered them to halt and identified himself. "Who are you?" he asked.

The men gave their names—William R. Mason, superintendent of the Porter Fuel Company, and Joseph Vanderweide, a mine employee.

"What are you doing with that shotgun?" Callaghan asked.

"This? Uh—hunting rabbits, that's all," Vanderweide said. "Why? What business is it of yours?"

"You'll find out," Callaghan said. "Let me have that gun, and you drive that rig into Durango. I want to ask you a few questions."

About 5 miles outside Durango they met the sheriff and the county coroner heading for Hesperus. "We got an anonymous report that a man had been murdered by these guys," the sheriff told Callaghan, pointing at Vanderweide and Mason. "We were just going out to investigate."

Vanderweide and Mason were formally arrested and lodged in the county jail in Durango. At first they denied knowledge of Walker's killing. Then Vanderweide claimed that he and Mason were out rabbit hunting and had discovered Walker sitting near the shaft on Mason's homestead. According to Vanderweide, Walker had threatened them with his revolver, an argument followed, and Vanderweide shot Walker with both barrels of the shotgun at a distance of about 10 feet. They stuck to the story despite the fact that Walker was shot in the back.

The State of Colorado claimed priority in the case and indicted Vanderweide and Mason for first-degree murder. They were tried in State Court at Durango. The jury, after deliberating for only 20 minutes, returned a verdict of not guilty!

In a report of the trial, Agent Callaghan included this significant comment: "The acquittal was no doubt due to the intense feeling against all Government agents in that region at the time, caused by the scores of indictments which had been returned by the Government against individuals who had been used as dummies by the big lumber and coal companies in the filing of false claims."

Callaghan also had this to say: "It was afterwards learned from a confidential source close to William R. Mason that their purpose in dropping the rope to the bottom of the shaft and making us prisoners was to keep us there until they could return to Hesperus, procure some dynamite, and return to blow up the shaft, obliterating all traces of Harper, Chapson, and myself, and claiming that whoever had descended the shaft had encountered a gas pocket which, through carelessness, was exploded by candles. The party furnishing this information refused to testify in court."

Following the acquittal, Mason and Vanderweide were rearrested outside the courtroom by U.S. Marshals and held for a Federal grand jury on a charge of conspiring to interfere with the rights of a citizen, there being no statute at that time covering assault on or murder of a Government agent. The two were tried in Federal Court at Pueblo, Colorado, where the defense counsel pleaded double jeopardy, arguing that no evidence used in the State's murder trial could be introduced in the Federal case. The motion was sustained by the Court, and the Government was compelled to dismiss its case.

The same judge whose ruling set the killers free later dismissed 1,400 indictments against offenders who had filed false claims to defraud the Government.

The Vanderweide-Mason case was but one in a long line of land fraud investigations. The Homestead Act, passed in 1862, threw public lands open to entry, and although many families braved the wilderness to establish homes and farms, greedy men stripped the forests, wasted oil and coal, and took possession of public water-power sites for private use. Cattle barons, through dummy claimants, turned their herds loose to graze on lands intended to be farmed.

In 1891 Congress authorized the President to withhold timberlands from entry, which helped to save some of the great forests.

Wholesale abuses continued until Theodore Roosevelt decided to crack down. Secret Service agents were sent into Colorado, Wyoming, Utah, Montana, New Mexico, Idaho, and Nebraska to expose the frauds and recover huge areas of stolen lands.

The agents were seriously handicapped by the fact that these states were only sparsely settled, and much of the land under investigation was owned or controlled by wealthy and powerful interests—railroad tycoons, cattle barons, mine owners, lumbermen—many acting in concert with influential public officials, both Federal and State. In other words, the principal offenders were the men who controlled the ranches and industries in the affected states.

Veterans of the Civil War and the Spanish-American War, and widows of such veterans, were paid expenses plus $50 to $100 to file homestead claims for land which they then turned over to the wealthy conspirators. In one case Agent Lucien Wheeler donned old clothes and ambled into a big ranch at Ellsworth, Nebraska, that was allegedly acquired by fraud. He sought out the ranch foreman, Charles C. Jamison.

"I'm broke," Wheeler told him. "I was put off the train in Ellsworth. I understand I might make a little money by filing a homestead claim and turning the land over to you."

Jamison shook his head. "Not right now," he said. "The Government is after us. Later, maybe. Sorry."

The outstanding Nebraska land fraud case involved Bartlett Richards and William G. Comstock, rich cattlemen whose holdings covered about 176,000 acres (275 square miles), all acquired through dummy entrymen. To get the land these men had sent agents through the Middle West to find 40 or 50 people who had never exercised their rights to apply for homesteads. Once assembled, these potential homesteaders were placed aboard a chartered railroad car and taken to the Land Office at Broken Bow, Nebraska, to file on the land desired by Comstock and Richards. As soon as title was granted, the land was deeded to the cattlemen, the claimants were paid off and sent home.

The Secret Service dug up strong evidence to prove these charges and arrested Comstock and Richards, who were brought to trial in Omaha, but only on a charge of subornation of perjury. The trial lasted 2 weeks. The verdict: Guilty. The sentence: Ten hours to be served in the custody of the U.S. Marshal.

Comstock and Richards, with the U.S. Marshal and the U.S. Attorney who prosecuted the case, immediately "served" their sentence in the swank Omaha Club. A week later, after a report of the incident reached President Roosevelt, he fired the prosecutor and the marshal.

The Secret Service, in co-operation with the General Land Office, succeeded in uncovering other land frauds in Nebraska, and in recovering more than a million acres of stolen land in that state alone.

In Idaho the trail led to prominent and powerful politicians and involved jury bribes and prejudiced jurors. The prominence of the landholders did not frighten the Secret Service men, and one of the people they indicted and prosecuted was a U.S. Senator, together with 10 other defendants, including a former Governor of Idaho. The Senator was tried in October 1907, in Boise, Idaho, for conspiring to defraud the Government of valuable timberlands. The jury deliberated for only 10 minutes, then acquitted the Senator.

In Oregon another Senator and a Congressman were prosecuted.

The power and influence of the landgrabbers in the various states was soon felt in Washington itself, where Congress raised the cry that the Secret Service was investigating matters that were no business of the Treasury Department. The legislators suggested strongly that the Secret Service should not be investigating members of Congress, that its agents should be restricted to work which related only to the Treasury, and that action be taken to prevent other departments of the Government from borrowing Secret Service men from the Treasury to conduct all kinds of investigations.

President Roosevelt thoroughly disagreed and delivered a long and forceful message to Congress in defense and in behalf of the Secret Service and its fearless and impartial enforcement of the law. In part he said:

> The chief argument in favor of the provision (to restrict the work of the Secret Service) was that the Congressmen did not themselves wish to be investigated by Secret Service men. Very little of such investigation has been done in the past; but it is true that the work of the Secret Service agents was partly responsible for the indictment and conviction of a Senator and a Congressman for land frauds in Oregon. I do not believe that it is in the public interest to protect criminals in any branch of public service, and exactly as we have again and again during the past seven years prosecuted and convicted such criminals who were in the Executive Branch of the government, so in my belief we should be given ample means to prosecute them if found in the Legislative Branch. But if this is not considered desirable a special exception could be made in the law prohibiting the use of the Secret Service force in investigating members of the Congress. It would be far better to do this than to do what actually was done and strive to prevent, or at least to hamper, executive action against criminals by the Executive Branch of the government.
>
> . . . I must honestly ask, in the name of good government and decent administration in the name of honesty and for the purpose of bringing to justice violators of the Federal laws wherever they may be found, whether in public or private life, that the action taken by the House last year be reversed.

Congress disregarded the President's appeal and curtailed the activities of the Secret Service by providing in its appropriation act that no funds allotted for the work of the Service could be used except in connection with the suppression of counterfeiting and other matters relating to the Treasury Department. All investigations of the Western land frauds by the Secret Service were discontinued immediately.

The President sought a new way to utilize the services of the experienced investigators of the Secret Service to investigate matters that were not related to the Treasury Department. At his instigation 8 Secret Service agents—George M. Kennoch, Irving Sauter, George Kraft, Louis P. Elsmere, Charles Dolan, Frank Wallace, Edward Chaims, and Edward J. Brennan—were officially transferred to the Department of Justice on July 1, 1908, forming the nucleus of an investigating force that, years later, was to become the Federal Bureau of Investigation (FBI).

The ban on the jurisdiction of the Secret Service still stands—but in 1915, with a war raging in Europe and with German spies and saboteurs plotting to violate the neutrality of the United States, President Woodrow Wilson saw fit to lift the restriction temporarily and to call on the Secret Service to undertake a difficult task. Its outcome was to startle the nation and the world.

$$\circ \ 10 \ \circ$$

The Brown Leather Bag

In 1914 a war flared in Europe, a struggle that was to embroil many nations in what history now calls the First World War. The United States, not yet involved, sought to mind its own business, and President Woodrow Wilson issued a proclamation of neutrality which included this statement: "No person within the territory and jurisdiction of the United States shall take part, directly or indirectly, in said wars, but shall remain at peace with all the said belligerents and shall maintain a strict and impartial neutrality."

As a neutral power the United States continued its commerce with both Germany and the Allies, a policy sanctioned by historical tradition and international law. America had every right to sell goods to any and all purchasers on a cash-and-carry basis, including munitions and other war matériel.

Among the belligerent powers, Great Britain and France controlled the seas, and since Germany herself could not obtain war goods in the United States and get many of them past the fleets of her enemies, the Germans sought desperately to prevent her opponents from replenishing their own stockpiles from American sources. There were two ways to attack this problem—sabotage and propaganda in the United States.

It was evident that both methods were being used soon after President Wilson's proclamation was made. Stories in certain magazines and newspapers sought to gain the sympathy of the American people for the German cause. Labor strikes were called in factories producing the goods of war. Subtle efforts were made to spark new legislation that would be beneficial to the Fatherland. The phantom offensive was taking effect, and the Allies were beginning to realize it. So was Woodrow Wilson.

It was obvious to the President and others that the neutrality of the United States was being violated. The necessity for counteraction and

The Chiefs of the United States Secret Service, 1865 to date.

Chief Baughman congratulates Historian Walter S. Bowen (*right;* co-author of this book) on his retirement after forty years in the Service. (*Photo, Tom White, U.S.S.S.*)

Chief Baughman (*left*) presents a gold Secret Service badge to Retiring Assistant Chief Harry Edward Neal (co-author of this book). Secretary of Treasury George Humphrey is on the right. The gold Secret Service badge is held by only four or five others, one of whom is the President. (*Photo, Tom White, U.S.S.S.*)

Bomb carrier developed by the Secret Service to transport bombs and explosives with maximum safety.

All Secret Service agents are expert in the use of all types of firearms. Here some of them are at target practice

All U.S. paper money is made at the Bureau of Engraving and Printing in Washington, D.C., where a skilled engraver is shown at work.

In the Bureau of Engraving and Printing new counterfeit bills are analyzed for the Secret Service.

Principals in the Philadelphia-Lancaster Counterfeiting Conspiracy.

Chief Baughman, through the barred window of his office, can keep an eye on the White House.

Agent Frank Burke (deceased) who seized the plot-packed briefcase from Dr. Heinrich Albert, described in Chapter 10, is shown on the day he retired, shaking hands with Secret Service Chief Frank J. Wilson.

Agent William H. Houghton (later placed in charge of the New York District), who took a major part in the Teapot Dome investigation (see Chapter 11).

Secret Service Agent Myles McCahill (in straw hat) is vigilant as President Wilson decorates an American soldier's grave on Memorial Day, 1919, at Suresnes near Paris, France.

(*Above*) At Casablanca during World War II, President Roosevelt dines with Harry Hopkins (hatless) and Generals Mark Clark (*left*) and George Patton (*right*). The three watchful jacketed men standing nearby are Agents Beary, Deckard, and Rowley.

(*Below*) On July 16, 1951, President Truman signs the bill defining the powers and duties of the U.S. Secret Service. Standing, left to right: E. H. Foley, Under-Secretary of the Treasury; Don Hansen, Assistant to General Counsel of the Treasury; U. E. Baughman, Chief, U.S. Secret Service; Harry E. Neal, the Assistant Chief of the Service; James J. Rowley and Gerald Behn, Special Secret Service Agents in charge of the White House Detail. Seated with President Truman is Secretary John Snyder.

Composite enlargements of Washington and Lincoln portraits from (*right side*) genuine and (*left side*) counterfeit bills.

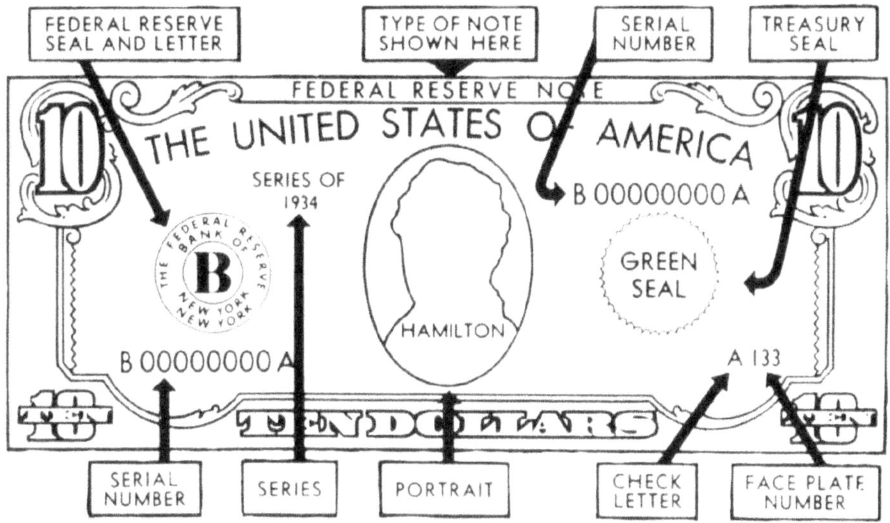

Diagram of a $10 Federal Reserve note showing the important features of paper money.

WARNING: DO NOT CASH A CHECK UNLESS ENDORSED IN YOUR PRESENCE! KNOW THE ENDORSER!

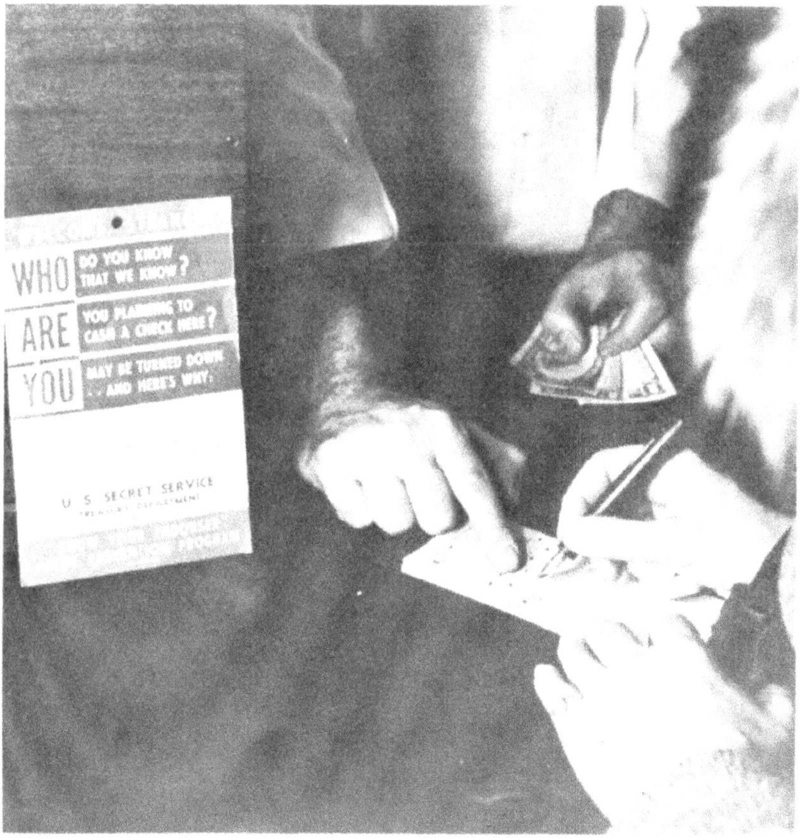

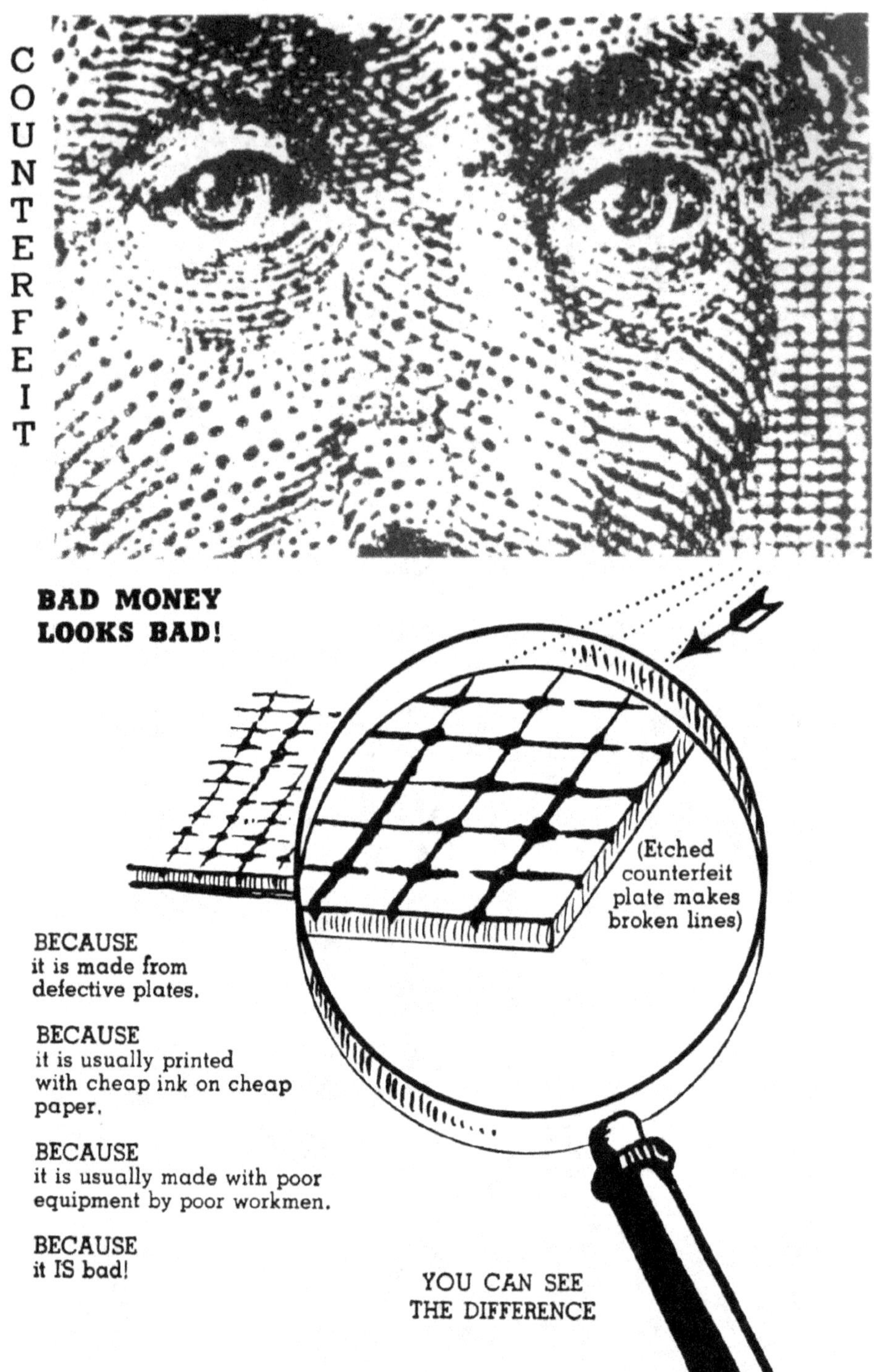

Enlargement of part of the Lincoln portrait from a counterfeit five-dollar bill.

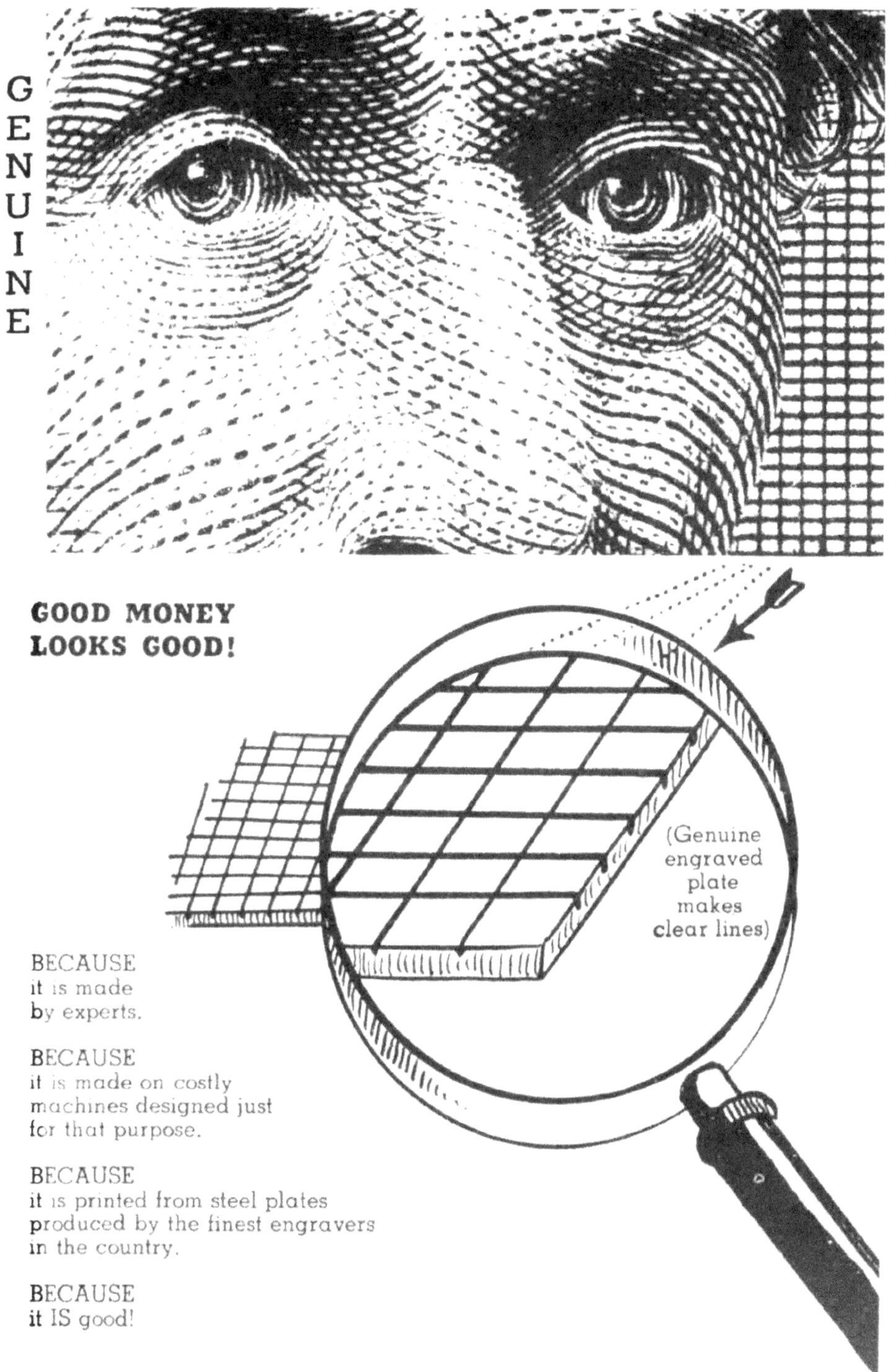

Enlargement of part of the Lincoln portrait from a genuine five-dollar bill.

The U.S. Secret Service Chief rides in the lead car of a Presidential procession, flying the Stars and Stripes and the Secret Service flag. Four agents of the Service walk at the four corners of the President's car with its Presidential flag.

At President Eisenhower's Inaugural Parade, January 21, 1957, his car is protected at the four corners by vigilant Secret Service agents. Other agents walk and ride directly behind.

for suppression of the underhanded activities grew to such proportions that Wilson lifted the Congressional restrictions on the Secret Service and ordered Secretary of the Treasury William Gibbs McAdoo to send Secret Service agents into action against the plotters.

William J. Flynn, then Chief of the Service, promptly established a Counterespionage Unit in New York, headed by Agent Frank Burke and staffed by ten carefully picked investigators. Burke was rather short and stocky, with light brown hair parted in the middle, and wore spectacles which rimmed Irish eyes that could twinkle or drill, as occasion demanded. He was shrewd, bold, and fearless, and completely dedicated to his job.

Chief Flynn also assigned agents to maintain surveillance over the German Embassy, a palatial red-brick mansion on Massachusetts Avenue near Thomas Circle in Washington, and to shadow certain Embassy officials and visitors, including Capt. Franz von Papen, the German military attaché.

In New York City, one prominent German under surveillance was George Sylvester Viereck, editor of a periodical called *The Fatherland.* Although no direct suspicions centered on Viereck, he was shadowed in the belief that persons active in espionage and propaganda might visit or associate with him, thus providing leads for further Secret Service investigation.

On Saturday, July 24, 1915, Agent Frank Burke sat in his shirt sleeves writing a daily report at his desk on the top floor of the Customhouse Building at the Battery. From the windows he could look across the shimmering harbor at the Statue of Liberty and Staten Island. Haze misted the docks and smokestacks on the New Jersey shore, for it was a hot, humid, lazy day, a good day to be off the baking concrete streets. Burke, however, was not destined to enjoy the slight breeze that wafted in from the harbor, for a telephone call sent him out on an assignment that was to make history.

The call came from another Secret Service agent, William H. Houghton, whose job it was to keep Viereck under surveillance. Houghton, like Burke, feared nothing and was devoted to law enforcement. Of medium height, he had sandy hair, a small sandy mustache, and a quiet manner that left him unruffled in many a tight situation during his thirty-odd years in the Secret Service.

Houghton reported that he had followed Viereck to the building at 45 Broadway and suggested that Burke join him there in case Viereck emerged with other persons. The building at 45 Broadway was at that time owned and occupied by the Hamburg-American Steamship Line, and it would have been unwise for the Secret Service to make guarded inquiries about any of the building's occupants.

Burke joined Houghton immediately, and the pair kept watch on the building entrance. Since it was Saturday afternoon, lower Broadway was virtually deserted and the sun-roasted streets were as quiet as a beckoning finger. At 3 o'clock Viereck came out with another man who carried a slightly bulging brown leather brief case.

Viereck's companion was about 50 years old, tall and slender, with close-cropped graying hair. His cheeks were branded with old dueling scars worn proudly as evidence of his youthful years at Heidelberg, and he walked stiffly and ramrod-straight in the haughty manner of the Prussian aristocracy.

It would make a better story to say that this stranger had earlier been identified as an important cog in the German propaganda machine and that the Secret Service had been on his trail for weeks. The truth is, however, that neither Burke nor Houghton had ever seen him before, did not know who he was, and had no knowledge of his importance or of his relationship with Viereck or others. Only after the dramatic adventure that was just beginning did they discover that this man was Dr. Heinrich Friedrich Albert, Privy Councillor of the German Government, who had entered the United States officially as a commercial attaché of the Germany Embassy.

Dr. Albert and Viereck walked to the Rector Street elevated station and boarded a Sixth Avenue train bound for Harlem. Burke and Houghton boarded the same train. The Germans sat together on a cross-seat in the center of the car. Houghton took a cross-seat directly opposite, and Burke sat down immediately behind Viereck and Albert. Albert held his brown bag in his lap. Burke tried to listen to their conversation above the rumble of the train, but they spoke in German, which he could not understand.

When the train halted at the 23rd Street Station, Viereck said good-by to Dr. Albert and left the car, followed by Agent Houghton. Burke remained to keep an eye on Albert.

Just before the car doors closed at the 23rd Street Station a young lady stepped aboard and sat down in the seat vacated by Viereck, next to Dr. Albert, who was closest to the window. She carried a book which she promptly opened and began to read.

Apparently Albert was en route to his living quarters at the German Club, located at 59th Street and Central Park. To get there it was necessary for him to leave the Harlem train at 50th Street and take a shuttle train that ran between 50th and 59th Streets. As they rode, Burke noticed that Albert removed the brief case from his lap and placed it on the seat between his body and the window side of the car. The German then took a paper from his coat pocket and began to read.

As the train pulled into the 50th Street Station the doctor was still reading, and he seemed oblivious to the fact that the train had stopped. Just as it was about ready to move, he glanced out of the window, saw the station sign, and realized that this was where he wanted to get off. He sprang out of the seat and shouted at the train guard, "Wait! Wait! I get off here! I get off!"

As he dashed frantically toward the door, the girl who had sat beside him called out, "Hey, wait! You forgot your brief case."

Evidently Albert did not hear her, for he ran out of the door and was on the station platform before he suddenly halted and turned, an expression of great anxiety on his face. In that instant Burke made a fateful decision. He reached over the back of the seat and seized the brief case.

"That's mine!" he said to the startled girl. With the case, Burke headed for the door at the front end of the car, noting that Albert was trying to re-enter the car through the rear door. Albert, it seemed, was having some difficulty, for his path was barred by a very fat woman who stood in the doorway asking a question of the train guard, and the German was making a desperate effort to push past her. When finally he succeeded and rushed to his former seat, the girl with the book pointed at the seat in back and said, "The man who was sitting there took the brief case. He went out the other door."

Several other passengers had alighted from the train, and Burke made himself as inconspicuous as possible by mingling with them. He saw Albert "come tearing out in a hurry, greatly disturbed." The doctor was between Burke and the exit stairway, and Burke knew it would be folly to make a break for the street at that moment. Instead, he walked calmly to the station wall, stuck a cigar in his mouth and pretended to light it, blowing out one match after another as though the wind were the culprit. With his body he held the precious brief case tight against the wall, partly covered by his coat. The train rumbled out of the station.

Albert glanced hurriedly at all the people on the platform, then whirled and rushed down the stairs to the street. There was no other train in sight which Burke might board, and he figured that it would be disastrous to wait on the platform any longer, so he walked rapidly to the stairway and descended to the sidewalk below.

On the street Burke saw Dr. Albert "with panic on his face," looking at pedestrians in all directions. Suddenly the German saw Burke and the brief case. He let out a wild yell and dashed in Burke's direction.

Again Burke made a split-second decision. A Sixth Avenue trolley car was approaching, headed uptown. It was one of the so-called "open" cars then popular, a car with running boards on each side and open seats extending the entire width of the vehicle. Burke ran and jumped on the running board of the moving car, near the conductor. Albert was racing to catch up, shaking a clenched fist and screaming at the top of his lungs.

"See that man?" Burke said to the conductor. "He's crazy—stark, raving mad! He's just stirred up a lot of trouble on the elevated station and if he gets aboard this car you're going to have more headaches than you can handle."

The conductor took one good look at the wild-eyed, fist-shaking, shouting Dr. Albert and decided that Burke was telling the truth. He called loudly to the motorman, "Hey, Joe, step on it! Don't stop, Joe —don't stop!"

The motorman looked back, saw the frantic Albert, nodded and speeded up the car, which soon outdistanced the doctor and turned west on 53rd Street.

At Eighth Avenue and 53rd Street Burke hopped off and boarded a downtown trolley, riding "as far as the carbarns a few blocks down, where the car stopped for an unusually long time." Burke alighted and went to a nearby drugstore, where he telephoned Chief Flynn, then in New York, and told him what had happened.

"Don't move, Frank," Flynn ordered. "You stay put in that store until I get there."

Flynn drove to the store in his car, picked up Burke and the brief case, and went to the Secret Service office in the Customhouse Building. Together they opened the bag and made a cursory examination of its contents—cursory, because virtually all the documents it contained were in German, which they could not read. It seemed obvious, however, that the papers were of vital importance, and Chief Flynn promptly telephoned Secretary McAdoo, then on vacation at North Haven, Maine. McAdoo requested that the case and its contents be brought to him immediately.

Meantime, agents reported that there was consternation in the German Embassy in Washington, and also at 45 Broadway, New York. Apparently the Germans suspected that a British spy had seized the brief case, but they had a weak hope that it had been stolen by an ordinary sneak thief, because on the following Monday, July 26, a pathetic little advertisement appeared in the New York *Evening Telegraph:*

> LOST: On Saturday, on 3:30 Harlem Elevated train, at 50th Street Station, brown leather bag, containing documents. Deliver to G. W. Hoffman, 5 East 47th Street, against $20 reward.

When Flynn and Burke delivered the brief case to Secretary McAdoo, he was stunned when a translation of the German documents provided incredible revelations of the vast and bold operations of the German propaganda and sabotage machine.

There was indisputable evidence that Albert was the top financial agent of the Imperial German Empire in the United States—and a total of $27 million had been deposited in various American banks for his use. The doctor, it appeared, had been spending about $2 million a week to buy sabotage and propaganda.

Plans and correspondence showed that Albert and his spies had incited strikes of longshoremen, of munitions workers, and of employees of other plants manufacturing goods of strategic importance to the Allies. The strikes were engineered by Capt. Franz von Papen, the German military attaché, with the co-operation of certain labor leaders.

In one case Albert, through dummy purchasers, had actually bought a Bridgeport, Connecticut, munitions plant which made artillery shells that were sold to the British and the Russians. The company proposed to accept orders for the ammunition, but never to make shipment, or to furnish defective shells that would be useless against the Germans.

Albert's plans called for his purchase of American newspapers and magazines, through which he proposed to influence public opinion in favor of his government. He invaded the Chautauqua Circuit with professional propaganda literature, and financed motion pictures with a pro-German slant.

A movement was under way whereby the Germans, through Albert and Von Papen, would corner the supply of liquid chlorine, used for poison gas warfare, and would also attempt to acquire the Wright Airplane Company and its aircraft patents. Another organized movement was designed to deprive England of her supply of cotton from American sources.

One of the most audacious of Albert's plans revealed that the Kaiser and the German General Staff intended not only to drive the United States into the European war, but also to invade this country. In actively prosecuting this aim, Albert had personally prepared a gigantic plan for the military occupation of the United States. Briefly, some 85,000 German soldiers were to be landed suddenly on the New Jersey coast, out of reach of any of our coast protective facilities. The landing was to be directed and protected by the German Navy, and was to be so co-ordinated that the United States would have no fleet in the vicinity strong enough to resist the invasion at that time.

The plan included detailed statistics showing that it was necessary for New York City to replenish its food supplies about every 5 days. The invading Germans were to cut off New York from the rest of the country within 24 hours, to starve the metropolis into submission; then, with 75 per cent of the wealth of the entire nation concentrated in New York, and to be captured by the Germans, this occupation would cripple all effective resistance. The first invasion wave would be promptly reinforced by a second, and the plan presupposed that the United States could thus be brought to its knees within a reasonably short time.

Accurate and abundant information regarding U.S. coastal defenses was among Albert's papers, including maps of defense stations and strategic military positions along the entire east coast.

The contents of the brief case also disclosed that top officials of the Kaiser's government, supposedly friendly toward the United States, were actively supporting the intrigue. No less a person than Theobald von Bethmann-Hollweg, Chancellor of the German Empire, was among the plotters—the same Bethmann-Hollweg who won dubious fame in 1914 by declaring that the German guarantee of Belgium's neutrality was nothing but "a scrap of paper."

Another discovery unearthed in the brown leather bag was an official and secret German code which was of tremendous value to the United States. Among other documents which the U.S. Government intercepted and decoded, thanks to this find, was a wireless message sent by the Kaiser's Foreign Minister to the Mexican Government, urging an immediate invasion of the United States by Mexico in collaboration with German troops to be landed on Mexican shores.

Dr. Albert's associates in executive capacities in Germany and the United States included Hugo Schmidt, western representative of the Deutsche Bank of Berlin, Hugo Schweitzer, a German-American chemist, S. Sulzberger, a banker of Frankfort, Germany, and Herr Wartzoldt, trade representative of the German Government in the United States. The doctor also carried on personal correspondence with friends in Germany, and one of these, named Trautmann, assigned to the Foreign Office, sent a long letter to Albert dated April 23, 1915, which expressed a rather gloomy outlook about the war. Because much of Trautmann's letter was prophetic, a part of it is worth quoting here:

> The whole war will end in Europe losing her domination of the world. America will be infinitely enriched and will become world banker at 7, 8 and even 10 percent interest. Japan will become mistress of Eastern Asia and Europe will be poorer by three hundred billions. This mighty change in the whole world will, in my opinion, first show itself in the sharpest form when we again have peace. The European people will have to make further preparations, for that this war, which must remain more or less undecided, will not be the last which we will have to fight is something of which everyone here is convinced.

Within 24 hours after reviewing the contents of the brief case, Secretary McAdoo sent both case and papers to President Wilson at the White House. The President immediately ordered that investigations of neutrality violations be intensified and, after conferring with McAdoo, agreed that the American public must be made aware of the extent and seriousness of the German plots.

To expose the Germans completely, and to disclose their machinations to as many people as possible, McAdoo talked with Frank I. Cobb, at that time editor of the New York *World*. Cobb was told the entire story and was informed that he would be permitted to publish all of the Albert documents in the newspaper, *provided* he would keep secret the manner in which they were obtained. Excited by the scoop of the decade, Cobb readily agreed and promptly began to make front-page history with banner headlines and illustrations of many of the incriminating papers. The patriotic Americans who had been fooled by Albert's underlings learned about their mistakes by reading the red-hot stories in the *World*—and promptly moved to sever all connections with those who had beguiled and betrayed them.

True to his word, Cobb never revealed how the papers were obtained or how they had come into his possession. In later years more than one individual "admitted" that he was the genius who had acquired the Albert brief case—and even in recent years *The Saturday Evening Post* published (in good faith) one factual article by a man who gave an account of his adventures, telling how he managed to get the bag from the German agent. Soon afterward the *Post* printed a short notice saying that the facts were not as reported in the article. The first time the real story was ever told in print was 1931, when Secretary McAdoo included an account of it in his autobiography, *Crowded Years*.

In December 1915, only a few months after the Albert episode, President Wilson demanded that the German Ambassador send Captain Franz von Papen back to Germany, because *officially* Von Papen was responsible for the intrigues aimed at violating the neutrality of the United States. Dr. Albert, on the record, was merely a finance expert and a commercial attaché, and he denied that any of his activities were inimical to the United States. Von Papen returned to Germany, later to become Chancellor under President Paul von Hindenburg, and Vice Chancellor under Adolf Hitler. In later years he served Hitler as Ambassador to Austria and Ambassador to Turkey. On April 10, 1945, just before the end of World War II in Europe, Von Papen was captured by American troops and tried with other Nazis as a war criminal. He was acquitted but was tried again in 1947 in a German de-Nazification court and convicted of committing crimes against his country. Although he was sentenced to serve 8 years in prison, he was confined for only a few months before he was released because of his age (69) and the fact that he was seriously ill.

On April 6, 1917, after the Germans deliberately sank many American ships, the United States entered the war against Germany. German Am-

bassador Johann Heinrich von Bernstorff was recalled to Berlin, and with
him went Dr. Heinrich Albert, whose usefulness as a propaganda director
in the United States had virtually ended when Secret Service Agent Frank
Burke grabbed his brief case and got away on a trolley car. Albert subsequently became Secretary of the Treasury of the German Republic.

Frank Burke retired from the Secret Service in 1942 and went to live
in Coral Gables, Florida, where he died on February 2, 1943. As this was
written, William H. Houghton, who also retired, after spending most of
his adult life in the Service, is living in Glendora, California.

When World War I had ended, George Sylvester Viereck summed up
the brief case affair in three succinct sentences. "The publication of the
Albert papers was a catastrophe," he said. "A veritable nest of intrigue,
conspiracy, and propaganda reposed placidly in the portfolio. Its loss was
like the loss of the Marne."

After the war the Secret Service was once again restricted to Treasury
Department investigations, but another President, Calvin Coolidge, was
to order the Service into action on another special mission—the investigation of a scandal that jarred the nation, a deal in oil lands called
Teapot Dome.

○ 11 ○

Teapot Dome

The exposure of crooked politicians and cattle barons in the Western land frauds had effectively spiked the good work of the Secret Service, yet in 1922 President Calvin Coolidge and some of his advisers decided to call on the Service again to make an important and delicate investigation which could not be entrusted to the Department of Justice, and because they considered the Secret Service to be completely incorruptible.

"Teapot Dome" was to become a synonym for chicanery, fraud, greed, and deceit.

Teapot Dome was the name given to an oil-producing area in Wyoming once known as Irish Park. Before 1909 various oil companies drilled wells there, but as extensive development of the field began, President William Howard Taft closed the public lands to private exploitation and in 1912 he issued an Executive Order which set aside certain land areas as "Naval Petroleum Reserves." Reserve No. 1 (38,969 acres) was at Elk Hills, No. 2 (29,341 acres) at Buena Vista, both in California, and Reserve No. 3 (9,481 acres) was at Teapot Dome, some 40 miles north of Casper, Wyoming.

These oil lands were intended to be held by and for the Navy, to provide oil for fuel if and when needed in a wartime emergency.

The closing of the reserves to private development exasperated certain big oil promoters and producers, who were anxious to exploit the areas for themselves. Among these were Harry F. Sinclair and Edward L. Doheny, both of whom had made fortunes in petroleum.

Pressures were brought to bear by some of the oil tycoons on President Woodrow Wilson and Secretary of the Navy Josephus Daniels to open the reserves to private interests, but Wilson and Daniels stood firm. Through lobbying and propaganda, subtle and otherwise, the oil promoters took another approach, claiming that if the reserves were not developed, the Government would lose a great deal of oil which would simply drain from these areas into active private oil fields adjoining the reserves. By letting private interests work the reserves, they said, the oil would not be lost through drainage, and the Government would profit from its leases.

Apparently there was good foundation for the drainage argument, and in 1920 the Secretary of the Navy was authorized by Congress to lease, develop, or operate the reserves if he decided that such action was necessary to protect their oil. As a result, the Navy Department permitted a few small operators to work the fields, but no big-scale operations were allowed by the Wilson administration.

When Warren G. Harding succeeded Wilson as President, his Cabinet appointments included Senator Albert B. Fall of New Mexico as Secretary of the Interior and Harry M. Daugherty as Attorney General. Fall, a native of Kentucky, sometime cowboy, gold prospector, schoolteacher, and lawyer, was a close personal friend of Harding's. Daugherty, a lawyer and small-time politician, was the man who had induced Harding to run for the Presidency.

In May 1921, less than 3 months after Fall became Secretary of the Interior, he prevailed on the President and the Secretary of the Navy, Edwin Denby, to transfer control of the Naval Petroleum Reserves from the Navy to the Interior Department. On its face this seemed a reasonable request, in line with the responsibility of Interior to preserve the natural resources of the nation, but behind the scenes it was the first major official move in a fortune-hunting conspiracy.

The next move came in November 1921, with another transaction which was not originally related to Teapot Dome, but which was to become a very important factor in the conspiracy. A Texas oil producer, Col. A. E. Humphreys, agreed to sell 33,333,333⅓ barrels of crude oil to oilmen Harry F. Sinclair, Harry M. Blackmer, James E. O'Neil, and Col. Robert W. Stewart for $50,000,000, or $1.50 per barrel. Blackmer was chairman of the board of the Midwest Refining Company, O'Neil was president of the Prairie Oil and Gas Company, both firms being affiliated with the Standard Oil Company, headed by Stewart.

The purchase of oil from Colonel Humphreys was to be made by a firm known as the Continental Trading Company, Ltd., of Toronto, Canada, Henry Smith Osler, president. However, Colonel Humphreys said he had never heard of this organization, and he wanted a firm guarantee of payment for his oil. Accordingly, the contract was guaranteed by Blackmer (Midwest Refining Company), O'Neil (Prairie Oil and Gas Company), Sinclair (Sinclair Crude Oil Purchasing Company), and Stewart (Standard Oil Company of Indiana), and the deal was closed.

Colonel Humphreys had never heard of the Continental Trading

Company, Ltd., because it was "limited" indeed—a brand-new firm, created in thin air to fatten the bank accounts of the conniving oil barons. Their scheme was simple. They bought the oil through this dummy corporation of their own creation for $1.50 a barrel, then sold the same oil to their respective companies for $1.75 a barrel, turning a neat profit of $8⅓ million for themselves at the expense of their stockholders, and without spending a dime. Henry Smith Osler, "president" of the fake company, was merely a Toronto attorney who had done legal work for some of the American oilmen.

The profits from the Humphreys purchase were invested in U.S. Liberty bonds paying 3½ per cent interest, and the bonds were delivered to Osler, who was to distribute them to the four purchasers at various intervals.

The Continental Trading Company began its "business" on November 17, 1921. At the end of November, Secretary Fall sent word to Edward L. Doheny in New York that he, Fall, was now prepared to borrow money from Doheny. Doheny had his son, Edward, Jr., withdraw $100,000 in cash from the son's own brokerage account and carry the money from New York to Washington, where young Doheny personally handed it to Secretary Fall, who counted it in Doheny's presence.

In December 1921 Fall made a trip to his Three Rivers Ranch in New Mexico, during which he bought—for cash—another ranch adjacent to his property. Also in December, Harry F. Sinclair paid a visit to Fall at the latter's Three Rivers home.

In April 1922 Senator John B. Kendrick of Wyoming received a telegram from B. B. Brooks, president of the Rocky Mountain Oil and Gas Producers Association, Casper, Wyoming, protesting the private development of Naval Petroleum Reserve No. 3 at Teapot Dome, and the proposed letting of a contract to Harry F. Sinclair or other persons without opportunity for competitive bidding. Rumors about such a contract had already appeared in the press.

Senator Kendrick immediately offered a Senate resolution (which was passed) asking the Secretary of the Interior and the Secretary of the Navy to tell the Senate whether or not such negotiations were pending and whether competitive bidding would be invited.

The surprising answer astounded the nation. It came, not from Fall, but from the Assistant Secretary of the Interior, who told the Senate in a letter dated April 21 that the Government had already leased the entire Teapot Dome reserve to the Mammoth Oil Company on April 7, 1922, for 20 years. The Mammoth Oil Company had been incorporated February 28, 1922, under the laws of the State of Delaware, by Harry F. Sinclair, its sole stockholder.

At the end of April the Senate adopted a resolution authorizing its

Committee on Public Lands and Surveys to investigate leases on Naval Oil Reserves and to report its findings and recommendations to the Senate. The committee asked the Secretary of the Interior for copies of pertinent documents and correspondence, and to justify the execution of the lease. Fall forwarded copies of a great number of papers, and the committee began its preliminary examination.

Despite this development, Secretary Fall dispatched his son-in-law, M. T. Everhart, on two different trips to collect money from Sinclair. The first "collection" consisted of $198,000 in the $3\frac{1}{2}$ per cent Liberty bonds which had come to Sinclair from Osler as part of the Continental Trading Company deal with Colonel Humphreys. The second, made a short time later, comprised another $35,000 in these bonds and a "loan" of $36,000 in cash.

Although the shadow of the Senate investigation was sure to darken Fall's office and reputation, in June 1922 he leased the whole of Naval Petroleum Reserve No. 1 at Elk Hills, California, to Edward L. Doheny —from whom he had already received $100,000.

The Senate Committee, after studying available documents, began to ask many disturbing questions. Early in 1923 Fall and Sinclair made a trip to Europe, ostensibly so that Sinclair might discuss possible oil concessions with the Russian government. Fall was to act as "counsel" for Sinclair, and the latter gave him $25,000 to cover his expenses. On March 4, 1923, after returning from this trip, Albert Bacon Fall resigned as Secretary of the Interior.

In October 1923 the Senate opened hearings to probe more deeply into the leasing of the oil reserves.

The first act of a tense drama was about over. It has been said that a good play "opens with a situation, progresses to a predicament, and finishes with a wow!" The predicament was about to unfold.

Witnesses testified that Fall had not paid taxes on the Three Rivers Ranch for some 10 years, but that in 1921 and 1922 he had suddenly bought the adjoining property for $91,500 and had made improvements in his holdings at a cost of $175,000 to $200,000.

Fall told the committee that he bought the property next to his ranch with $100,000 he borrowed from Edward B. McLean, Washington newspaper publisher. Mr. McLean, questioned by Senator Thomas J. Walsh of Montana, said he had given Fall checks totaling $100,000, but that Fall later returned the checks uncashed, saying he had obtained the money elsewhere.

"Elsewhere" turned out to be Edward L. Doheny, who told the committee that he had "loaned" $100,000 to Fall because of their long friendship and because of financial reverses Fall had suffered.

The Senate finally decided that an all-out investigation should be conducted, and passed resolutions in 1924 directing the President to cancel leases of oil and incidental contracts for the naval reserves and to appoint special counsel to conduct a thorough investigation to institute civil suits or take other necessary action to protect the interests of the United States.

President Harding had died. His successor, Calvin Coolidge, appointed as special counsel former Senator Atlee Pomerene of Ohio, and Owen J. Roberts, a Philadelphia attorney (who became Associate Justice of the Supreme Court in 1930).

Pomerene and Roberts wanted "the very best investigators" to unearth the facts they needed. Senator Walsh cautioned them not to use agents from the Department of Justice because Attorney General Harry M. Daugherty was under investigation by another Senate committee and Senator Walsh was convinced that Daugherty's agents could not be trusted. Pomerene, Roberts, and President Coolidge then decided that they would use agents of the U.S. Secret Service, who were considered to be completely honest and highly efficient investigators.

Roberts discussed the problem with Chief W. H. Moran. "We want men of intelligence and skill," Roberts told him. Moran assigned four experienced agents to work with and for Roberts and Pomerene. William R. Jarrell of Seattle, a one-time prospector, would see what he could turn up in the Teapot Dome area. Thomas B. Foster of San Francisco, noted for his tenacity and thorough research, was to cover Texas and New Mexico to unearth information about Fall. Michael P. Bolan, Jr., and William H. Houghton of New York would conduct investigations in the East. (Agent Jarrell's findings are not of significance in this account.)

The agents first read all the testimony that had been given to the Senate committee, and they started out with one handicap. The actions they were to investigate had occurred in 1921 and 1922, which meant that possible leads were already 2 or 3 years old. Also, it was reasonable to assume that the principals had taken steps to conceal any incriminating evidence.

Agent Foster, knowing that Fall transacted most of his banking business in El Paso, Texas, visited the First National Bank there and examined the deposit slips in Fall's account. On June 11, 1923 Fall was credited with twenty-five $1,000 Liberty bonds—undoubtedly representing the $25,000 he had been paid by Sinclair for his "expenses" on the trip to Russia. The bonds, it seemed, had come from the Exchange Bank of Carrizozo, New Mexico, which was near Fall's Three Rivers Ranch. It was also Foster's next stop.

The Exchange Bank of Carrizozo was in bankruptcy, and when Foster walked in he found only one man there—A. D. Brownfield, assistant to the receiver in bankruptcy. Brownfield was cordial enough until Foster identified himself as a Secret Service agent and said he wanted some information about Fall's banking business. Brownfield was noticeably worried and upset, though he tried to hide his nervousness.

"I don't see how I can help you, Mr. Foster," he said. "I'm not the receiver, I'm only his assistant. Judge Meacham is the receiver, and he's out of town. You'd better talk with him when he gets back."

A smile came over Foster's cherubic face. "I think you can probably help me," he said. "All I want to do is look at Mr. Fall's account records."

Brownfield looked quickly at a filing cabinet in the corner of the room, then turned back to Foster. "I—I wouldn't have the authority to show you any of the account transcripts," he said.

"In that case, I'll have to get a subpoena or court order."

Brownfield tried to laugh. "Well, I guess you could do that, but—well, as a matter of fact, Mr. Foster, the transcript of Mr. Fall's account isn't here. It was—uh—it was moved out with a lot of other records."

"Oh? Where was it moved to?"

"To? Oh! Why, Judge Meacham took care of that. You'll have to talk with Judge Meacham."

Brownfield's earlier worried glance at the filing cabinet had not been lost on the observant Foster. The agent suddenly rose from his chair, strode to the cabinet, and yanked open a drawer. "It won't hurt to look around," he said.

As the startled Brownfield jumped up, Foster's quick eye spotted a folder with the name "Fall, Albert B.," which he promptly lifted out.

"You can't do that!" Brownfield cried, snatching the folder from Foster's hand. "You have no right."

"Very well," Foster said. "How do we arrange for me to look in that folder?"

"We—I'll have to call Judge Meacham at Alamagordo."

"All right. Call him, then. Right now."

Brownfield nodded and started for the adjoining room, the folder in his hand. "Where are you going?" Foster asked.

"The only working phone is in another room," Brownfield answered. "I'll go with you."

"I'd rather you didn't. I'd like to talk to the judge privately."

"Very well—but in that case, you leave that folder out here where I can keep an eye on it."

Torn between two choices, Brownfield hesitated for a moment, then nodded and placed the folder on his desk; then he walked to the next room and closed the door. No sooner was the door shut than Foster opened the file. There were a lot of figures, and he noted instantly that many entries were numbers of Liberty bonds, including numbers of the bonds recorded at the First National Bank of El Paso. Others had come from the First National Bank of Pueblo, Colorado—a new lead.

Seizing an envelope on the desk, Foster began feverishly to scribble the bond numbers from the account record. Many were in sequence, which made the recording faster. As he was jotting down the final entry Brownfield came back and saw Foster, his pencil, the envelope, and the open folder. Angrily Brownfield rushed toward the desk, banged the folder shut, and picked it up.

"Give me that paper," he said.

"Oh, no," Foster said. "What did Judge Meacham say?"

"I couldn't get Judge Meacham. You're not going out of here with that paper until the judge says it's all right." Brownfield advanced threateningly, one hand extended toward the agent.

Foster kept the desk between him and his opponent. "You're making a big mistake, Brownfield," he said. "Remember that I'm representing the Federal Government here. And if you want to put things on a personal basis and get tough, I can get tough, too. Try me if you want to find out."

Brownfield decided not to accept the offer. Foster put the envelope in his pocket and walked out of the bank. The envelope was of major importance. If Brownfield reached Judge Meacham, the judge might compel Foster to return the scribbled transcript and Foster would have to obey—unless, of course, he was unable to do so. He went directly to the post office, put the envelope into another which he addressed to himself at the post office box number used by the Secret Service in El Paso, and mailed it.

Foster later learned that Brownfield was a friend of Fall's and was the brother-in-law of Fall's next-door neighbor, whose ranch Fall had acquired.

Following his latest lead, Foster traveled by train to Pueblo, Colorado. Sometime during the overnight trip his brief case with all his notes (but *not* with the transcript of the Fall account) was stolen by a person or persons unknown.

At Pueblo, Foster's mail included a startling letter from Chief Moran. In effect it said: "We have learned that you are being followed by agents of the Bureau of Investigation and the Burns Detective Agency, who seek to ascertain the progress and scope of your investigation. I suggest you avoid keeping written notes and that you submit all reports via registered mail."

At the bank in Pueblo, Foster interviewed L. T. Rule, cashier, who was most co-operative. Rule disclosed that in May 1922 Fall's son-in-law, M. T. Everhart, had deposited $233,500 in $3\frac{1}{2}$ per cent Liberty bonds in Fall's account, and that some of the bonds had been sold by the Pueblo bank and by banks in Colorado, Texas, and New Mexico. Foster obtained a transcript of Fall's account, which he sent to Roberts and Pomerene with a suggestion that they ask the Treasury to identify the original bond buyers.

Later that day Agent Foster returned to his hotel room and found his suitcase opened, his clothes strewn around the floor, and his bedding mussed, apparently by someone seeking to recover the Carrizozo transcript.

In Washington, Roberts and Pomerene took Foster's latest information to Chief Moran to trace the bond numbers. Some 25 Treasury clerks in the offices of the Register of the Treasury, the Treasurer of the United States, and the Division of Loans and Currency were assigned to search the records.

The bonds in which the Secret Service was interested had been included in a shipment to the Federal Reserve Bank of Atlanta in 1917 and had eventually been sold to the Southland Steamship Company of Savannah, Georgia.

At the New York offices of this company, Agent Michael P. Bolan, Jr., soon learned that the bonds had been sold to the Chase National Bank of New York. At the Chase Bank Bolan found that the bonds had been received April 10, 1922, and 2 days later had been sold to Salomon Brothers & Hutzler, 60 Wall Street, New York City.

Bolan was joined by Agent William H. Houghton, who had been working in Philadelphia on other leads. En route to New York by train, Houghton recognized a Burns Detective Agency operative, and at the Pennsylvania Station in New York it was evident that the Burns man was following Houghton. Thanks to his own experience in surveillance, he had little difficulty in shaking the shadow before he met Bolan.

Together these agents, by permission, scanned scores of correspondence files and account books in the storage warehouse of Salomon Brothers & Hutzler. The dusty and tedious search paid off, for they found a record of $100,000 in Liberty bonds sold to the Dominion Bank of Canada on April 13, 1922. The serial numbers were the same as those found by Foster in Fall's bank account in Pueblo.

At the New York office of the Dominion Bank of Canada, Agent Houghton asked Manager C. S. Howard about this bond purchase. Howard sent a clerk to get the necessary records, and while they waited, Howard asked Houghton why he wanted the information. Houghton sparred with words until the clerk returned and handed Howard a slip of paper. When the manager did not seem inclined to co-operate, Houghton calmly reached over and took the paper out of his hands. It showed that the bonds had been bought by the bank for the Continental Trading Company, Ltd., of Toronto. The order had been placed by the law firm of Osler, Hoskin and Harcourt.

Houghton sped to Toronto, but at the address of record he could find no listing for the Continental Trading Company. At the law offices of Osler, Hoskin and Harcourt he finally interviewed H. S. Osler.

Yes, Osler said, the Continental Trading Company, Ltd., had been organized by him, and the only other officers of the company were clerks in his law firm. The explanation was simple, he said. As an attorney he had been given charge of a large estate, and he created the Continental Trading Company as a device to avoid litigation. He had used the estate funds to buy $100,000 worth of Liberty bonds so that the estate would not be compelled to pay taxes on this sum.

Osler explained that he was a big-game hunter and that just before going to Africa on a hunting trip in 1922 he had dissolved the Continental Trading Company and sold the $100,000 in bonds, because the affairs of the big estate had been settled satisfactorily. Unfortunately, he claimed, he could not remember who had bought the bonds—and of course the records of the company had been destroyed. Houghton returned to New York.

Back in El Paso, Texas, Agent Foster picked up the envelope with the Carrizozo bond numbers and submitted them with his report. At the Treasury in Washington, Chief Moran established that the 25 bonds in Fall's account at the Carrizozo bank had been shipped to the Federal Reserve Bank of Chicago. There Agent Bolan traced them to the First Trust and Savings Bank, Chicago, to the First National Bank of New York, to Rhoades & Company, New York—and to the New York Branch of the Dominion Bank of Canada on April 13, 1922.

This time the Dominion Bank refused to tell the agents anything without authority from the bank's president in Toronto. Bolan and Houghton went to Toronto and talked to the president. He was polite, but reluctant, and the agents spoke bluntly.

"You can authorize our inspection of the books in New York," they said, "or you can surrender them under a Federal subpoena."

The banker instructed his New York office to show the agents the account of H. S. Osler.

While in Toronto the agents called on Mr. Osler to get the total amount of "dividends" paid by the Continental Trading Company, Ltd. Osler insisted that he was helpless. The books had been destroyed, he could not tell what profits had accrued, or how any money had been invested beyond that used for the bond purchases.

The agents returned to Washington and discussed Osler's obvious evasion with Counsel Roberts and Pomerene. The counsel and agents then went to Toronto and questioned Osler, explaining the precarious position in which he now found himself. Thereupon Osler gave them a guarded and somewhat distorted account of the formation of the Continental Trading Company in connection with the purchase of oil from Colonel Humphreys. The whole idea, Osler said, was to avoid any litigation with landowners over the Humphreys lease, and if there was to be any such litigation he, Osler, thought it wiser to fight it out in Canada. Also, if the company did its business in the United States and kept its bank accounts there, no Canadian corporation tax would have to be paid.

In Denver, Colorado, Agent Foster interviewed Colonel Humphreys, who named the oilmen who had guaranteed the contract of the Continental Trading Company—Stewart, Sinclair, Blackmer, and O'Neil. In Ohio, Foster obtained a copy of the contract.

Colonel Stewart, questioned by Foster in Chicago, told about the Continental Trading Company and Osler, but made no incriminating admissions.

In El Paso, Texas, Foster was unable to get any admissions from Fall's son-in-law, M. T. Everhart, concerning the $233,500 in bonds which Everhart had deposited to Fall's account in the Pueblo bank. In later court proceedings Everhart hid behind the Fifth Amendment and refused to furnish any information about this deposit. Subsequently, however, Everhart told a Congressional committee that the bonds had come from Harry F. Sinclair. Everhart insisted that the bonds represented the purchase price of one third of the stock of the Fall-Everhart Tres Rios Land & Cattle Company, whose ranch property was to be turned into a swanky club. Though this story was generally regarded as a shallow fable, it was later (1928) accepted by a jury in the District of Columbia which acquitted Sinclair of a charge of conspiracy to defraud the United States in securing the Teapot Dome lease.

To prove how Fall obtained the bonds which Osler bought and distributed to Sinclair, Blackmer, O'Neil, and Stewart, special counsel wanted O'Neil, Blackmer, and Stewart to testify as to the numbers of the bonds they had received. Thus they could show the numbers of the bonds Sinclair had received and could make the connection between Sinclair and Fall. However, Blackmer and O'Neil fled to Europe.

Senator Walsh introduced legislation, which was enacted, giving U.S. consuls abroad the power to serve subpoenas on American citizens and to impose a maximum fine of $100,000 on any citizen who failed to respond. Joseph E. Murphy, Assistant Chief of the Secret Service, was given subpoenas for Blackmer and O'Neil and sent to Europe to find the pair.

Murphy arrived at Cherbourg on February 9, 1927, and learned that Blackmer had left Milan, Italy, for parts unknown, and that O'Neil had left Marseilles, France, early in January. Murphy trailed Blackmer to Monte Carlo, where Blackmer had grown a beard and was living under an assumed name. Monte Carlo had no American consul, and Murphy arranged with the State Department to appoint B. F. Hale, consul at Marseilles, as a temporary consul in Monte Carlo.

When Murphy and Hale prepared to serve Blackmer with a subpoena, they discovered he had checked out of his hotel and gone to the railroad station. They rushed to the depot and boarded Blackmer's train, aboard which Hale served the subpoena and asked for Blackmer's passport. Blackmer refused to surrender the passport until Hale threatened to have police take it by force. The oil magnate then gave up the passport, but said he had no intention of responding to the subpoena and would not return to the United States.

All clues as to the whereabouts of O'Neil were unproductive, and agents failed to find him.

In 1925 Harry Ford Sinclair was questioned on several occasions by Senator Thomas J. Walsh before a Senate committee, and on each occasion he refused to answer Walsh's questions. The Senate cited him for contempt and in March 1927 he was tried and convicted on this charge.

In June 1925 Federal Judge T. Blake Kennedy ruled that the Interior and Navy Departments were within their rights in leasing the naval oil reserves. The Government entered an appeal which was upheld by the Circuit Court of Appeals on the grounds that the Teapot Dome lease was fraudulently negotiated. The case went to the Supreme Court.

A trial was held in Washington on October 17, 1927, charging Fall and Sinclair with conspiracy to defraud the United States. After the jury was chosen, Sinclair hired the Burns Detective Agency to investigate members of the jury and to keep them under surveillance. One of the Burns operatives found this duty distasteful and secretly reported it to the Government, also revealing that if Sinclair was convicted it was planned to frame an official of the Department of Justice by claiming that he had shadowed the jury—an act that would constitute grounds for a mistrial.

The Secret Service was assigned to shadow the jury shadowers, and Assistant Chief Murphy and Agent Myles McCahill confirmed the Burns man's report. The Burns agents were housed in various Washington hotels, and the Secret Service men managed to get access to their rooms at the Capitol Park, the Pennsylvania, the Continental, and the Wardman Park. At the Capitol Park Hotel, Murphy and McCahill discovered copies of reports revealing conversations between the Burns men and some jurors, and the names of Burns operatives assigned to follow certain jurors.

Warrants were issued for Sinclair and his representative, Henry Mason Day. For tampering with the jury, Sinclair was sentenced to 6 months,

Day to 4 months. Both appealed, both lost. William J. Burns, head of the detective agency, was convicted for contempt, but his conviction was later set aside by the Supreme Court. Burns's son, Sherman, was fined $1,000. Sinclair was subsequently sentenced to serve 3 months for contempt of the Senate and to pay a fine of $500. In all, he served 7½ months in prison and was also assessed $358,340.53 in taxes. Sinclair was acquitted on the charge of conspiracy to defraud the Government, and he could not be tried for bribery because the statute of limitations outlawed any such prosecution.

In 1928 Fall's son-in-law, M. T. Everhart, testified before the Senate committee, admitting for the first time that Sinclair had handed him, Everhart, $198,000 in Liberty bonds which Everhart then delivered to Fall. Except for $2,500 which Fall kept, the bonds were deposited by Everhart in the Pueblo bank where Agent Foster had discovered the deposit in 1924.

In October 1929 Albert B. Fall went to trial for accepting a bribe from Edward L. Doheny in connection with the lease for the Elk Hills Naval Petroleum Reserves. Fall was convicted and sentenced to serve a year in jail and to pay a fine of $100,000. He lost an appeal and served 9 months and 19 days in the New Mexico State Penitentiary at Santa Fe. He was unable to pay his fine, and a judgment for $100,000 was entered against him. This was the first prison sentence served on a felony conviction of a Cabinet officer in the history of the country.

Edward L. Doheny was tried March 12, 1930, for bribing Fall, but was acquitted by a jury, despite the fact that Fall had been convicted of accepting a bribe from Doheny!

Harry M. Blackmer remained in exile until September 22, 1949, when he returned to Denver at the age of 81 and was there charged with tax evasion and perjury. He had already paid a fine of $60,000 for failing to answer his subpoena, and on the tax charges he paid the Government $3,713,118.70. The perjury charge was dropped.

James E. O'Neil never did come back to the United States, but the Government collected $540,000 from his holdings as a tax liability. O'Neil died in France at the age of 64.

Colonel Robert Stewart was acquitted on charges of perjury and contempt, but was assessed $506,300.47 as tax liability.

The closing paragraph in a report in the Secret Service files reads: "The Service was highly complimented by the Special Counsel and by Senator Thomas J. Walsh of the Senate Committee, for the character of the work performed."

The character of the work performed in another unusual investigation also brought praise from members of Congress. This case involved, of all things, a fly. . . .

∘ 12 ∘

The Fly

In 1929 a fly smaller than an ordinary housefly was responsible for the destruction of thousands of tons of Florida fruit and vegetables and for the expenditure of millions of dollars by the Federal Government and the State of Florida. The fly was also a suspect in one of the most unusual investigations ever made by the U.S. Secret Service.

In March 1929 J. C. Goodwin, a nursery inspector employed by the State of Florida, visited the experimental station of the U.S. Department of Agriculture at Orlando. When he prepared to leave on March 30 he asked if he might take with him several grapefruit from the trees at the station, since they appeared to be as fine as any grapefruit he had ever seen. He was given several and took them to his home, where he placed them in his refrigerator.

A few days later he took out one of the grapefruit and cut it open. Instead of the firm and juicy interior he expected to find, he saw several larvae which had eaten their way through much of the pulp. Goodwin suspected that the larvae might be those of the Mediterranean fruit fly, but since he was not sure he sent them to the experimental station with a report of his discovery. The experimental station sent the larvae by airmail to the Department of Agriculture in Washington, and they were shown to an entomologist at the National Museum, who definitely identified the maggots as those of the Mediterranean fruit fly.

The Mediterranean fruit fly *(Ceratitis capitata Weid)*, according to the Department of Agriculture, is one of the world's most destructive fruit pests. It attacks citrus fruits and more than 200 other fruit and vegetable crops. Originally a native of Africa, the fly has become a notorious world traveler, making commercial fruit production difficult or impossible in some foreign countries. It had never been identified as gaining a foothold in the United States until 1929.

The female fly punctures the fruit and deposits her eggs just beneath the skin. The eggs hatch into larvae which burrow into the fruit, feed, and develop. Such fruit spoils and usually falls to the ground.

After positive identification of the larvae in Washington, representatives of the Department of Agriculture's Plant Quarantine and Control Administration, the Bureau of Entomology, and the Florida State Plant Board met in Orlando with Mr. Wilmon Newell, Plant Board Commissioner, together with fruitgrowers, shippers, and newspapermen, to announce and discuss a campaign of eradication of the fly. An emergency fund of $50,000 was released by the State, and $40,000 by the U.S. Department of Agriculture. On May 1 a fruit fly quarantine became effective, and on May 2 Congress made available $4,250,000 to fight the insect. At the same time the State of Florida appropriated $500,000 in the same cause.

It was agreed by State and Federal officials that starvation of the fly would contribute to its eradication. This meant the elimination, in infested zones, of all host fruits and vegetables in a stage of ripeness to be attractive to the fly. It also meant the use of a sweetened poison bait to be sprayed on the citrus trees and elsewhere at frequent intervals.

To do these jobs a large force of men was quickly recruited. Where 138 field inspectors were employed in April 1929, 750 were on the rolls by March 1930. There were 460 quarantine inspectors on the job in May 1929, as against 642 in January 1930. Laborers, who did the spraying and other menial jobs, numbered more than 5,000 in August 1929. Obviously not many of these men had any expert knowledge of the fruit fly, of poison spray, or of horticulture in general.

As the campaign progressed, a move was under way in Washington to ask Congress to appropriate $26,600,000 to the Department of Agriculture to carry on the emergency work. Apparently there was some opposition to this sum, because in a report of the Chief of the Plant Quarantine and Control Administration for the year ended June 30, 1930, he indicated that a revised estimate of $15,381,000 was sent to the Budget Bureau, approved by President Herbert Hoover, and sent to Congress in December 1929.

Congress, however, did not rush to approve the request, and for good reason. Congressman Will R. Wood, Chairman of the House Committee on Appropriations, had been bombarded by letters of protest from various owners of large citrus groves in Florida, complaining that their fruit crops had been and were being unnecessarily destroyed and that their trees had been badly damaged by wrongful use of poison sprays. Their livelihood was at stake.

Congressman Wood finally approved an emergency interim appropriation of $1,290,000 to continue the control program. He decided to look further into reasons for the complaints he had received, so he approached several Cabinet members to assign investigators to get the facts. They pleaded shortages of qualified personnel and gave other excuses for staying out of what might be a political bombshell. The Secretary of the Treasury, however, had no such fears. He put Wood in touch with Chief W. H. Moran of the Secret Service and instructed Moran to make whatever investigation was necessary.

Congressman Wood explained the situation, furnished the names of the complaining fruitgrowers, and made only one stipulation. Because the appropriation request for $15,381,000 was awaiting Congressional action, the Secret Service men must conclude their investigation within 10 days.

On December 16, 1929, Assistant Chief Joseph E. Murphy kept an appointment in Jacksonville, Florida, with five Secret Service agents from southern districts—George H. Brodnax, Carl Dickson (later Assistant Chief), John C. Marsh, Henry F. Tyson, and Robert F. Perry. Murphy delivered to Brodnax, as leader of the group, a bundle of affidavits and letters from the grove owners. Together the men roughed out a plan of operation, set up headquarters in Orlando the same day, and went to work.

There was little question but that the Mediterranean fruit fly and its larvae had been found in some 20 counties in the Florida citrus region—but there were certain circumstances that struck the investigators as peculiar. For instance, a thorough investigation had earlier been made of fruit at the experimental station from which came the grapefruit in which the larvae were first found, but no other larvae and no flies could be located. Larvae were discovered, however, in a grove about three fourths of a mile from the experimental station, and in groves in other counties.

At first some growers were reluctant to talk with the agents, claiming that any criticism of the Plant Board might result in revocation of their shipping permits. The agents assured them that there would be no such repercussions, and gradually the Secret Service men obtained statements from 150 witnesses.

In one case a Florida Plant Board field inspector had discovered some larvae in one grapefruit—the only larvae found in the entire grove. When he reported this to the grove owner, preparatory to destroying the entire crop, the owner looked at the grapefruit.

"This fruit didn't come from my grove," he told the inspector. "I don't raise this kind of fruit here. I'll give you a thousand dollars if you go through my trees and show me another grapefruit like it." The challenge was not accepted.

In Eustis, Florida, one irate vineyard owner told the agents that State Plant Board employees had come to his place, condemned and picked 5 tons of grapes and buried them in the ground. The very next day a different Plant Board group visited his farm, learned about the grapes, and shook their heads sympathetically. "Too bad," they said in effect. "There wasn't any reason those grapes couldn't have been shipped."

In Sanford, the owner of 640 acres of fruit trees and vegetables reported that the Plant Board had declared both beans and cowpeas to be hosts of the fruit fly, and as such they were subject to destruction. Accordingly, they destroyed his extensive crops of these vegetables, but a short time later declared that neither beans nor cowpeas were hosts and were not subject to destruction or quarantine. In addition, the board's spraying teams doused his hundreds of citrus trees with so much strong arsenic spray that the trees and fruit were seriously damaged.

The arsenic spray was a sore point with numerous other growers. Agents determined that the State Plant Board's instructions to its men, based on advice from the U.S. Department of Agriculture, were to spray from $\frac{1}{2}$ to 1 pint of the poison on the body of each tree, where it would attract and kill any of the flies. The growers, however, said that it was common for the inexperienced crews to spray from $1\frac{1}{2}$ to 2 gallons over each tree, causing extensive damage to the tree and ruining the fruit.

When the eradication campaign began, the Plant Board, in co-operation with the Department of Agriculture, set up three zones, numbered 1, 2, and 3. Zone 1 included the actual infestation area and covered 1 mile in all directions (later changed to 5 trees in all directions from an infested tree). Zone 2 covered a distance of 9 miles from Zone 1 in all directions. Zone 3 was a "noninfested" area.

When inspectors found an infestation of the fly or larvae, the infested grove was placed in Zone 1 and all other groves within a distance of 1 mile were condemned accordingly. If the property line of a grove in Zone 2 happened to extend into Zone 1, the fruit in the Zone 2 grove was destroyed, even though the trees themselves were inside Zone 2. In Zones 1 and 2 all trees, whether infested or not, were to be sprayed at least 12 to 16 times with a solution composed of 200 gallons of water, 8 pounds of arsenate of lead, 5 gallons of syrup, and 25 pounds of sugar. (The arsenic was later reduced to 4 pounds.) Trees in noninfested Zone 3 were sprayed 4 times with the poison.

The complaints about the spray damage were well founded, for the investigators themselves visited many groves in the infested regions and had a good look at the injured trees and spoiled fruit.

The agents were told by a Plant Board official that inspectors and others were forbidden to trespass on any owner's property without first informing the owner of the intended visit. Investigation, however, showed that in some cases the spraying teams had failed to notify the grove owners of intended visits and had even driven tractors over property fences to make entry "by the back way."

In a later hearing a small property owner, Mr. T. M. Arnold of Conway, Florida, told a Congressional committee about a Plant Board group that visited his holdings. The dialogue that follows is taken from official records:

One day, said Mr. Arnold, a man drove up to his place in a car with a placard on the windshield reading, "State Plant Board."

"Is this Mr. Arnold?" the visitor asked.

"Yes, sir, this is he."

"We have come down here to tell you what we are going to do."

"Is that right?"

"Yes."

"What are you going to do?" Arnold asked.

"We came down here to dig up your guava trees, your peach trees, your plum trees, your fig trees, and in fact everything on your place that is a host plant to the fly."

"Who said you were?"

"Well," the man answered, "we are representing the U.S. Department of Agriculture."

"To what extent does your authority run?"

"I am authorized to do that."

"Do you mean to tell me that you are a duly authorized agent of the Federal Government, authorized to go around here and enter people's premises, trespass on them, and destroy their property like you have been doing?"

"Yes, sir."

"I demand to see your credentials."

"Brother, I am sorry to say that I cannot produce them."

"Let me tell you something," Arnold said. "Neither the State of Florida nor the Government of the United States has got one dime invested in these premises. I bought this stuff and I paid for it. I have my deed to it and my abstract. I pay the taxes on it and I live on it, and the Constitution of the United States of America guarantees to me the right, as an American citizen, to protect my property—and I will protect it, sir. Now you come here with the authority that you say you have and demand to destroy my stuff. The first man that goes down there on such authority as that and destroys what I have got, I will drill a hole through him!"

There was no more argument, and the visitor went away. About a month or 6 weeks later, Arnold declared, he was sitting at a table writing a letter after dinner when his wife came in from the yard.

"Did you know that there is a bunch of Negroes down there at the east side of the place just slaughtering everything there is on your place?" she asked.

Arnold got up, went to his bedroom, picked up his .38 caliber Smith and Wesson revolver, put a handful of extra cartridges in his pocket and went out, holding the gun in plain sight. When he came to within 60 yards of the labor crew, one of the men yelled, "Boss, there come white folks with a great big pistol, that long!" He started to walk away.

"Hold on, boy," Arnold said. "You're the one I want to see. Come back here." The man came back, but the others started to leave in Indian file until Arnold called, "Hold on, there—come back here."

When they all came back he said, "I want to know what you are doing here, destroying my property like this, trespassing on my property?"

"Cap'n," the spokesman said, "we wasn't coming in here, only the white folks sent us in—the boss man sent us in here."

"Where is he?"

"He's up yonder in that grove, eating oranges."

"You'd better get him down here."

The laborer hollered for the boss, who came down promptly. "What does all this mean?" he asked.

"Yes," Arnold said, "tell me what does all this mean—a man entering my premises without any permission, without my knowledge or consent, to destroy what I have got?"

"Am I on your property?" the boss asked.

"You are."

"I did not know it."

"Let me tell you something," Arnold said. "You get this bunch of Negroes that you have got here and you gather up every tool that belongs to you and your department, and you load them in that truck out yonder and you get to hell out of here and you stay out when you get out!"

As the laborers walked away Arnold called, "Boys, I'm going to let you get off here this time without any trouble, but if you come back here any more, somebody is going to be hauled out of here."

"Cap'n," one answered, "if you just won't shoot us this time we sure to God ain't going to come back."

Soon after this incident a Plant Board spraying crew showed up at the Arnold farm to spray Arnold's trees with the arsenic poison. When Arnold saw the crew, he said, he approached the leader and objected to any spraying of his trees. "I don't want my two horses, my mule, my chickens, and my dog to be poisoned with that stuff," he said. "I don't want a drop of that stuff put on my place, and it isn't going to be. You see the road that you got in here on?"

"Yes, sir," the crew leader said.

"Well, you turn this outfit around right here, and you get to hell out of here and stay out when you get out!"

They got out.

Several months later a Plant Board official made an affidavit that he and a foreman of the cleanup section had called on Mr. Arnold, explained the purpose of the work, and "on request of Mr. Arnold" grubbed up and pruned back some guava bushes. Also, the leader of the spray crew made an affidavit that he and his men were "operating in the neighborhood of Mr. T. M. Arnold's property. To the best of my knowledge and belief, Mr. Arnold's property was sprayed with the regulation bait spray at regular intervals. . . . No record was made of the spraying on the Arnold property, as at that time all blocks of citrus under five acres in extent were included under miscellaneous reports."

The Secret Service men learned that the last Mediterranean fruit fly seen in the citrus region was discovered on August 4, 1929, although fly larvae were found up to and including August 27, 1929. No other larvae were seen until November 16, 1929, when a Plant Board inspector visited an orange grove 9 miles west of Orlando. He made a statement that an orange dropped from a tree at his feet, and that when he cut open the orange he found 4 fruit fly larvae in it. A careful search was made of the remainder of this grove, but not one larva nor one fruit fly could be located.

These developments later led Congressman Robert G. Simmons, of the Appropriations Committee, to point out what he called "an important chain of coincidences." In questioning Dr. Wilmon Newell of the Plant Board, Mr. Simmons said: "Here is a peculiar characteristic of the fly you have not discussed. He appeared in Florida three days after a member of the Legislature proposed to introduce a bill to abolish the Plant Board. Then your last infestation was in August, just as the budget was considering the request for $26,000,000. Then you found nothing until November, when Congress was getting ready to consider the question of the appropriations for this eradication work."

Some of the fruitgrowers claimed that they had seen what they called "jumping maggots" in Florida for several years—maggots like those of the fruit fly, although they did not identify them as such. However, there are larvae of other flies that are similar to those of the Mediterranean fruit fly, and it is possible or even probable that these were what the growers had seen.

There were strong suspicions among the growers that the fruit fly larvae had been deliberately "planted" in some groves, to insure continuation of the quarantine and the eradication campaign, which was providing work for so many men in this period of depression. Agent Brodnax, in his report, wrote: "I found it to be general rumor that larvae had been planted. It would appear that this rumor is well founded, although I was not able to definitely establish a specific case of planting. Many instances are cited of the finding of a single larva in one piece of fruit, coupled with the failure to find larvae on the same tree, on the ground beneath the tree, or in the remainder of the particular grove."

The agents did, however, obtain an affidavit from one former State Plant Board employee to the effect that while he was supervising a work force destroying host fruits and vegetables, a Plant Board inspector gave him two small bottles, one containing what the inspector said were maggots of the fruit fly, the other containing alcohol. The inspector was anxious to quarantine a grove owned by a woman at Fort Christmas, so he instructed the foreman to take one of the maggots from Bottle No. 1 and put it in the alcohol, making it appear that he had found the larva in the grove. The foreman said he carried out his instructions, and the grove was quarantined.

Agents took a sworn statement from another former Plant Board employee who said that on or about November 12 he overheard a conversation between two officials, one of whom said: "What do you think about it? Word has passed that there must be another infestation found within ten days or there will be something doing." Four days later the lone orange with the 4 larvae was discovered—the last maggot in the campaign.

The agents established that there were about 8,300 "fly traps" in existence in the various groves—devices that were inspected regularly to see whether or not Mediterranean fruit flies were caught. They also examined records which showed that from 28 to 36 inspectors of the U.S. Department of Agriculture Experimental Station reported on twice as many specimens of larvae and host plants in 1 month as did 600 inspectors of the State Plant Board.

In the campaign to eradicate the fly, growers were forbidden to ship citrus fruits to certain sections of the country without heat-processing or precooling. Many complained that such processing ruined the taste, caused the fruit to decay, cracked the peel, and sapped the natural acids. One shipper said his processed fruit was returned by markets as being unfit to eat.

In addition to the tons of fruit and vegetables destroyed in groves and fields, about 500,000 crates of oranges and grapefruit—noninfested, but which came from allegedly infested groves—were destroyed.

Some of the growers told agents that they believed the whole business had been conceived by rivals from California, though there was no proof that this was so. One owner whose 700 acres of fruit trees had been ruined by spray was in favor of reasonable control by the U.S. Department of Agriculture, but not by the Florida State Plant Board, and he told agents that he and other growers would protect their property the next year with shotguns if necessary.

The agents had been instructed to interview the growers, and in an attempt to be impartial the investigators also interviewed officials of the State Plant Board. Agent Brodnax reported: "While conferring with A. C. Brown, assistant to Dr. Newell, he gave us the names of several large growers and packers who are against the State Plant Board. We advised him that we did not want the names of growers who were against the board, but would like to have the names of some of the large growers and shippers who were in favor of, or friendly to, the board. He could not give us the name of a single grower or shipper, although we made this request several times."

In fairness it should be said that following the Secret Service investigation the Secretary of Agriculture made a special statement to the press concerning the fruit fly eradication campaign. The statement declared that the Department had been greatly embarrassed by repeated attempts to stir up discontent in Florida, and that it was expected that the fruit growers would not submit to regulations without some friction. According to the Secretary, many organizations of growers and farmers in Florida "supported the administration wholeheartedly and forwarded several commendatory resolutions."

"There can be no doubt as to the gravity of the infestation," the Secretary declared. "Tests made with cyanide gas netted as high as 400 flies on one tree. The total number of infested properties, as revealed by subsequent counting, ran to nearly 1,000. These were spread through 21 counties."

The Secretary branded as ridiculous any implication that the outstanding citizens who served without pay as heads of the Florida State Plant Board were responsible for the appearance of the fly, or used the fly to save the political life of the Board. He pointed out that two of the Board members were growers of citrus fruits and that all had their homes and businesses in Florida. It should be made clear here, however, that most of the difficulties accrued from actions of the several hundred inspectors and several thousand laborers who were in the Board's employ, and not directly from the citizens who administered its activities.

"In the view of our entomologists," the Secretary's statement continued, "the abandonment of the work now would be a calamity, would mean that the money already expended has been wasted, and that the fly, if and when it reappears, would spread without hindrance to the enormous damage of the whole South, Southwest, and West."

As a result of the Secret Service investigation and the Congressional appropriation hearings that followed it, the President recommended to Congress that instead of the $15,381,000 requested for the period December 15, 1929 to July 1, 1930, there be appropriated $6,902,404 to carry on the work until November 30, 1930. Of that amount, $1,500,000 was to be set aside as an emergency reserve. Evidently the Congress did not approve the request, for all field inspections were halted March 27, 1930, "on account of scarcity of funds."

The regular appropriation bill for the year beginning July 1, 1930, included only $1,740,000 for the Mediterranean fruit fly work, and an emergency fund of $1,500,000 to be used if the President decided that infestations of the fly justified the expenditure of this money. Actually none of the emergency fund was used, and on June 30 the Department of Agriculture returned an unspent balance of $500,000 of the $1,740,000 appropriated. In other words, the year's expenditures totaled $1,240,000.

In all, the eradication campaign cost $7,513,136.91. Of this amount $6,764,364.47 came from Uncle Sam, $385,032.33 from the State of Florida, and $363,740.11 from counties, civic organizations, and the like.

It would appear that the Secret Service and the House Appropriations Committee, with the economies achieved by the Department of Agriculture, saved the American taxpayer more than $14 million and perhaps averted violence. Although property damage was extensive, the State Plant Board did put Florida oranges and grapefruit back on the grocers' shelves by rubbing out a tiny winged enemy—the Mediterranean fruit fly.

Another kind of enemy, however, was preparing to weaken the economic blood stream of the nation by circulating some of the most deceptive counterfeit money ever produced. . . .

∘ 13 ∘

Did the Russians Counterfeit Our Money?

In the cold war, as well as the hot, counterfeit money can be a potent weapon—a dangerous, destructive, silent saboteur.

Early in May 1928 a number of new counterfeit $100 bills were detected in a bank in Houston, Texas, having been spent in a gambling house by unknown persons. Indications were that the bills had been brought into the United States from abroad through the port of Galveston or Houston. From that time the notes appeared singly, or in pairs or threes, at widely separated points, but none could be traced beyond the individuals who deposited them in banks where they were detected.

Detection of the notes was difficult because they were among the finest counterfeits ever made. When they appeared in 1928, the paper money of the United States was considerably larger and more ornate in design than it is today. The flaws in the counterfeit hundreds were decidedly minor, and to aid bank tellers in identifying the bills the Secret Service issued detailed descriptions with sketches showing enlarged portions of the design in which imperfections could be seen on close examination. The most glaring defect was on the back of the bill, which portrayed five mythological human figures, three seated and two standing. One of the seated figures had an outstretched left arm and a left hand which held a small branch. On the genuine bill the tip of the thumb definitely overlapped the stem of the branch. On the counterfeit the thumb barely touched the stem.

The paper on which the counterfeits were printed was, like the genuine, impregnated with two rows of coarse red and blue silk threads (in today's currency smaller and finer colored threads are scattered throughout the paper). An analysis of the paper by the Bureau of Engraving and Printing, made at the request of the Secret Service, showed that in some respects the paper was superior to that used in printing genuine notes.

The counterfeits were not surface-printed, as most are, but had been produced from expertly engraved plates with first-class technical equipment.

In July 1929, for economy reasons, the United States officially reduced the size and standardized the designs of its paper money, thereby saving thousands of dollars in paper and printing costs, while increasing production at the same time. The large-size notes were still circulating, however, and were retired gradually as they reached the Treasury from banks in the normal course of business.

Considering the highly deceptive quality of the counterfeit $100 bills, the Secret Service was somewhat puzzled by the fact that only a few thousand dollars' worth appeared in circulation, mostly in Europe, which indicated that the notes had originated abroad and were being passed overseas. In January 1930 the Reichsbank-Direktorium, Berlin, Germany, informed the Secret Service that some $25,000 in these counterfeits were in circulation in Berlin and that some consideration was being given to declaring American $100 notes of this issue nonnegotiable and to bar them from the Berlin Bourse, or exchange. The suggestion was not adopted. The Secret Service decided that an investigation in Europe was in order.

It was discovered that $24,000 in the counterfeit $100 notes had been sold to the Deutsche Bank in Berlin by the private banking house of Sass & Martini, which allegedly received the bills from a man giving his name as Franz Voigt. The address which Voigt had given the bank proved to be fictitious. The Secret Service decided to check further and also to take a quiet and closer look into the operations of the Sass & Martini firm.

It appeared that this bank was operated by two men from the United States, and the Secret Service commenced inquiries into their backgrounds. The Berlin newspapers, learning that a quantity of counterfeits had been traced to Sass & Martini, published sensational stories, and the Berlin police began an independent investigation which resulted in the unexpected closing of the bank and the disappearance of its two operators.

The Secret Service was able to learn that Franz Voigt's real name was Franz Fischer, and although he was not located, there were indications that he had left Germany for Russia.

The circulation of the counterfeit $100 notes became spasmodic and infrequent until December 23, 1932, when Thomas J. Callaghan, Special Agent in Charge of the Chicago office of the Secret Service, received a telephone call from the Federal Reserve Bank of Chicago asking that he come there at once.

The Federal Reserve officials showed Callaghan 35 of the counterfeit $100 bills received in deposits from the Continental Illinois Bank and Trust Company, 25 more from the Harris Trust & Savings Bank, and 2 others from the Northern Trust Company.

Callaghan took the notes to his office, issued warnings to all banks in Cook County to be on the watch for the counterfeits, and initiated inquiries at the banks from which the 62 notes had come. In the midst of this action he received a telephone call from the First National Bank of Chicago saying that a man had just presented $10,000 in old-style $100 bills to be exchanged for small-size currency. When the teller told the man the notes would have to be examined, he claimed he was merely representing someone else and left the bank, saying that he would return with his friend.

Two agents were sent to the bank, and they identified the bills as counterfeits. The man who presented them, whom we will call Fred Goodrich, apparently did so in good faith, for he had furnished his name and an address at which the agents located him. He stuck to his story about representing another man by the name of Goldberg, but was unable to produce Goldberg. He was arrested and arraigned, and at intervals the skeptical agents called on him to ask more questions. A week later Goodrich said he had decided to tell them the truth.

A personal friend had introduced him to two men who were supposedly bootleggers. They showed him a package of $10,000 in $100 bills, told him that this was cash they had received in their bootleg operations, and that they wanted to get it exchanged for the new small-size currency. They would pay him a commission of 2 per cent. They could not afford to make the exchange openly, they said, because they might become involved with the Treasury Department for failure to pay income tax on this hoard which they had kept in safe-deposit boxes.

Goodrich, a former bank teller, examined the notes, saw nothing wrong with them, and took the $10,000 to the First National Bank, where he received $10,000 in new currency. He returned to the hotel and delivered the money to the two men, who then asked if he would exchange another package of $10,000. He agreed, and it was this second trip to the bank that resulted in the call to the Secret Service.

Agents located the alleged bootleggers, who confirmed the story. It was one of these men who had cashed the 62 counterfeits that Callaghan had picked up at the Federal Reserve Bank, and this man said he had also cashed $10,000 more in good faith at other banking institutions.

The men claimed to have received the money from a friend named Irving, who told them that it came from a bootlegger who was afraid to change it for fear of getting into trouble with the Treasury. Their commission was to be 5 per cent.

The agents questioned Irving, who brought them further along a trail that finally led to a Chicago private detective whose name (fictitious) was Harry Laufter. In tracing the deal to Laufter, the agents recovered $40,000 in counterfeit $100 notes which the men in the "parade" had not yet exchanged. Laufter, it seems, had originally delivered $100,000 to be cashed.

Laufter readily told the Secret Service that he had received the $100,-000 from a personal friend, one Enrique Dechow von Buelow, with a now-familiar story—the money represented the "take" in bootleg deals by members of the old Arnold Rothstein gang in New York who could not afford to appear openly in the transactions.

With private-eye caution, Laufter had first lent samples of the bills to two reputable attorneys, asking that they determine whether or not the bills were genuine. The attorneys returned the notes to him saying that they had established that they were not counterfeit.

The detective then approached a friend, who approached a friend, who approached other friends, thus leaving the trail that ultimately led the Secret Service back to Laufter.

Laufter revealed that Von Buelow was acting in concert with, or for, a New York obstetrician, Dr. Dmitri Valentine,* who had apparently delivered the money to Von Buelow for disposition. At Von Buelow's request, Laufter had already telegraphed $2,700 to the doctor in New York and had delivered several thousand dollars personally to Von Buelow, for Dr. Valentine.

When word first reached Laufter that the bills were counterfeit (and before he was questioned by the Secret Service), Laufter sent a distress call to Von Buelow in New York City, asking him to rush to Chicago. Von Buelow told Dr. Valentine about the call.

"Don't worry about it," the doctor said. "If something has gone wrong, my people will take care of things. You go out and see what he wants."

Von Buelow met Laufter in the LaSalle Hotel in Chicago, where the detective gave him the bad news that the money was bogus. Von Buelow flew back to New York and relayed the story to the doctor.

Dr. Valentine was noticeably upset. "There is only one thing left to do," he said. "We have to get away—fast! We have to go to Europe."

"Europe!" Von Buelow was startled. "Why do we have to go to Europe? What happened? Did you know the bills were no good?"

"There's no time for explanation," the doctor said. "We have to take the first ship we can get."

"No! Why should I go to Europe? I took the bills in good faith. Besides, Laufter is my friend. I'm not going to run out on him."

* Dr. Dmitri Valentine is a fictitious name. The man has served a prison sentence and is now gainfully employed, and the authors have no wish to add to his disgrace.

"Don't be a fool!" the doctor said, and he took a letter from his inside pocket. "Here, read this."

Von Buelow read it. The letter was typewritten, signed "Joe," and bore a Boston postmark. *"We will expect you to straighten out anything you have messed up,"* it said, *"or we will deal with you in no maybe way."*

"Who wrote this?" Von Buelow asked. "Who's this Joe?"

"Never mind," the doctor replied. "He's with the people that gave me the money. And they mean what they say."

"You told me that if anything was wrong, your people would take care of things. I'm in a bad spot. So are those guys in Chicago. What about them?"

"The hell with them!" the doctor said. "We've got troubles enough to take care of ourselves."

"Well, you can do what you want. I know one thing—I'm not going to Europe."

Dr. Valentine took out his wallet and extracted several bills which he handed to Von Buelow. "Here's two hundred dollars," he said. "Take this and go to Canada—to Montreal. I'll meet you there, in the Mount Royal Hotel. I'll register in the name of Brill. Then we'll decide what we're going to do."

Von Buelow took the money. "All right—but I'm not going to Europe."

At about 7 o'clock that evening, as Von Buelow approached the entrance to his apartment house, a tall, heavy man stepped out of the shadows and blocked his path. "You are Von Buelow, yes?" the man said.

"That's right."

"We want you to get out of the country."

"Who are you? Who's 'we'? I don't understand."

"Dr. Valentine has told you. You are going first to Canada, then to Europe." The man glanced around furtively, then drew something from his overcoat pocket. Von Buelow could see the reflection of the street light on the blue steel of a revolver barrel. The stranger put the gun away and said quietly, "If you do not do as we say, we blow your brains out. You understand now?" He walked away rapidly.

In his apartment Von Buelow telephoned Laufter and told him of developments. Laufter suggested that Von Buelow meet the doctor in Montreal as planned and try to persuade him to get enough genuine money to make reimbursement to the banks for the counterfeit bills that had been exchanged. Von Buelow agreed and fled to Canada, registering at the Mount Royal Hotel.

The next morning he met Dr. Valentine in the coffeeshop. "I've arranged to get you a passport for Europe," the doctor said.

Von Buelow pleaded with him to get enough cash from his "people" to pay the Chicago banks for the counterfeits, but Valentine branded the idea as ridiculous.

"What's to become of Laufter, then?" Von Buelow asked.

"Who cares? Let him go to hell." The doctor pulled his chair closer to Von Buelow's and in a low voice went on: "Tomorrow you will leave for St. Johns to board a ship. I will bring your papers tonight."

When Von Buelow returned to the lobby he was met by the same tall stranger who had accosted him near his New York apartment. "Tomorrow you are going to St. Johns," the man said. "Now you will go to your room and stay there until morning."

Von Buelow stayed in his room until nearly 1 o'clock that afternoon, pacing the floor, smoking cigarettes, looking out of the window, sitting in a chair, lying on the bed, seeking a way out of his dilemma. Finally he packed his suitcase, then cautiously opened the door to the hall. Not a soul was in sight. He took the suitcase and went to the elevator, riding to the lobby. If there was any attempt to stop him, he would make a commotion that might frighten away his potential abductors. He paid his hotel bill and asked the cashier about the bus schedule to New York, then walked to the street. He hailed a taxicab and told the driver to take him to the airport. As he entered the cab he looked around carefully. No one seemed to be following or watching him.

By this time the Secret Service had pieced together the story about Von Buelow and Laufter, and from the latter they learned that Von Buelow had gone to the Mount Royal Hotel. A telephone call was made to the Royal Canadian Mounted Police, who immediately tried to take Von Buelow into custody, only to find that he had just checked out.

The R.C.M.P. called the Secret Service in New York. "Your man asked the hotel cashier about a bus schedule to New York. He's probably on the New York bus right now," they reported.

From its investigation the Secret Service had established that Von Buelow had been a German aviator, and this one piece of information led to a shrewd deduction by New York agents. Would an aviator be likely to take a bus on a long trip, or would he fly—provided, of course, that he could afford air travel? Agents were sent to the bus terminals in New York City, but strictly on a hunch two agents were dispatched to Newark Airport to await the arrival of a plane then en route from Montreal.

When the plane landed, the agents waited until all passengers had alighted and were walking away; then one of the agents in a loud voice called, "Hey, Von Buelow!"

Only one passenger turned in response to the call, a short, dapper young man in a blue suit. It was Von Buelow. The agents took him to New York.

The German readily made a complete statement about the entire affair, but was unable to reveal Dr. Valentine's whereabouts unless the doctor was still in the Mount Royal Hotel. He wasn't. Agents* visited his offices, his home, and other places in New York without finding him, but they let it be known that he was wanted by the Secret Service.

Within 24 hours Dr. Valentine surrendered himself to the New York Secret Service agents. He denied all knowledge of the counterfeit money, branded Von Buelow's statements as lies, and refused to co-operate in any way. "His lies were so obvious that it was pitiful," one Secret Service man said later. "Too bad he's so scared."

Agents did learn that Dr. Valentine was born September 25, 1898, in Odessa, Russia, and came to the United States on July 4, 1907. He had a profitable medical practice in New York, was a member of the staff of a prominent hospital, and at one time had been an active member of a Communist clique known as "the Lovestone Group."

Dr. Valentine was subsequently returned to Chicago for prosecution on the counterfeiting charge, was convicted, and on May 25, 1934, was sentenced to serve 15 years in a Federal penitentiary and to pay a fine of $5,000.

Von Buelow testified for the Government and was not imprisoned.

The Secret Service did not consider the matter closed, for strenuous efforts were made to determine where Dr. Valentine had received the $100,000 in counterfeit $100 bills. All leads ran into blank walls—and it was not until September 30, 1939, that an article published in *The Saturday Evening Post* helped to solve the mystery.

The article was entitled "When Stalin Counterfeited Dollars," and it was written by W. G. Krivitsky, identified as a "former general in the Red Army."

According to Krivitsky, Soviet Russia in its 1928–1932 Five-Year-Plan spent so much money abroad for machinery and industrial supplies that there was a serious shortage of foreign exchange in Moscow. "And this in turn," Krivitsky wrote, "led to what may be called Stalin's Five-Year Counterfeiting Plan, a bold experiment launched with the printing of about $10,000,000 in bogus United States currency."

"The source of the bogus money was never a mystery to the man in the Kremlin," the article continued. "The headquarters of the counterfeiting industry was located in the deepest recesses of the Soviet Secret Service. The distributors of the fake currency were Soviet agents."

According to Krivitsky: "Three years before the discovery of the transactions in Chicago, a serious failure had occurred in Berlin. There the private banking firm of Sass & Martini had been acquired in a de-

* Including Harry Edward Neal, co-author of this book.

vious manner by the Soviet Government for the express purpose of exchanging in bulk the spurious $100 bills."*

When the size of U.S. paper money was changed in 1929, the Russians evidently decided that their counterfeit fortune could not be used as planned, since they feared the old-style bills would attract more than usual attention and might therefore be more readily detected. Krivitsky claimed that he was assigned by the Soviet Government to "liquidate the affair and to have the outstanding currency shipped back to Moscow."

One recollection of Krivitsky's was a brief meeting in Vienna with Franz Fischer, alias Voigt, who had negotiated a quantity of the $100 notes through the ill-fated Sass & Martini Bank in Berlin. Fischer was on his way back to Moscow. "He was effectively disguised, wore a false mustache, and cut a melancholy figure," Krivitsky recalled.

"I am a finished man," Fischer told him.*

Krivitsky also mentioned a meeting in Vienna with a Soviet representative from America named Nick Dozenberg, and implied that Dozenberg had some connection with the counterfeiting operation.

Nick Dozenberg was arrested December 9, 1939 for obtaining a passport under false pretenses, and on a plea of guilty was sentenced to serve 1 year and 1 day in Lewisburg (Pa.) Penitentiary, where Dr. Valentine was also serving his 15-year sentence.

After Krivitsky's story appeared, Dr. Valentine wrote an urgent letter to Frank J. Wilson, then Chief of the Secret Service, saying that he wanted to give some important information to the Service. Wilson sent Assistant Chief Joseph E. Murphy to the prison to talk with Valentine.

The doctor told Murphy that he had indeed received the $100,000 in counterfeits from Nick Dozenberg. When Dozenberg came face to face with Valentine in prison, the doctor pleaded with him to tell the truth in the hope that the Government might then shorten Valentine's sentence. Dozenberg, he said, had laughed in his face, angering Valentine to the point where he decided to tell the whole story.

"That's what you should have done when you were first arrested," Murphy told him. "For all we know, you may simply have read Krivitsky's story in the magazine."

In 1949 the Committee on Un-American Activities of the House of Representatives, 81st Congress, held hearings regarding Communist espionage and questioned Nick Dozenberg and Dr. Valentine. They established that Dozenberg had worked for the Soviets in Moscow, in Rumania, in China, and in Germany, and was at one time a member of

* From the article, "When Stalin Counterfeited Dollars," by W. G. Krivitsky. Copyright 1939 by *The Saturday Evening Post*. All quotations used by permission.

the Soviet military intelligence organization. Dozenberg furnished no information about the counterfeit money.

Dr. Valentine, however, spoke his piece. Frank S. Tavenner, Jr., the committee counsel, mentioned the counterfeiting case (which had been reported to the committee by the Secret Service) and said, "Suppose you tell us the entire story about Dozenberg's connection and your connection with that counterfeit enterprise."

"Well," the doctor answered, "Dozenberg had been passing that money all over the world and he proposed to me that I should help him in getting this money converted in large blocks. At that time I was acquainted with a German, Hans von Buelow. . . . The proposition given to him was that he should help pass the money. . . ."

"What was the purpose of passing these counterfeit bills?" Mr. Tavenner asked. "What was to be done with the money?"

Said Valentine: "The money which I was to get, part of it I was going to turn over to Dozenberg, who would finance himself, his enterprises, and part of it was to go to the Lovestone Group."

The Case of the Counterfeit Hundreds was finally marked "Closed" in the Secret Service files, but it had an interesting epilogue. W. G. Krivitsky, author of the magazine exposé, was subsequently found dead in his room in a Washington hotel under somewhat mysterious circumstances. Metropolitan police conducted an investigation, but the available facts and evidence warranted only one conclusion—suicide.

Death and threats of death are of great concern to the Secret Service in the discharge of its greatest responsibility—the protection of the Presidents of the United States. . . .

° 14 °

Protecting the Presidents

In 1835 President Andrew Jackson attended a funeral in the Capitol Building in Washington. As he prepared to leave, a man with a wild look in his eyes dashed out of a crowd of spectators in the corridor, jabbed the barrel of a muzzle-loading pistol against the President's chest, and pulled the trigger. The gun failed to fire.

Quickly the attacker yanked out a second gun, aimed it at Jackson's heart, and tripped the hammer. The second gun also failed to fire.

After these few seconds the startled President whacked the assassin with his cane, and men in the President's party then disarmed him and delivered him to the police. At police headquarters the two pistols that had misfired were tested again and again. Not once did either gun fail to shoot, and experts declared that the odds against two successive misfires by these weapons were perhaps 100,000 to 1.

This was the first recorded attempt to kill a President of the United States while in office.

On March 4, 1865, when Abraham Lincoln was inaugurated for his second term, an actor named John Wilkes Booth tried and failed to force his way through a line of Capitol police officers guarding the route of the Presidential procession. Booth later said that he had lost a good chance to kill the President that day. After General Lee surrendered to General Grant at Appomattox on April 9, 1865, Booth, an ardent supporter of the Confederacy, conceived a maniacal plot to murder Lincoln and some members of his Cabinet.

On April 14, 1865 Booth discovered that Mr. and Mrs. Lincoln would attend a play at Ford's Theater that evening. As an actor he was well-known in the theater and was not questioned when he wandered backstage that afternoon. He bored a hole in the door that led to the private box the Lincolns would occupy, so that if for any reason he could not open the door he could shoot through the opening.

At 10 o'clock that night he went to a nearby saloon, drank some brandy, then entered the rear door of the theater and went directly to the hallway outside the President's box, barring the hall entrance behind him. A guard who was supposed to be on duty was in a nearby saloon. Booth peeked through the hole in the door. The President, Mrs. Lincoln, and their friends were enjoying the play.

Booth took a 6-inch brass-barreled derringer and a knife from his pockets. Cautiously he opened the door to the box, and with a weapon in each hand he stepped to the President's chair, held the gun close to Mr. Lincoln's head, and fired. He dropped the gun, struck down another occupant of the box with the knife, leaped over the front of the box to the stage, and limped into the wings, later escaping on a waiting horse. He was trailed to a barn not far from Washington and was shot and killed several days later. The President was carried to a house across the street from the theater, where he died within a few hours.

In 1881 James A. Garfield was elected to the Presidency. A religious fanatic named Charles Guiteau who, without being asked, had made campaign speeches supporting Garfield, sought a reward for his "help" in getting Garfield elected. He demanded that the President appoint him as American Consul in Paris. The President referred him to the Secretary of State, who told him that there were no open diplomatic posts to which he might be appointed.

For weeks Guiteau pestered the White House and the State Department without success. He had spent most of his money and gradually became obsessed with the notion that God had chosen him to "remove" the President. He bought a revolver and spent considerable time in target practice. When he decided that he was proficient in the use of the gun, he began to shadow Mr. Garfield. One Sunday morning he went to the President's church and noted that the President sat near an open window through which a gun could be fired at Garfield's head. He decided to kill the President on the following Sunday morning as he sat in his church pew.

During the week the newspapers announced that Mr. Garfield would leave Washington on Saturday. This killed Guiteau's plans for the church murder. On Saturday he arrived at the railroad station ahead of the Presidential party, his gun in his pocket ready for use. When the President arrived he walked close to Guiteau, but he was accompanied by Mrs. Garfield, and the assassin decided not to go through with the plan in deference to her.

When the President returned to Washington, Guiteau found other opportunities to shoot him, but failed to do so for one reason or another until he read once again that Garfield was to leave town. Guiteau waited at the depot until the President arrived. Garfield walked toward him on the way to the tracks. As soon as the President passed him, Guiteau drew his gun, aimed at the center of Garfield's back, and fired twice. Instantly Guiteau gave himself up to a police officer, demanding that he be taken to the city jail and given protection from any mob that might assemble.

The President died some 3 months later, and Guiteau was subsequently executed for the murder.

On September 6, 1901 President William McKinley faced a receiving line in the Temple of Music at the great Pan-American Exposition in Buffalo, New York, where he was shaking hands with thousands of people who had heard him make a speech the day before. In the stream of well-wishers, Death walked in the person of a thin, dark Polish man named Leon Czolgosz, whose right hand was covered with what seemed to be a crude bandage, held close against his chest as though the hand were injured. Actually the "bandage" was a handerchief that concealed a small loaded revolver.

When finally it came his turn to shake Mr. McKinley's hand, Czolgosz put out his left hand and at the same time pointed the other at the President's chest and fired twice. The President swayed and was held by his startled friends. Instantly several men jumped on the assassin and began to beat him until Mr. McKinley gasped a plea to them to show mercy.

At first it was hoped, even expected, that the President would survive, but on September 14, eight days after the shooting, he collapsed and died.

Leon Czolgosz was tried, convicted, and executed for the murder, and then Congress decided that action should be taken to protect Presidents of the United States against such attacks. No such formal protection had ever been provided, and it was still on an informal basis that Congress asked the Secret Service to furnish the necessary protection. No extra funds were provided for this duty until 1903, when formal authorization for safeguarding the President was included in the Secret Service appropriation act.

On June 23, 1913 Congress authorized the Secret Service to protect "the person chosen to be President" (President-elect), and on June 12, 1917 the protection was extended to members of the President's immediate family. Today the Secret Service protects the President, members of his family, the President-elect—and the Vice President "at his request," the latter authorized by Congress in July 1951.

Since 1901 Secret Service agents have safeguarded Presidents at home and abroad. They were with Theodore Roosevelt when he broke precedent and went to Panama, the first American President to set foot on foreign soil while in office. Agents protected Woodrow Wilson when he went to Europe after World War I. They were with Franklin D. Roosevelt in South America, Casablanca, Teheran, Yalta, Canada and Mexico, and with President Harry S. Truman in Potsdam and other places outside the continental United States. Secret Service men protected President Eisenhower when he made his historic journey to the Korean war zone as President-elect, and at the 1955 "summit" meeting in Geneva.

In 1959 the Secret Service sent agents to Europe to plan for President Eisenhower's visits to Germany, France, and England, and later for his unprecedented 22,370-mile journey to 3 continents and 11 countries. As in the U.S., he was always only a few feet away from Secret Service agents, whose alert eyes were constantly on the hands and faces of the throngs of people who gave the President such a cordial welcome. Such occasions place every Secret Service agent under terrific tension, for he knows that even a bouquet of roses tossed at the President by an innocent child might conceal a deadly bomb, yet the agent must ever be tactful and courteous—and inconspicuous.

When trips such as this are completed without incident and without harm to the President, few public tributes are ever paid to the Secret Service, which is probably as it should be; but let even a minor injury befall the President in some swift incident in a crowd, and watch for an avalanche of criticism and condemnation to thunder down on his protectors.

As this is written, plans are being made by the Secret Service to protect President Eisenhower during his proposed 1960 visit to Russia to accept an invitation extended by Nikita Khrushchev, who spent several days in the United States as the guest of the Government in September 1959. Agents will travel to Moscow and other Russian cities several days in advance of the President's arrival to work with Russian security officers in planning the precautions to be taken to safeguard Mr. Eisenhower during his stay.

Since 1901, during visits of foreign dignitaries to the United States, the Secret Service has had the honor of safeguarding such notables as the King and Queen of England, Queen Wilhelmina and Queen Juliana of The Netherlands, Sir Winston Churchill, Madame Chiang Kai-shek, Princess Martha of Norway, and scores of other foreign rulers and diplomats. Today, however, the protection of such dignitaries is provided by representatives of the Department of State. At such times as an important foreign visitor is in the company of the President, the Secret Service co-operates with the State Department's Security Division in the protection of both visitor and host, as was the case when Chairman Khrushchev spent time with the President in 1959. Incidentally, the head of the State Department's Security Division was formerly an agent of the White House Detail of the Secret Service.

Although no President has been harmed since the Secret Service began its protective duties in 1901, there have been assassination attempts. Franklin D. Roosevelt, for instance, had a close call on February 15, 1932, when, as President-elect, he spoke to a large crowd in Bay Front Park, Miami, Florida.

After his talk the President sat in his car chatting with Anton Cermak, then Mayor of Chicago, who stood on the pavement facing Mr. Roosevelt. Giuseppe Zangara, a demented Italian immigrant, jumped up on a seat in the middle of the throng and fired 5 shots at the occupants of the car. One bullet grazed the hand of a Secret Service agent and struck Mayor Cermak. Each of the four others found a separate human mark.

In telling of the tragedy later President Roosevelt said: "I looked around and saw Mayor Cermak doubled up and Mrs. Gill [who was shot in the stomach] collapsing. Mrs. Gill was at the foot of the bandstand steps. She was slumped over at the bottom. I called to the chauffeur to stop. He did—about fifteen feet from where we started. The Secret Service men shouted to him to get out of the crowd and he started forward again. I stopped him a second time, this time at the corner of the bandstand about thirty feet farther on."

"I saw Mayor Cermak being carried," the President continued. "I motioned to have him put in the back of the car, which would be the first out. He was alive, but I didn't think he was going to last. I put my left arm around him and my hand on his pulse, but I couldn't find any pulse. He slumped forward."

Praising the quick action of the Secret Service agents, Mr. Roosevelt said: "The agents did one quick and clever thing. When they got Zangara up from the ground they saw the car in which Vincent Astor and Raymond Moley were riding, two cars behind mine. It had just started out. They threw Zangara on the trunk rack and three policemen sat on him all the way to the hospital. They had to go to the hospital because inside the car was the fellow who had been shot in the head [Detective William Sinnott of the New York Police Department]."

Zangara failed to shoot the President, which he had set out to do, but he had wounded 5 people including Cermak, who later died. Zangara was electrocuted the following month.

The next spectacular assassination attempt came on November 1, 1950, when two Puerto Rican Nationalists, Griselio Torresola and Oscar Collazo, converged on Blair House, diagonally across the street from the White House. President Harry S. Truman and his family were in temporary residence in Blair House because the White House was under major repair.

Torresola approached Blair House from the west, Collazo from the east. In a police booth near the west side of the house was Pvt. Leslie Coffelt of the White House Police Force, a uniformed arm of the Secret Service. Without warning Torresola whipped out an automatic pistol, aimed it point-blank at Coffelt, and fired. Although he was only one or two heartbeats away from death, Coffelt managed to draw his gun and shoot Torresola in the head, killing him.

Meantime Collazo had opened fire on the police officers guarding the front entrance of the house. One officer, shot in both legs, went down but lay prone on the road, shooting at the attacker. Another, with a Secret Service agent (Floyd Boring), was firing at Collazo, who was partly protected by an iron fence that caused bullets to ricochet, but within the time it takes to read this paragraph Collazo was seriously wounded and collapsed on the sidewalk.

President Truman, in a bedroom on the second floor, appeared at the window to see what was going on. The Secret Service agent signaled and shouted at him to get out of sight, which he did.

Leslie Coffelt died, but two other White House Police officers were critically wounded and recovered. Collazo, the surviving attacker, was sentenced to be executed, but President Truman later commuted his sentence to life imprisonment.

The abortive attempt would never have succeeded, even if the attackers had shot their way past the White House Police on the street, for armed Secret Service agents stood at their posts inside the house prepared for just such an emergency.

On rare occasions there may be hazardous situations which are beyond the control of the Secret Service. In 1943, for example, President Franklin Roosevelt was secretly escorted aboard the U.S.S. *Iowa*, considered at that time the most powerful battleship afloat, bound for the historic Teheran-Cairo conferences. During a routine antiaircraft drill at sea on the morning of November 14 there was a sudden explosion close to the ship. From loudspeakers came the cry. "This is not a drill! This is not a drill!" Was the *Iowa* being attacked by Nazi U-boats? Instantly the Secret Service men made ready to take the President off in a lifeboat if necessary.

A few moments later the escort vessel, the U.S.S. *William D. Porter*, providing an antisubmarine screen at starboard, reported that she had accidentally fired a live torpedo in the direction of the *Iowa*. Captain John L. McCrea, on the *Iowa*'s bridge, saw the wake of the projectile, promptly heeled his battle-wagon to port, and watched the torpedo miss the ship by a bare 20 feet. But for Captain McCrea's maneuver, the torpedo would have struck the *Iowa* directly below the President's quarters.

Admiral Ernest King ordered an immediate investigation, which resulted in the court-martial of a seaman, but when it was established that the torpedo had been fired by accident the sailor was not punished, except for a stern reprimand.

People who attend functions at which the President appears, or who sometimes see him riding in his car, with Secret Service men close behind or walking beside the automobile, have little or no knowledge or appreciation of the careful planning which has preceded his public appearance, nor are they aware of the specialized training the Secret Service agents have undergone to qualify them for the vital job of safeguarding the life of the Chief Executive.

The security precautions taken by the Secret Service are designed to afford maximum protection with a minimum of interference with the freedom of action expected by and of a President in a democracy. In public gatherings every effort is made by Secret Service agents on Presidential protection duty to be as inconspicuous as possible, and it is only rarely, and usually by accident, that agents are seen in newspaper or magazine photographs of the President.

A group of picked agents, known as the White House Detail, accompanies the President whenever he leaves the White House, and remains with him wherever he may go. When necessary, the Detail is strengthened by the temporary assignment of additional agents from field offices.

When the President travels from Washington to some other city, agents are sent to his destination well in advance of his arrival to make plans for the visit. This advance work is practically always done in close co-operation with local police departments, without whose assistance an effective security program would be virtually impossible.

The Secret Service advance men and the police map out the best routes to be traveled by the President and his entourage. If several stops are to be made for brief appearances by the President, a certain amount of time is allotted for each stop, to fit a schedule laid out by the White House staff or perhaps by the President himself.

If the President is to stay overnight at a hotel, the agents ascertain the identities of other guests who will occupy rooms near his quarters. They investigate hotel employees who will have access to the President. The agents also set up plans for a perimeter of protection that must be surprise-proof and flexible enough to allow a quick response to any emergency. Screening points are established to give authorized persons access to the protected area and to keep out those who have no good reasons to enter it. An agent will walk in advance wherever the President is scheduled to walk, the elevators and cables will be carefully inspected, and arrangements will be made to receive and inspect all packages intended for delivery to the President.

Duty stations, or posts, will be marked on a floor plan or sketch, so that in a later briefing each agent will understand clearly where he is to be placed, what he will be expected to do, and will also know the locations and duties of other agents, for the success of the protective program depends on the teamwork of all agents participating in it.

If the President attends some social function where formal dress is expected (such as the Inaugural Ball), some of the agents will don white-tie-and-tails and mingle with the guests, always managing to be reasonably close to the President.

Crowds that gather to see the President in parades or elsewhere are usually orderly—but the Secret Service must consider that even friendly throngs can be danger sources. For instance, a potential assassin may lurk among hundreds or thousands of men, women, and children. Some unforeseen incident might bring on a stampede which could block streets or trample innocent people. If an attack should be made on the President, the well-meaning spectators might unintentionally prevent Secret Service agents or police from reaching the attacker.

If the President is to lead a parade, agents and policemen patrol the roofs of buildings along the parade route. If unusually large crowds are expected, the Secret Service may call on the Armed Forces to station troops along the line of march.

When the President plans an extended summer (or winter) vacation, the Secret Service inspects the building and grounds where he will stay, laying out whatever security precautions seem warranted.

When he goes to church the agents arrive well in advance of the services (sometimes the day before), make a careful search of the building from cellar to roof, and arrange to place men in strategic positions, including some to be seated in pews near "The Boss," which is the unofficial and informal manner in which the Secret Service agents (among themselves!) refer to the President.

When the President travels by train, the agents arrange with railroad and local police to patrol tunnels, overhead bridges and viaducts, and sometimes may send a pilot engine over the tracks in advance of the Presidential train.

Protecting the President when he is in residence in the White House is obviously much less nerve-racking than when he is in strange quarters. In Washington the first line of defense against intruders or those who seek audience with the President to air their personal grievances or to settle some fancied grudge is the White House Police Force, a unique organization.

As early as 1860 a few officers of the Washington Police Department were detailed to protect the White House and its grounds. Although the responsibility for protecting the President rested solely with the Secret

Service after 1901, not until 1922 did the Chief of the Service have any direct control over these uniformed policemen.

In 1922 Col. C. O. Sherrill of the U.S. Army, chief military aide to President Warren G. Harding, urged the enactment of legislation to create a separate White House Police Force. Some people argued that it would be better to assign soldiers to guard the White House and grounds, but this proposal had several disadvantages. Use of a military organization would mean frequent changes of military personnel, and newly assigned men would be unable to recognize members of the White House staff, important official visitors, and the many officers of Government who transact business frequently at the Executive Mansion.

Moreover, a military force would give the White House the atmosphere of a military establishment or of a stronghold with a "palace guard" which might make it comparable, in the public eye, to certain heavily guarded domiciles of foreign rulers. In other words, the use of soldiers to protect the White House in peacetime would not be in keeping with the popular conception of the democratic way of American life.

On September 14, 1922 an act creating the new White House Police Force became law. It specified that the force was "under the sole control of the President and under the direct supervision of such officer as he may designate." As his designated supervisor of the force, the President named Colonel Sherrill, who was also Director of Public Buildings and Grounds. Colonel Sherrill named Maj. O. M. Baldinger, junior military aid to the President, to supervise activities of the force.

Early in 1930 President Herbert Hoover recommended that all phases of Presidential protection be placed under the control of one head. Acting on this recommendation, the Congress directed, by the Act of May 14, 1930, that the Chief of the Secret Service supervise and control the White House Police Force.

Today the Force, supervised by one officer under the direction of the Chief of the Secret Service, is responsible for the protection of the White House and grounds, while the Secret Service is charged with the protection of the persons of the President and members of his family.

Members of the White House Police Force are recruited from the Metropolitan Police Department of Washington. They are required to take special training in firefighting, first aid, crowd control, self-defense, dealing with the mentally ill, and the use of all types of firearms. The Force boasts a collection of scores of trophies won in important pistol matches, and members of its Pistol Team are among the finest marksmen in the world.

One little known but vastly important segment of the Presidential protection work is the Protective Research Section of the Secret Service.

This is a group of specialists located in the Executive Offices Building, next door to the White House, who read, analyze, and classify threatening, obscene, and scurrilous letters addressed to the President or to members of his family.

Among the tons of letters sent to the President every year are thousands which are referred to the Secret Service for various reasons. The Service is first and foremost interested in those which threaten bodily harm to the President or his family, but many letters that are craftily worded to make only implied or veiled threats are also given top priority for investigation.

Long experience has shown that most threats or implied threats are made by persons who are mentally unbalanced, but this fact in itself magnifies the danger, since the man or the woman with a warped mind and a fancied grudge will be more likely to carry out the threat than will a normal individual.

Frequently people write to the President in strong language because they are in violent disagreement with an expressed statement or policy. The Secret Service—and the President—considers that it is the privilege of every American to voice his disapproval of the actions of his Government, and no letter writer need fear any investigation simply because he writes critical letters to the head of the nation. Only when such letters include direct or indirect threats of bodily injury, or when they are obscene, are they of interest to the Secret Service—and also the post office inspectors, who work closely with the Treasury agents in cases of this nature.

The Protective Research Section maintains thousands of specimens of handwriting, handprinting, typewriter characters, writing paper, watermarks, inks, and other reference materials for comparison purposes. In one case a threatening letter, sent to a member of the President's family, was typed on what had been a business letterhead. The printed portion of the original had been cut off, but the letter was postmarked in New York City. Secret Service agents identified the kind of paper used, obtained a list of purchasers of the stationery, and began the drudgery of narrowing down suspects. Eventually they came to one of the country's biggest steamship lines. An agent, posing as a typewriter repairman, obtained samples of numerous typewriters used in the firm's offices, and finally found one that exactly matched the characteristics of the threatening letter.

The male employee who generally used the typewriter was questioned by the agent in the presence of his supervisors and soon admitted that he was the author of the threat. It appeared that he had no intention of carrying it out and that he was mentally upset over personal difficulties. He was promptly discharged by the company, and arrangements were made for him to receive psychiatric treatment which he should have had long before.

Since the Secret Service began its protective duties, its agents have had opportunities to see Presidents of the United States merely as human beings, living as individuals and not as symbols, men who can laugh and joke, or play cards, or golf, or who worry about their wives and children and grandchildren, or who have stomach-aches and head-aches and colds and trouble with their teeth—men who are concerned with the fate of the nation and also with the little things that make them simply people like the rest of us.

Through the years Secret Service agents may have overheard private conversations or witnessed meetings or activities which could make headline news, yet each agent keeps a closed mouth and a memory which is conveniently forgetful where significant events are concerned. There have been, however, amusing or serious or exciting occurrences which throw considerable light on the human side of the Presidents and the Secret Service as well. . . .

• 15 •

Secret Service Scrapbook

President Theodore Roosevelt, always enthusiastic about outdoor exercise, liked to rise early and hike for several miles, often through Washington's Rock Creek Park. Occasionally he took great delight in making a sudden morning appearance wearing boots, striding swiftly out of the White House for his walk, leaving the agents no time to change shoes, even if they had boots available. Then, in the park, Teddy would slosh through Rock Creek and wade through tangles of underbrush, grinning as he watched the agents splash through the stream soaking their shoes, socks, and trousers.

One of the most delicate Presidential assignments came when Woodrow Wilson courted an attractive widow, Mrs. Edith Bolling Galt, who was destined to become the second Mrs. Wilson. Mrs. Galt and Miss Helen Bones, the President's cousin, visited a secluded estate in the New Hampshire wilderness, where Mr. Wilson subsequently joined them.

The late Richard L. Jervis, then in charge of the White House Secret Service Detail, later recalled the touchy task. "The courtship was difficult for us," he said. "The couple would go hiking through the forest, and although we didn't want to watch their every move, this was something we had to do. I discussed our duties privately with the President and found him altogether reasonable. 'I quite understand what your duties are,' he said, 'and you must perform them as best you can—remembering, however, to let your conscience be your guide!'"

President Wilson, like other White House occupants, enjoyed playing golf—but Dick Jervis remembered that he did not care for the customary male foursome, for refreshments at the "nineteenth hole," or for any kind of wagering. When he did not play alone, his golfing companions were Mrs. Wilson (a better golfer than her husband) and Adm. Cary Grayson, his Naval aide and White House physician. In the summertime, however, the President liked to get up at 4 o'clock in the morning and go to the Washington Golf and Country Club, just across the Potomac in Virginia, for 18 holes, returning to the White House ready for work at 7 o'clock! Jervis, who accompanied him, had to rise about 3 o'clock and usually went without breakfast.

One morning (at a later hour) Jervis was walking the course with the President and Mrs. Wilson when, strolling past a dense wooded area toward the 12th hole, they were startled by an earsplitting explosion. A great cloud of smoke billowed above the trees nearby, and a huge tree stump came hurtling down not far from the trio. Jervis dashed into the woods and found a farmer who said he was clearing out some old stumps. He had never before used dynamite and had actually set off enough in the single charge to blow up the Washington Monument!

Two days later the President instructed Jervis to determine how and to whom dynamite was sold, and to propose to the proper authorities that they require dealers in explosives to teach buyers how to use them correctly.

In 1918 President and Mrs. Wilson (and their Secret Service escort) went to France for the historic Paris Peace Conference. After the conference the President and First Lady visited other European countries, including England, where they were to be guests of the King and Queen at Buckingham Palace. Arriving in London by train, the Americans were met by the King in an impressive display of pomp and ceremony. Here an incident occurred that called for quick thinking by the Secret Service, as well as an abundance of tact.

As Agent Jervis later told the story: "Outside the railroad station, where the party was to ride in gilded royal carriages, there was some confusion about precedence. The carriages were magnificent conveyances. A gay-liveried driver and footman sat up high, the King and Queen and the President and Mrs. Wilson occupied the two seats built between heavy gold-plated springs, with two palace servants on a high seat at the rear. I had arranged for the Secret Service detail to occupy the carriage immediately behind the President's, as usual—but while we were getting the President and Mrs. Wilson seated in the royal carriage some of the prominent British officials, including David Lloyd George and Lord Balfour, strode out and climbed into our vehicle. If they remained there the Secret Service would have to find transportation some distance back in the procession, out of sight of the President's carriage, where agents would be helpless in an emergency. Walter Ferguson and Arnold Landvoigt, two of our agents, stood close by me waiting for instructions. Each of these men looked distinguished and important. I led Ferguson to the second carriage and introduced him to the British occupants as the personal aide to the President, explaining that arrangements had been made for him and his associates to ride in this conveyance. Lloyd George and the others smiled and quickly clambered out. We found them another carriage further back and they joined the royal party upon arrival at the palace."

On some occasions Presidents have assigned Secret Service men to unusual tasks. Once President Warren G. Harding was invited by Mr. Carl Fisher, a Florida realtor, to go fishing with a stag party on a tiny island off the Florida coast. The guests arrived at the island during the late afternoon and planned to fish the next morning. Just after dinner, however, the President complained of a stomach-ache and decided to go to bed. He vigorously opposed suggestions to call a doctor from the mainland. In a little while he summoned Agent Jervis to his bedroom.

"Dick, I want you to do something for me," the President said.

"Certainly, Mr. President."

"The boys were going to have a poker game tonight. I don't want them to call it off on my account, and I've told them you will play in my place."

Jervis grinned. "Yes, sir. Uh—does that mean I'm on my own, or am I to split my wins or losses, or are you staking me?"

Laughing, the President answered, "It means you're to sit in the chair they have for me—and from then on you're on your own."

Jervis nodded hesitantly. After all, the President's friends were millionaires, and Jervis could see himself as a Government employee whose entire salary might be consumed by a pair of Jacks. As though reading his thoughts, the President said: "Now don't worry about it. Just listen to me a minute. When the game starts, come out fighting. Watch General [Charles G.] Dawes, and don't take him too seriously unless he draws more than two cards. Then be careful. Gorse, of the National Geographic, might be a little nervous—but look out for him if he gets a good pile of chips. You won't have any trouble with our host, Carl Fisher—but keep your eyes open for Al Lasker, that advertising duck from Chicago. All right?"

"Yes, sir. All right."

Jervis won $240 and Mr. Harding's cheerful congratulations.

On another occasion, when Harding visited his home at Marion, Ohio, farmers, factory workers, businessmen, housewives, and children formed lines four abreast to shake hands with the President. In the line Jervis spotted an elderly man whose weathered face was partly hidden behind a shaggy widespread red beard. He wore rough overalls, a crumpled blue denim workshirt open at the neck, and carried a wooden box about 8 inches square.

Jervis approached him and said in a quiet voice, "What's in that box, Mister?"

The bearded man glared at him. "None of your damned business," he answered.

Jervis showed the man his badge and identified himself as a Secret Service agent.

"In that case, sonny," the man said, "I'll tell you that I'm an old friend of Warren Harding's and this is a little present for him."

"All right," Jervis told him. "If you'll give the box to me, I'll see that it's delivered to him and I'll tell him you brought it. What's your name?"

Without another word the man turned and began to walk away rapidly, clutching the box under one arm. Jervis caught him by the arm and, despite his protests, took him away from the line and had him open the box. It contained a small but whole cheese. Jervis explained that an inspection of packages was essential to safeguard the President and said again that he would deliver the cheese, but the man refused and took it away.

Later that day the President summoned Jervis to his quarters. "What's this I hear about you interfering with a man who wanted to make me a present of some good cheese?"

Jervis told him what had happened.

"That man and I have been friends since we were boys," Harding said sternly. "Now he operates a cheese factory. All he wanted was to give me some of his cheese. What was the harm in that?"

"No harm, Mr. President—and I'm sorry your friend was offended. Frankly, he didn't look so good to me, and I was concerned about the package, especially when he tried to get away when I questioned him. I was only doing my job—and I think I should tell you that I'd do the same thing again in similar circumstances."

The President's stern expression was swept away by his laughter. "I know you would, Dick," he said, "and that's what I would want you to do. I just thought I'd tell you not to be concerned about what happened today. It's all in the game, and I'm fully aware that everything you boys do is done in my behalf, so let's forget about the cheese, eh?"

On Warren Harding's death while in office, the leadership of the nation became the responsibility of Vice President Calvin Coolidge, a Yankee with a nasal twang, a granite face, and a penchant for keeping his mouth shut. Old-timers in the Secret Service tell many stories about Mr. Coolidge—stories like the one recalled by Harvey Ingley, now retired, but who spent many months as a member of the White House Detail and who later headed the Forgery Section of the Secret Service.

Harvey was on duty in the Black Hills of South Dakota, where the Coolidges were spending a vacation on the shores of a lake. Harvey had been on the night detail outside the lodge where the President stayed, and one morning as his shift ended Harvey went to the lake shore, only a few yards from the lodge entrance, and began to fish. Within a few minutes he had landed a 3-pound black bass which he unhooked and placed on the grass. Some 10 minutes later he saw the President emerge from the lodge, dropped the fishing tackle, and went to meet him. With a terse greeting Cal walked to the shore, eyed the bass, picked up the fishing rod, and flicked the line into the water. "Who caught that?" he asked, nodding at the fish.

"I did, Mr. President," Harvey said. "Just a few minutes ago."

Edmund Starling, then Agent in Charge of the White House Detail, came out shortly and approached the President. He saw Cal with the pole, saw the bass on the ground, and said brightly, "Congratulations, Mr. President. That's a nice catch."

Without taking his eyes from his line, the President answered gruffly, "I didn't catch it."

Starling looked surprised. "You didn't? Who did?"

Cal gazed at Starling, then at Ingley, and jerked his head toward the latter. "He *says* he caught it."

Mr. Coolidge thoroughly enjoyed fishing, and on occasion he invited agents of the Detail to fish with him. One day he was accompanied in a trout stream by Agent John J. FitzGerald (now retired), himself an expert flycaster. Both wearing waders, the President and FitzGerald moved slowly along the stream, and gradually FitzGerald, intent on his casts, drew out in front of Cal.

Above the gurgle of the stream he heard the President's twang: "Fitzie! Fitzie!"

Fitzie turned, ready to dash to Mr. Coolidge's assistance if necessary, although other agents were along the banks. "Yes, Mr. President?" he called.

Cal beckoned broadly with one arm for FitzGerald to get behind him. "Remember," he said, "*I'm* the President!"

Not all Secret Service experiences behind the scenes are happy ones. During Mr. Coolidge's first year in the White House his younger son, Calvin, 15 years old, contracted blood poisoning from a blister on his heel, which developed while playing tennis. Critically ill, he was sent to Walter Reed Hospital, and the President and Mrs. Coolidge moved there to be near him. During the first night at the hospital the President was called back to the White House, and Agent Jervis went with him.

"While we were there," Jervis recalled later, "he asked me to come into his private office, a rather unusual request. While he signed some papers I walked to the window and waited. When he had finished he sat thoughtfully flicking the corners of the pages of a book on his desk. We were the only ones in the office, and it was very quiet. This was the first and only time I ever saw the President so shaken. Presently he looked at me and in a voice so low that I could barely hear it he said, 'Dick, do you—do you think Calvin will die?' "

"I hope he won't, Mr. President. We're all praying for him."

When they returned to the hospital young Calvin was in a coma, and there was a screen around his bed. The President went in and stood looking down at the pale face of his son until Mrs. Coolidge took her husband by the hand and led him across the hall to their rooms.

Agent Jervis kept vigil in a chair just outside the President's quarters. In about half an hour the door opened. Mr. Coolidge came out in his nightclothes and walked again to the boy's bedside, standing there silently for several minutes. Once again Mrs. Coolidge came, and without a word led him back to his room.

"This happened four times during the night," Jervis remembered. "I know how he must have yearned to see the boy open his eyes and recognize him. Once the President stopped directly in front of me, his eyes looking into mine. His face was grim and his eyes were dry— dry and sad."

Young Calvin died the following night, and the President's manner changed. He gave curt orders to the Army officers, doctors, hospital attendants, packed his belongings himself, and returned to the White House with Mrs. Coolidge.

President Coolidge's successor was Herbert Hoover, who, like his predecessors, was appreciative of the work of the Secret Service in his behalf. Mr. Hoover, incidentally, subsequently employed a one-time Secret Service agent, Lawrence Richey, as his personal secretary. As this is written the two are still together and are close friends.

One of the most humorous exchanges of official telegrams was made in connection with a trip to South America taken by Mr. Hoover. When he was scheduled to return to the United States, the then Chief of the Secret Service, William H. Moran, decided to assign field agents to meet and assist the Presidential party. Chief Moran sent a wire to an agent in Texas directing him to meet the White House Detail at Miami, Florida.

The Texan wired this reply: "JUST HAD ALL MY TEETH EXTRACTED. NEW PLATES NOT READY YET. BELIEVE IT INADVISABLE REPORT MIAMI."

And the Chief sped his answer: "REPORT MIAMI AS DIRECTED. YOU ARE TO PROTECT THE PRESIDENT, NOT TO BITE HIM."

Secret Service agents have had frequent brief glimpses into the lives of the great and near-great which tear away the glitter of fame and reveal hearts that beat as our own. One agent recalls a story about Pandit Jawaharlal Nehru of India, who was attending a monetary conference in the United States a few years ago.

While the meeting was in progress, a messenger arrived with an envelope for Mr. Nehru and was escorted to the Secret Service man, on duty at the entrance to the conference room. "This envelope," the messenger said, shaking it significantly, "contains a message of vital importance for Prime Minister Nehru. Can you see that it is delivered to him at once?"

The agent said that he could. He took the envelope to the conference table and handed it to the Indian statesman, who opened it and read the message on the single sheet of paper it contained. He crumpled the paper in his hand, threw it to the floor, pushed back his chair, and quickly hurried from the room. Apparently the message had indeed been urgent.

When the conference ended and the members left the room, the agent noticed the crumpled note still lying on the floor near Mr. Nehru's chair. He decided that because it was important he had best destroy it or return it to the Prime Minister. He picked it up and noticed that the message was in English, written in a longhand scrawl. It said, "Your wife's shoes are in the car, and you have the keys."

The President protected by the Secret Service for the longest time was Franklin Delano Roosevelt, who served three full terms and part of a fourth. Escorting Mr. Roosevelt entailed unusual situations and problems because of his paralysis, but he always seemed to consider his affliction as a nuisance rather than a handicap.

Agents who made advance arrangements for Mr. Roosevelt's many trips and visits had to plan ramps on which his wheel chair could roll, and if he was to make a speech on an outdoor platform the agents usually had a ramp built next to the stage so that the automobile with the President could be driven directly to it. America's plunge into World War II presented many new and unusual problems for protecting a President who could not walk.

Within minutes after the Japanese attack on Pearl Harbor was known, the then Chief of the Secret Service, Frank J. Wilson, summoned members of his staff to his offices in the Treasury Building to make immediate emergency plans for protecting the President and his family in case of an enemy air attack.

At the Chief's request, Treasury officials ordered Vault No. 14, one of a number of strongholds in the Treasury's dungeon-like subbasement, to be cleared out ready for occupancy.

Agents from various field offices were ordered to Washington to augment the White House Detail. All leave for Secret Service personnel, including the White House Police Force, was canceled.

Agents promptly confiscated White House press credentials from all German, Italian, and Japanese correspondents—about 20 altogether—

including 3 seized from foreign newspapermen who had boarded a train for New York City.

Within the next 2 days an engineering survey was made of Vault No. 14 and other vaults in the Treasury, and experts decided that Vault No. 1 would be a safer haven than No. 14. In Vault No. 1 were stored 700 million silver dollars, and $1,800,000,000 in gold certificates, all of which were moved to other strongholds. Vault No. 1 was strengthened with extra steel beams and reinforced concrete, was equipped with an air-filtering system, a separate generator, an escape hatch, a dozen telephone lines, a stove, and a refrigerator. A bedroom and an office were prepared for the President, and desks were furnished for members of his staff. A bunk was installed above each desk and could be folded back against the wall when not in use.

The Treasury Building was just across East Executive Avenue from the White House, but if it became necessary to transport the President to the vault shelter the agents would have to take him out-of-doors. In an actual air raid, such exposure would be dangerous. Therefore, plans were made to construct a bomb-resistant tunnel leading from the White House to the Treasury subbasement.

Ground for the tunnel was broken on December 13, 1941, and digging was carried on around the clock. When the tunnel was finished, the President was taken through it to the Treasury shelter, with which he was highly pleased.

On December 11, 1941, the date Germany and Italy declared war on the United States—and vice versa—Chief Wilson was directed to assemble a special guard force of 200 special officers and 125 Treasury agents in New York City, under the direction of James J. Maloney, Agent in Charge of the New York Secret Service District, and later Chief of the Service. These men were assigned to seize and protect the files, papers, and other property of enemy-alien firms in the New York area. Throughout the United States other Treasury investigators checked on business firms owned by alien Germans, Italians, and Japanese.

A two-way radio network was established for quick communication between Chief Wilson and agents in automobiles in Washington, and between the Chief and the White House Detail. The network was set up and maintained by a detachment of the U.S. Army Signal Corps. To provide liaison between the Signal Corps and the Secret Service, Agent George J. McNally (the same McNally who investigated Hitler's counterfeiting plot) was commissioned a Second Lieutenant and assigned to the White House Signal Detachment. As this is written McNally is a Lieutenant Colonel and commanding officer of the Detachment, which keeps the President in touch with any part of the world at all times, wherever he may be.

Vault No. 1, the Presidential shelter, figured in a now-it-can-be-told story that would have created headlines when it happened. On February 16, 1942 the third Selective Service call was issued, requiring men between the ages of 20 and 44 to register for the draft. The draft for this registration was to be held on March 17, 1942. To protect the capsules containing the registration numbers, two Army officers asked the Secret Service if the capsules, together with the historic "goldfish bowl" from which they were to be drawn, could be placed in a Treasury vault until March 17. The Secret Service agreed, and on March 12 the capsules and bowl were lodged in a Treasury vault (not Vault No. 1) by the Army officers, in the presence of agents. The bowl and capsules were in a securely sealed container when they were delivered, and in addition, the door to the vault was locked and sealed.

Two days later the Secret Service received a telephone call from one of the Army officers who had delivered the capsules. The officer said that he had received in the mail, anonymously, two of the official draft capsules containing Nos. T-5498 and T-6430. He and two associates brought them to Chief Wilson's office immediately.

Because the other capsules were in a sealed container, it was reasonable to assume that the two sent to the officer had been removed before the container was sealed—or that they were extra capsules prepared and sent by some practical joker. The only way to find out was to count the capsules in the container.

The Army officers retrieved the bowl and capsules, which were then taken to Vault No. 1, the shelter, to be counted. There should be a total of 7,000 capsules. The officers broke the Army seal and emptied the capsules out on the carpeted floor. The three officers and a member of the Chief's staff* began to count, putting the capsules in piles of one hundred.

When the count reached 6,700, the men paused and looked at each other. "Let's be extra careful now," one of the officers suggested.

Slowly they continued the count of the remaining capsules. When it came to 298 the men sat back and heaved sighs of relief, for with the 2 capsules received in the mails, the total of 7,000 was accounted for. How the 2 capsules became separated from the others, or who mailed them, remains a profound mystery. If some reader knows the answer, the authors would be happy to hear from him.

The war took President Roosevelt on trips totaling hundreds of thousands of miles—cross-country inspection tours, conferences at Casablanca, Teheran, Yalta—grueling journeys made under great tensions and terrific pressures. After his return from the Yalta Conference in

---

* Harry Edward Neal, co-author of this book.

February 1945, wan and bone-tired, he went to Warm Springs, Georgia, for a sorely needed rest. This was to be his last journey alive. On April 12, while posing for a portrait being painted by Mrs. Elizabeth Shoumatoff, Mr. Roosevelt put one hand to his forehead and mumbled, "I have a terrific headache." The next moment his head drooped, and he was unconscious. Secret Service Agent James M. Beary, later appointed Agent in Charge of the Washington Field District, grabbed the emergency telephone and summoned Dr. Bruenn, the President's physician, who was at a swimming pool about 2 miles away. Dr. Bruenn examined the President and telephoned Admiral McIntyre at the White House, who promptly called Dr. James K. Paullin, a noted heart specialist in Atlanta. Dr. Paullin sped to Warm Springs, but there was nothing he could do when he arrived. The President was dead.

The Secret Service, fulfilling its prescribed duty, immediately assigned a group of agents to protect the new President, former Vice President Harry S. Truman.

Although the interment of Mr. Roosevelt at Hyde Park, New York, was private, Mrs. Roosevelt personally invited the members of the White House Detail to join the small funeral company, considering them as friends who had accompanied the President on his pilgrimages all over the world.

After some 12 years of escorting a President who was generally confined to a wheel chair, members of the White House Detail found a decided change in the enthusiastic mobility of President Truman. Without warning, he would grab his hat, stride out of his office, and say, "I'm going to the Capitol for lunch." The agents had to scramble to keep up with him, but within a few days they were prepared for whatever quick moves he might make.

Mr. Truman enjoyed rising early and taking long morning walks—and the agents (as well as newspapermen and photographers) got their exercise whether they enjoyed it or not. Generally Mr. Truman was accompanied by James J. Rowley, Special Agent in Charge of the White House Detail. Jim Rowley, a Secret Service veteran, is a husky, handsome Irishman from New York who chased counterfeiters and check forgers in the field before he was assigned to the White House Detail in the late 1930's. A first-class investigator, intelligent, tactful, resourceful, and courageous, Rowley is an outstanding asset to the Secret Service. His devotion to his job has probably deprived his own family of his company on more holidays, weekends, nights, and special occasions than is the case with any other agent.

During Mr. Truman's walks, agents would remain a few steps behind him unless he invited them to stay by his side, which he frequently did. One morning as an agent walked beside him up 16th Street in

Washington the President said: "Here comes old Johnny Smith. I haven't seen him for months. Let's see if he recognizes me."

The agent noticed an elderly man approaching. When they were practically abreast of him, the man glanced casually at the President and at the Secret Service man, then looked away, and continued on past them. The President chuckled as he turned and called out, "Hey, Johnny! Aren't you speaking to your friends these days?"

Johnny stopped and looked around. His face brightened with recognition as he smiled, walked back to the President with his right arm outstretched, and said cordially: "Well, *Senator!* How are you? Where have you been keeping yourself?"

On one occasion the President and an agent returned from a hike by way of Treasury Place, which brought them to the southeast side of the White House grounds. They saw one of Washington's many whitecapped sightseeing guides talking to a group of tourists who looked through the fence at the White House.

"Come on," Mr. Truman said to the agent. "Let's find out what he's telling 'em."

They crossed East Executive Avenue and stood quietly in the rear of the group. The guide was pointing out various windows in the White House. "You see that first window from the right on the top floor? That's the President's personal study." The President kept nudging the agent with his elbow, because most of the guide's statements were wrong!

As they prepared to leave, the President looked down and saw the scrubbed freckled face of a little boy, probably 8 or 9 years old. The youngster was ignoring the remarks of the guide and was squinting intently at Mr. Truman. The President merely smiled at him and walked away with the agent. As they strolled toward the White House the President looked back two or three times, and each time he saw the boy standing a little apart from the crowd, still staring at him.

"I wonder if he recognized me?" the President said.

No one will ever know.

° 16 °

The Badge, the Klan, and Coxey's Army

From 1865 to 1960 the Secret Service had only 13 Chiefs:

1. William P. Wood....1865–1869
2. Herman C. Whitley..1869–1874
3. Elmer Washburn 1874–1876
4. James J. Brooks.......1876–1888
5. John S. Bell.............1888–1890
6. A. L. Drummond....1891–1894
7. William P. Hazen....1894–1898
8. John E. Wilkie.......1898–1911
9. William J. Flynn....1912–1917
10. William H. Moran..1917–1936
11. Frank J. Wilson.....1937–1946
12. James J. Maloney..1947–1948
13. U. E. Baughman...1948–

The career of William P. Wood has been set out in an earlier chapter. When Wood resigned on May 5, 1869, he was succeeded by Herman C. Whitley, an Assistant Tax Assessor in the Internal Revenue Bureau for the Fifth District of Virginia.

Oddly enough, Whitley had never applied for the job and was not aware of his appointment until one Sunday morning when he had just finished breakfast at his home in Lynchburg, Virginia. He picked up the newspaper and scanned the headlines, one of which startled him: "Col. H. C. Whitley Selected for Chiefship of the Secret Service."

The story must be a reporter's mistake, he decided, and would have to be corrected the next day. Throughout that Sunday he was approached by various friends and associates offering congratulations, and in the next day's mail came a letter from the Secretary of the Treasury notifying him of the appointment and asking that he come to Washington at once. He arrived there on May 13 and delivered his resignation from the Internal Revenue Bureau to the Commissioner of Internal Revenue.

"I wish you'd change your mind, Herman," the Commissioner said. "If it's a question of money, I can arrange to raise your **salary.**"

As Whitley later wrote about this meeting, he said, "I'm sorry, Commissioner, but I'd rather be Chief of the Secret Service than President of the United States."

The Commissioner escorted Whitley to the office of Secretary of the Treasury George S. Boutwell. Boutwell had made a careful search to find a suitable replacement for Chief Wood. In a casual discussion of the problem with Maj. Gen. Benjamin Butler, Commander of the Department of the Gulf during the Civil War, Butler suggested Whitley as a possibility.

"I had a chance to observe him for some nine years," the general said. "He was good at scouting, good at sniping, and one of the best cavalry leaders I had to fight those rebel guerrillas. He has plenty of initiative, a lot of git-up-and-go, and I think he's well equipped for the job you want done."

Whitley came out of the war as a lieutenant colonel, with a decoration for distinguished service. As a civilian he became a detective in the Internal Revenue Bureau, rooting out moonshiners in Kansas and Illinois for three lively years, after which he was appointed Assistant Tax Assessor in Lynchburg.

Anyone who saw Whitley would never forget him. Still in his forties, he stood 6 feet 10 inches tall. He had deep furrows in his forehead, a black mustache and neatly trimmed beard, and ice-blue eyes as steady and penetrating as those of an eagle.

As the new Chief, Whitley shook up the Service, firing some men, appointing replacements. He established a new system to keep a complete record on every counterfeiter—name, age, aliases, description, dates of arrests and dispositions, method of operation, and criminal specialty (engraver, printer, dealer, passer, etc.).

Whitley adopted a new method of promotions, based on merit. He appointed an Assistant Chief (the first) and expanded his office force so that he could keep a tight control over field operations.

In Wood's time each agent (then called "operative") was required to submit to Washington a general report of his activities four times each month. Whitley ordered agents to forward reports weekly that would account for their actions every hour of every day. A typical report, written in longhand, would begin: "I got up at 5:30 A.M., ate my breakfast, left home at 7:00, arrived at the office at 8:00. At 8:30 I went to the First National Bank. . . ." The report would conclude, "I returned home at 10:00 P.M., and at 11:30 I went to bed." Twelve to sixteen hours represented the usual working day, and there was no extra pay for overtime.

One of Chief Whitley's major accomplishments was the furnishing of official credentials to agents. In the early days the Secret Service investigators operated "on their faces"—they had no badges, no commissions, no guns unless they possessed or bought their own. They were equipped only with handcuffs. In a few instances they carried letters written on Treasury Department stationery, identifying them as Secret Service agents, but this was not the universal practice, and agents frequently found bankers or others reluctant to talk with strangers about clues or suspects in criminal cases.

In June 1871 a smooth and eloquent individual named Ira W. Raymond appeared in the San Francisco office of the Secret Service and introduced himself to Agent in Charge Henry F. Finnegass, saying that he had been appointed to administer the affairs of the Secret Service in the California District and also was to represent the Department of State in that area. Raymond took from his pocket an official Government envelope from which he extracted written documents ostensibly signed by the heads of the State and Treasury Departments, confirming his statements.

"Tomorrow," he told Finnegass, "I shall expect you to give me a complete report of the property under your control, including any contraband you are holding as evidence. Also, I will need a set of keys to your office vault."

Finnegass was surprised and puzzled. Why had not the Chief informed him of Raymond's appointment and arrival? Somehow Finnegass felt there was something wrong, and with the thoroughness of the investigator he was, he sent a telegram to the Chief asking for confirmation of Raymond's statements. The answer was not long in coming—Raymond was an impostor, unknown to the State and Treasury Departments.

With local police, Finnegass promptly took Raymond into custody. In his luggage they found numerous forged papers and letters. It developed that he had written to the Secretary of State and the Secretary of the Treasury about trivial matters, and that his letters were acknowledged by them in brief longhand notes. With chemicals he had removed the bodies of the letters, leaving the signatures of the Cabinet officers, and had substituted the messages constituting his "appointment." At an appropriate time he intended to steal whatever was of value in the offices, and also proposed to continue to use his forged letters "to good advantage."

Raymond pleaded guilty and was sentenced to the California State Prison.

To forestall the success of other schemes such as this, Chief Whitley initiated plans to issue distinctive badges and printed credentials to all members of the Secret Service. Various designs for the badge were suggested and considered, but it was not until August 5, 1873 that the official badge was approved and issued.

It was in the shape of a five-pointed silver star, each point engraved with a lacework design similar in pattern to that appearing on the printed borders of our present paper money, and it carried the engraved inscription: "U.S. SECRET SERVICE." With his badge, each agent received a memorandum from Chief Whitley reading, in part: ". . . It has been deemed best that the cost price, $25, should be deposited by each officer (which amount will be deducted from your account for the current month), to be returned upon your retirement from the Service."

Engraved and printed credentials, called commissions, were prepared by the Bureau of Engraving and Printing and issued to agents on March 17, 1875. Today each agent carries the silver star and the commission (which bears his photograph and signature).

Whitley asked and received approval to move his headquarters to New York City, the bustling center of counterfeiting, forgery, smuggling, and other crimes. The executive records were sent to New York "in a small, black, leather-covered trunk." The Assistant Chief and a small corps of clerks remained in Washington, while Whitley set up headquarters at 63 Bleecker Street, New York City.

Whitley's administration saw a nation in turmoil and in growth. In the North and West there were spreading monopolies, new railroads, coal mines and gold mines, big ranchers and meat-packing industries. There were great abuses as well as notable achievements. The upright and the crooked, the saints and the devils jostled each other, and ruthless men fought for money and power. The South was straining to recover from its desolation, and was hindered by a growing "society" that called itself the Ku Klux Klan. It began about 1866 in Pulaski, Tennessee, as a loosely organized social group of young men who dressed in long white robes with white hoods that had openings for eyes, nose, and mouth, the openings ringed in red flannel. Horns jutted out from the front of the headpiece. A "nose" was 6 or 8 inches long, and a huge red tongue lolled out of the mouth, so arranged that it could be wagged about by the wearer's real tongue. Under this fake tongue was an opening to a leather pouch, so that when the robed figure demanded a drink of water he could pour a whole bucketful through the mouth opening and into the hidden pouch.

At first the Klan engaged in rather harmless mischief, but soon learned that its hooded costumes struck terror into the hearts of the superstitious Southern Negro, and the one-time pranksters gradually became menaces who sought to "discipline" the freedmen. Disgruntled Southerners saw in the Klan a chance to strike back at the North and at former slaves. Victims were threatened, beaten, or driven out of town. Many were maimed, several were lynched, with little or no reason.

Congress finally sent a special message to President Grant on December 5, 1870, condemning the Klan and in 1871 authorized the Federal courts to punish violations of civil liberty. The Attorney General asked that the Secret Service investigate the Klans in the Carolinas, Florida, Alabama, and Georgia. Eight agents were assigned to this difficult task, and within 3 years had rounded up and prosecuted 1,000 offenders. Prison sentences ranged all the way from 2 months for minor violators to 10 years for organizers and Klan leaders. The rampages of the hooded terrorists promptly declined, but were destined to be revived many years later. The Secret Service was never again assigned to investigate the Ku Klux Klan.

Whitley's efficient administration of the Secret Service ended under a cloud. In 1871 the government of the District of Columbia consisted of a Governor, a Board of Public Works, a Legislative Assembly, and a House of Delegates. The Board of Public Works supposedly had authority only over the streets and the roads, but actually it controlled the District government. The Board tore up streets and sidewalks for "improvement," planned and built extensive sewer systems, and spent millions of dollars in excess of the limits set by Congress—proceeding to raise the money by hiking taxes and incurring a large corporate indebtedness. Residents protested, charging that the taxpayers were being victimized by a "ring" of favored contractors and speculators.

Citizens led by Mr. Columbus Alexander made an official appeal to Congress, which created a special committee to investigate the charges. The committee, headed by Congressman Jeremiah M. Wilson of Indiana, worked from February 11 to June 16, 1874, recommending passage of an act to appoint commissioners for a temporary government of the District of Columbia. This plan was later made permanent by the Act of June 11, 1878.

While the investigation was in progress, certain account books of a real-estate operator named John S. Evans were produced in connection with testimony. Mr. Alexander noticed that the books were virtually new, and suspected that they were not Evans' true records.

Alexander's enemies arranged to have him approached with an offer to place the real books in his hands for use before the committee. Alexander was prepared to accept the offer and to pay a reasonable amount to cover any expenses incurred, but was not aware that his foes were behind the move.

The conspirators were to "plant" a fake set of books, then have them stolen and carried by the "thief" to Alexander's home at night, where Alexander would be arrested for receiving stolen property. They got a set of meaningless books belonging to John Evans and put them in a safe in the office of the U.S. Attorney, Richard Harrington, who was Secretary of the District government and counsel for the officials under investigation.

An "anonymous" letter was sent to the U.S. Attorney, warning him of the proposed theft. At the appointed time Harrington and two police officials watched the "burglar" blow open his safe and take the books. He instructed the officers to wait until the books were delivered to Alexander, then to arrest Alexander and the thief.

The burglar, followed by the officers, went to Alexander's home and rang the doorbell several times, but no one came to the door. The Chief of Police, ignorant of the whole plot, then took the burglar into custody.

The case created a sensation and resulted in another Congressional investigation, during which it was alleged that the plotters had obtained the name of the burglar from Chief Whitley. The conspirators were indicted and prosecuted in one of the most spectacular trials in the history of the District of Columbia. The jury deliberated for 45 hours, finally disagreed and was discharged. The case was never retried.

There was no proof that Whitley was involved in the conspiracy, but because his name was mentioned unfavorably in the testimony, the Secretary of the Treasury felt that his resignation should be requested. Whitley resigned on September 2, 1874. Simeon B. Benson, Agent in Charge of the Pennsylvania District, was named Acting Chief and served until October 2, when Elmer Washburn, Chief of Police of Chicago, Illinois, former Warden of Joliet Penitentiary, was appointed the third Chief of the Secret Service.

Before Elmer Washburn took over, the Solicitor of the Treasury made an investigation of the Secret Service. Despite some criticism of its management he recommended few changes, and the organization emerged with its reputation unscathed. The Solicitor's main findings: (1) The force of 32 agents was competent but too large (!); (2) the loyalty and efficiency of the agents should be rewarded by increases in pay; (3) the national headquarters should be returned to Washington; and (4), a share of the field work should be performed by U.S. Attorneys and U.S. Marshals. The latter recommendation was not approved.

The Chief's office was re-established in Washington, where Washburn occupied a high-backed padded swivel chair at an ornate walnut desk on the fourth (at that time the top) floor of the Treasury Building. Along one wall were two large safes filled with counterfeit money and other captured contraband. A massive sofa, a wardrobe, and a few small tables matched the heavy pattern of the desk. Hanging from another wall were some of the grotesque hoods and robes of the Ku Klux Klan, symbols of the successful investigations in the South. Near a wood-burning fireplace were rows of "WANTED" posters describing various fugitives from justice.

Adjoining the Chief's room was the headquarters office force—three male clerks, each about 19 years old, wearing smooth-pressed alpaca coats with black cotton wrist-guards. They crouched over their desks flourishing dip-pens, occasionally spitting into the brass cuspidors near each chair.

In the same room, perched on a 3-foot stool, a young lady copyist in a denim smock copied letters and reports in longhand. If duplicates were needed she turned them out on a copy press which, under pressure applied by a large wheel and worm gear, transferred impressions by sheer strength. In her spare time she was required to learn to operate the newfangled machine known as a Sholes-Glidden-Remington typewriter, intended eventually to replace the copy press and the longhand writing.

From this executive center Chief Washburn made several administrative changes in the Service and took a personal hand in rounding up certain persistent counterfeiters. No spectacular fireworks marked his Chiefship, but there was one major occurrence that took place during his incumbency. The Government began to print its own money.

From 1863 to 1875 National Bank notes had been produced by commercial engraving firms, except for the seal and serial numbers, which were affixed by the Treasury Department. In September 1875 the faces of National Bank notes were printed by a Treasury unit known as the First Division National Currency Bureau. The backs continued to be printed commercially. The First Division National Currency Bureau subsequently became what is today the Bureau of Engraving and Printing, where all U.S. paper money is produced.

On October 24, 1876 Elmer Washburn voluntarily resigned as Chief of the Secret Service, secure in the belief that the Service had achieved a higher level of public respect and efficient operation.

Washburn's successor had been Special Assistant Chief under Whitley and was the first to be appointed to the top job from the Secret Service rolls. James J. Brooks was born in 1824 in Birmingham, England, emigrated to the United States in 1848, and worked for a time building baby carriages.

About 1851, when thousands of people were heading West, young Brooks led a group of pioneers to the new frontier, traveling by rail, covered wagon, boat, and finally on foot to a settlement called Reed's Landing in Minnesota Territory. In 1854 he returned East, went back to England with his wife and two children for a visit, and the next year came back to settle in Newark, New Jersey, where Brooks again took up the making of baby carriages.

Interested in writing, Brooks did some newspaper work in Newark and later became a reporter for the Washington, D.C., *Chronicle*, where he specialized in reporting criminal cases. By 1859 he had won a reputation as a public defender through his reportorial sleuthing and outspoken defense of the underdog. So efficient were some of his investigations that he was offered—and accepted—a job with the Internal Revenue Bureau to hunt down and arrest violators of the tax laws.

In appearance Brooks did not fulfill the public conception of a law-enforcement officer. Only 5 feet 6 inches tall, weighing 155 pounds, he had mild, benevolent brown eyes, a high forehead, a wide prominent chin, and a prematurely white bushy mustache and white hair that gave him the air of an elderly clergyman. His actions belied his looks. Within 10 years he had caught and convicted so many revenue lawbreakers that his territory was extended to include most of the states east of the Mississippi and some to the West. He recovered millions of dollars for the Government and exposed graft and corruption in high places.

Brooks received many threats against his life, and on one occasion he was seized and beaten by 8 men, and was in the hospital for several weeks. The underworld put a price on his head—$500 to the men who would kill him. Two young hoodlums from Philadelphia's Fourth Ward sneaked up on Brooks while he was inspecting the books in a store. One shot him, one hurled a blackjack at his head. Both were caught and sent to prison. The bullet that struck Brooks cut away a portion of one lung and lodged in his chest. It was there for the rest of his life.

When he recovered from the wound he accepted appointment as Special Assistant Chief of the Secret Service, taking over as Chief when Washburn resigned.

One of Brooks's first acts as Chief was to compile and issue the first formal manual of instructions for agents, designated as "General Orders No. 4."

With a change of national administration and the election of President Rutherford B. Hayes, the new Secretary of the Treasury, John Sherman, was in some mysterious manner led to believe that the Secret Service was operating "for improper purposes." He set up a special committee to conduct a thorough probe of all Secret Service activity. The committee dug into every phase of the work—filing, accounts, reports, expenses, case load, personnel—everything. It had no criticisms to offer—only praise. Secretary Sherman later reported: "I do not find occasion to make any order growing out of the investigation. The Service on the whole seems to be satisfactorily performed, and I am not convinced that any material change would be beneficial to the public interest."

During the committee's investigation Chief Brooks recommended that legislation be drafted to give the Secret Service official recognition and authority. The money used for its operations was appropriated to the Treasury Department "for suppressing counterfeiting and other crimes." The Treasury decided that this was sufficient, but on August 5, 1882, the Appropriation Act for the fiscal year 1883 actually authorized funds for the "Secret Service Division" of the Treasury Department. Accordingly,

July 1, 1883 was the day the Secret Service was officially "christened."

Brooks did not believe in vacations for his men. In July 1883 he issued a circular indicating that certain agents had requested leave of absence, and saying that such leave was "not needed by a class of agents who for twelve hours of each day are actively exercising their functions of body and mind in the bracing air and purifying sunshine. . . . Hereafter, leave of absence can only be given without pay."

In 1885 Brooks offered his resignation to a new Secretary of the Treasury, who refused to accept it. He remained at the helm, but labored under a handicap which has plagued the Secret Service throughout its existence. A frugal Congress refused to appropriate more than one half of the cost of operating a first-rate law-enforcement agency. Brooks's requests for additional agents were ignored. His predecessors had been helped by Assistant Chiefs, yet Brooks was allowed no assistant. For the administrative work that had cost $11,500 a year before Brooks took over, he was authorized to spend only $3,500.

No wonder Brooks thought seriously about retirement. Besides his official handicaps, he still carried an assassin's bullet in his chest, and he had spent nearly a quarter of a century fighting the underworld. On June 30, 1888 he sent a memorandum to all personnel saying that Agent John S. Bell would act as Chief until February 15, 1889, when Brooks expected to retire. However, William Windom, who had been President Garfield's Secretary of the Treasury, was again named to that post, and he made a personal plea to Brooks to remain in the Service. Brooks finally agreed to stay as a "special agent" to carry on special investigations, and he was so engaged until February 16, 1893, when he retired.

As planned, however, John S. Bell formally became Chief on February 16, 1889. Bell had earned a reputation as an honest, fighting Chief of Police of Newark, New Jersey, before he became a Secret Service agent on June 22, 1885. A polished conversationalist with a congenial personality, Bell was big and muscular. He had a graying beard and mustache, was given to wearing 10-gallon cowboy hats, and available photographs of him show a decided resemblance to William F. ("Buffalo Bill") Cody. He was, in fact, an expert horseman, could throw a lariat as accurately as any cowpuncher, and could draw and shoot as fast as most frontier gun slingers.

Bell's administration was short-lived. There are no detailed records of the facts that led up to his resignation, but it appears that he was pestered by appeals of bankers, businessmen, and Federal prosecutors to send agents into areas where counterfeiting, forgery, and other offenses were prevalent, and that he was compelled to ignore the appeals because he did not have the necessary funds or manpower. Counterfeiting was increasing, the quality of counterfeit money was improving, other departments were clamoring for agents to make investigations for them, and there was a fast-growing need for more Secret Service men. Bell became increasingly insistent that the Secretary seek added appropriations from Congress, but the Secretary was not in sympathy with his appeal. Economy was the Government watchword.

Bell continued his arguments until one day the Secretary told him, "There's one way to get more money and to avoid a deficiency in your appropriation."

"What's that?" Bell asked.

"We could vacate the position of Chief for a year."

Bell did not immediately offer to resign, but evidently he decided that his fight was futile. He had done everything possible for the Secret Service, and he was now content to draw his pay and let nature and government take their course.

On June 2, 1890 Bell received a curt note from Secretary Windom: "Sir: Your services as Chief of the Secret Service will not be required from and after this date."

On June 3, 1890 Chief Clerk John Cowie was named Acting Chief and served as such for the next 7 months. Windom tried to interest Brooks in taking the Chiefship once again, but Brooks declined.

When word spread that the job was vacant, the Secretary's office was deluged with mail from applicants, and an influx of political stooges wore a path to Mr. Windom's office to ask for the appointment. Windom, however, made a careful check of men already in the Service to find a suitable successor to Bell, and finally chose Andrew L. Drummond, Agent in Charge of the New York District, who became Chief on January 2, 1891.

Drummond, a native of Lancaster, Pennsylvania, had shipped as a seaman on a transport carrying supplies to Union armies in the South during the Civil War when he was only 16 years old. Before the war ended he was conducting various investigations for the North and developed a fondness for detective work. Subsequently he opened a private detective agency in New York with his son, who later operated it alone.

In 1871 Drummond was offered an appointment in the Secret Service, cracked several major cases, and was made Agent in Charge at New York by Chief Brooks. He had been in the Service for 20 years when he was made Chief, and the appointment brought scores of letters of praise and congratulations from U.S. Attorneys, bankers, and other law-enforcement agencies with whom Drummond had worked in the field.

Drummond was rather stout, with gray hair, a "longhorn" gray mustache and bushy black eyebrows. Aware of deficiencies in the counterfeiting laws, Drummond launched a campaign to get new Federal legislation for more stringent protection of the currency, and to amend existing laws that offered loopholes to counterfeiters on trial. Before his departure as Chief, he had succeeded in getting 14 amendments toward these objectives.

During Drummond's administration the Secret Service was given a new duty—investigating frauds in National Banks—a function performed today by the Federal Bureau of Investigation. Congress appropriated money for the new work, but the amount was so small that it was absorbed in a few months, and although there were only 8 people engaged in this field the work had to be halted when the money ran out.

In this short period the Secret Service had already cracked down on several banks, and when the investigations stopped, the newspapers raised a loud cry for their resumption. So great was the public insistence that a "Committee of Fifty for a New Philadelphia" came forward with a voluntary loan to the Government to finance the bank investigations.

The Secret Service arrested directors of one bank for aiding bank officers to embezzle and misapply funds; arrested the president and cashier of another bank, in Muncie, Indiana, for making false reports to the Comptroller of the Currency; and arrested the president of one bank and the cashier of another for embezzlement and for making false entries in the books. The cases stirred up national interest because they included the first on record in which a director of a national bank was punished for complicity in wrecking a bank.

Drummond resigned as Chief on January 31, 1894, to return to his son's detective agency, leaving behind a record of progress, praiseworthy achievement, and constructive leadership.

Drummond's resignation brought the usual flood of applicants for the Chief's job, many bringing packets of letters of recommendation from Congressmen, Senators, local politicians, even from personal friends without "connections." The number of written applications received would have filled a small truck! By this time, however, a pattern had been set—the last three Chiefs of the Secret Service had been career men appointed from the ranks. Treasury Secretary John G. Carlisle decided to follow the pattern.

Examining the records of various field agents, Mr. Carlisle's attention was especially attracted to that of Agent William P. Hazen, a young investigator in the Cincinnati, Ohio, District. Hazen's father, Larry, had worked as a Cincinnati police officer and had later established the Hazen Detective Agency in Cincinnati, a business that grew and prospered for 10 years. Even the famous Pinkerton's Detective Agency pronounced Hazen's to be "an agency of the highest type." Young Bill Hazen worked as an investigator for his father and solved several important cases involving a variety of offenses.

Bill Hazen applied for appointment as a Secret Service agent, was accepted on May 26, 1893—and less than a year later, on February 1, 1894, he was summoned to Washington and placed in the top job.

One of Chief Hazen's first major assignments is of historic interest. The Panic of 1893 plunged the nation into a great depression. A man named Jacob S. Coxey was said to be assembling an "army" of unemployed in Ohio to march to Washington, where they would demand that Congress issue $500,000,000 in unsecured paper money to be spent in providing work for the idle by improving streets and roads. Fearing that this movement might induce disorder and violence, the Secretary of the Treasury asked Hazen to keep close watch on Coxey and his "army."

Hazen assigned two men, J. W. Cribbs and Schuyler A. Donnella, to join the movement in Ohio. On April 16, 1894 Cribbs's report included this statement: "I fell in line with the squad of James Burns, one of the marshals. I heard Coxey's speech. He said they would march down Pennsylvania Avenue in Washington a hundred thousand strong and ask Congress to pass a bill to issue bonds for the benefit of the laboring man, and to give the laborer $1.50 a day as a minimum wage for an eight-hour day. Marshal Brown followed with a speech lashing all political parties, saying that if there was any Heaven it was here on earth."

Both agents reported that Coxey's followers were "a hard-looking class of vagabonds, footsore and weary. They are completely unarmed, except for a few who have pocketknives. They all seem to feel they are martyrs in a great cause, and if interfered with by the officials they will make no resistance but will go to prison or any place they are put, in the interests of the working man."

If the army reached major proportions and plotted violence, the Secret Service would be prepared to act. However, Coxey's "invasion" of Washington was a flop. With less than 600 men, he reached the city on April 28 and on the morning of May 1 attempted a demonstration on the Capitol grounds, where police arrested him and many of his marchers for walking on the grass. Coxey was jailed until June 10, when he was released after being nominated in Ohio for Congress. Later (1931–1933) he served as Mayor of Massillon, Ohio.

Counterfeiting was on the upswing, and the Secret Service was plagued by an increasing use of new methods of reproduction, including lithography and photoengraving. In 1898 a new counterfeit $100 bill appeared in circulation in Philadelphia. In a description of the note which Hazen sent to banks, he wrote: "This is the most dangerous counterfeit known to the Secret Service. Its existence is considered so grave a menace as to warrant the recall of all notes of this kind from circulation."

Secretary of the Treasury Lyman Gage became deeply concerned and instructed Hazen to devote his full time to locating the makers of the counterfeit hundreds. Gage appointed Fred Brackett, Chief of the Appointment Division of the Treasury, to take over the Chief's administrative duties and also named a committee to investigate the affairs of the Secret Service, assuring Hazen that this was no reflection on his management.

Apparently the investigation was prompted by newspaper reports that the Secret Service had assigned 2 or 3 agents to safeguard the President of the United States and his family during their vacation at Gray Gables, Massachusetts. Such duty, said the newspapers, was decidedly unauthorized and improper, since the agents were paid with money appropriated for the suppression of counterfeiting. The records do not show by whose authority Chief Hazen sent the agents to be with the President.

On February 27 Hazen was notified that he was being demoted to the rank of agent, and he continued to work in that capacity until June 12, 1901, when he resigned.

Hazen's successor as Chief was one of the great criminologists of his time—John E. Wilkie—who started as a crime reporter on the Chicago *Tribune*, moved up to foreign correspondent, then editor. Slender, erect, distinguished in appearance, John Wilkie was to lead the Secret Service through fourteen of the most dramatic years of its existence.

Secretary Gage learned from Assistant Secretary Frank Vanderlip about this Chicago newspaperman who, as an ace crime reporter, had solved numerous criminal cases that had baffled police. Gage sent for Wilkie, offered him the Chiefship. Wilkie declined, saying that he was not qualified, but the Secretary insisted that Wilkie remain for a week or so to look into the activities of the Secret Service and then make up his mind. At the end of the week, on February 28, 1898, Wilkie accepted the appointment, and Secretary Gage was flooded with letters from all sections of the country congratulating him on his wise choice.

° 17 °

Triumphs for a Trio

Chief Wilkie's first task was to find the makers of the deceptive counterfeit $100 bills. He did not choose to leave this job entirely to his agents. He sent two men to Philadelphia, and he himself assembled a squad to be stationed with him in New York City, hotbed of the counterfeiting racket.

In New York and Philadelphia, agents inserted a "Help Wanted" advertisement in the *Inquirer*, offering attractive pay for experts in the photoetching business. Applicants furnished personal histories and were checked by agents as possible suspects. Among the Philadelphia applicants were two young men, Arthur Taylor and Baldwin S. Bredell—revealed by the investigation to be the owners of an engraving shop of their own, a shop with practically no visible clientele. The men's reputations, however, were unblemished.

When a rash of the counterfeit $100 bills appeared in Atlantic City, agents went looking for Taylor and Bredell and discovered that they had left for Europe. From photographs the two were identified as passers by some victims of the counterfeits. Weeks later the pair returned to the United States, but were not arrested immediately, for Chief Wilkie wanted them to lead his men to the plant, if possible.

They were followed to a cigar factory in Lancaster, Pennsylvania, owned by William M. Jacobs. Chief Wilkie went to Philadelphia, and from a friend in the cigar business he borrowed a dozen boxes of brands put out by the Jacobs firm. He turned them over to a specialist in the Service, William H. Moran (later Chief) and after a careful examination Moran reported that the Internal Revenue stamps on ten of the boxes were counterfeit. Moreover, the workmanship resembled that on the $100 bills.

Agents rented a house across from Jacobs' cigar warehouse and made daily observations. An office boy, about 14 years old, was seen to come out on the fire escape every day and do gymnastics. On the theory that the boy might be interested in becoming a circus acrobat, Assistant Operative Larry Richey (later a confidential secretary to Herbert Hoover) approached the boy casually on the street one day and indicated that he, Richey, was a talent scout for a circus. The boy was intensely interested and insisted on doing a few acrobatics for the agent. Richey suggested that he could get a better idea if the boy were dressed in circus garb, and made an appointment for him to come to the hotel the next day at noon—without saying anything to his boss.

Richey obtained adjoining rooms in the hotel. He had the boy undress in one, then go to the other to be measured for a costume by a "tailor." While the measurements were being taken, so was a wax impression of the key to the warehouse, which the boy carried in his clothes.

That night, armed with a search warrant, the agents unlocked the warehouse and found the complete plant for the counterfeit $100 bills—plates, presses, and all.

The next day Chief Wilkie and his agents raided the warehouse and arrested Taylor and Bredell as the counterfeiters. Jacobs and an accomplice, William L. Kendig, were also arrested and prosecuted. All four were convicted and each was sentenced to 12 years in prison. Two defense attorneys were arrested and convicted for attempting to bribe the Secret Service men. A few months later Taylor and Bredell were again prosecuted for making counterfeit money in their cells at Moyamensing Prison, and were sentenced to serve an additional 7 years.

Wilkie's next big assignment was the result of the war between the United States and Spain, when the War Department called on the Secret Service to track down Spanish spies. Wilkie organized an auxiliary force of Spanish-speaking agents and stationed them at strategic points throughout the nation.

Bits and pieces of information revealed that Spanish agents were swarming through Washington, Key West, New York, New Orleans, San Francisco and Seattle, and were guided by Señor Ramon Carranza, one-time military attaché of the Spanish Legation in Washington, who had been evicted from the United States before the outbreak of hostilities. Wilkie's agents located Carranza in Montreal, Canada. With the co-operation of the Canadian authorities, Carranza's activities were exposed, his emissaries in the United States were arrested, and Carranza was banished from Canadian soil.

After the war Chief Wilkie's help was sought in cracking down on naturalization frauds by which thousands of aliens, mostly in New York, were obtaining naturalization papers unlawfully. The agents learned that political ward heelers devised the scheme to gain voters for their parties (and also to collect "fees" from the aliens in the bargain).

The racketeers would approach ignorant foreigners with an offer to obtain naturalization papers on payments ranging from $5 to $15. Thousands of the aliens who could not pass the required citizenship examinations were willing to pay. The promoters would then get other people to impersonate the applicants, meet the requirements, and would furnish professional witnesses to identify each alien and certify as to the latter's length of residence.

Some of the professional witnesses appeared in 75 or 100 cases in the same court! The Secret Service established that nearly 5,000 men in Brooklyn had been unlawfully naturalized within 8 months, and in Manhattan another 4,000 had been "made citizens." In nearly all cases the agents discovered that the aliens could not speak, read, nor write English, and only a small number knew the dates of their birth or of their arrival in the United States. In 1903, of the 150,000 Italians in New York City, 40 per cent held fraudulent naturalization certificates.

With perseverance and patience the Secret Service uncovered many of the perpetrators of the scheme, including one who operated in collusion with the Clerk of the Court and who actually did his "paper work" in the Clerk's office. Since the Department of Justice was anxious to keep the investigations secret, details were not given to the press, and the Secret Service completed its important mission without publicity or fanfare.

Chief Wilkie's administration saw these developments and more—the smashing of the crooked Louisiana Lottery, the assassination of President McKinley, the "busting" of the notorious "Beef Trust" (a monopoly of meat packers), the exposure of the Western land frauds, and the resulting unreasonable restriction of the Secret Service because it had done an honest and efficient job. For 14 years, from 1898 to 1912, John Wilkie led the Secret Service in brilliant fashion through a great variety of criminal investigations. In 1912 he was offered the presidency of a public utilities company in Chicago, which he accepted, turning over the affairs of the Service to his successor, William J. Flynn.

Flynn was made Chief on December 18, 1912, on Wilkie's recommendation to the Secretary of the Treasury. This was another promotion from the ranks, for Flynn had spent 15 years in the Secret Service and had become Agent in Charge of the New York District. Before entering the Service he had been Warden of the Ludlow Street Jail in New York City, where he first became interested in counterfeiters, and even after he became Agent in Charge he insisted on leading his agents when they raided counterfeiting plants. He had also served as Chief of the Detective Bureau of the New York Police Department.

He was a natural leader, and all of his men had a warm affection for him. A patient listener and a good observer, Flynn relied on "horse sense" and a retentive memory to help solve many perplexing cases.

When Flynn was offered the Chiefship there arose a question of residence. Flynn was a native New Yorker and wanted to stay in New York, but he also wanted to be Chief. The Secretary finally compromised—headquarters of the Service would remain in Washington, but Flynn could live in New York and commute, though his salary as Chief would then be reduced by $500 a year.

Flynn stayed in New York most of the time, and mail from Washington to the field offices was frequently signed "W. H. Moran, Assistant Chief," or "W. H. Moran, Acting Chief"; and the Agents in Charge also received mail from New York signed by "William J. Flynn, Chief." One apocryphal story goes that a stranger came to Washington several times to see Chief Flynn, but always found that he was out of town. He mentioned this difficulty to a railroad official at Union Station in Washington.

"If you want to see Bill Flynn," the railroad man told him, "just stay right here. He's always taking a train out or getting off one from New York."

One of Flynn's major challenges was the rule of the Mafia in New York, and the story of his cleanup of the Black Handers has been told in Chapter 5.

The investigations of neutrality violations and the seizure of Dr. Albert's plot-filled brief case were also highlights in Flynn's administration. When the United States became embroiled in World War I, President Wilson issued an Executive Order establishing the U.S. Food Administration to control the supply and distribution of food and to prevent food monopolies and food hoarding. Herbert Hoover was appointed to head the new agency, and Mr. Hoover requested that the Secret Service be authorized to investigate all violations of the food regulations.

Agents investigated thousands of allegations of hoarding, excessive prices, speculation, evasion of regulations, and other reported violations. Many of the reports were made by housewives and other individuals against unpopular neighbors, without good foundation, but some cases did require drastic action against German sympathizers and would-be profiteers, involving revocation of licenses, heavy fines, and the closing of businesses for short periods. Generally, however, a warning was sufficient to correct minor violations.

Under authority of the "Trading With the Enemy Act," the War Trade Board, another wartime agency, controlled imports and exports of all food commodities. The Board made special requests that the

Secret Service be assigned "to investigate merchandise and commodities sold for export and their ultimate destination, and to investigate persons seeking to buy goods in this country (for export)."

Congress granted the authorization, and the Secret Service in the ensuing year investigated more than 1,800 individuals and corporations to determine whether or not they were trading with the enemy. On the basis of these investigations, scores of names were added to the "War Trade confidential consignors" list and there were numerous seizures by the Alien Property Custodian of unreported enemy-owned or enemy-controlled properties.

On December 31, 1917, William J. Flynn voluntarily resigned as Chief of the Secret Service to direct the activities of the Flynn Detective Agency in New York City. He had devoted 20 years of his life to the Service, 5 of them as its Chief. During his 5 years in the top job, Flynn and his agents arrested more than 2,000 counterfeiters, hundreds of check forgers, broke up the big German sabotage plot, helped to control food hoarding and profiteering, investigated irregularities in the newly organized Federal Farm Loan System, and uncovered numerous people and firms engaged in trading with the enemy. The work was done without sensational publicity and without any request by Chief Flynn for an increase in manpower.

On January 2, 1918, two days after Flynn resigned, William Herman Moran was appointed Chief, capping a Secret Service career that began in 1882 when Moran, at the age of 18, started work as a messenger in the office of Chief James J. Brooks. To close friends Moran was "Herman" rather than "Bill." Both his Irish-sounding name, Moran, and his German middle name, Herman, were misleading, for he was of Scottish extraction and a member of the choir of a Presbyterian church.

Moran's first promotion was from messenger to clerk, mostly because his fine Spencerian penmanship attracted the attention of his superiors in those days of handwritten records and correspondence. At night and on weekends he worked with field agents to learn all he could about investigative methods. After office hours he studied case files of criminals, gave careful attention to their various methods of operation. With encouragement from Chiefs Brooks, Bell, Drummond, Hazen, Wilkie, and Flynn, he became an expert on the art of engraving, the techniques of counterfeiting, the manufacture of genuine money and its flow in commerce and banking.

On December 16, 1897 Moran was appointed Chief Clerk. Ten years later, on July 1, 1907, he was Assistant Chief at the age of 43.

As Chief Clerk, Moran once solved a puzzle that later became a favorite story of President Theodore Roosevelt. In 1905 the Federal Government issued a periodical report of the estimated national crop production. Preparation of this estimate was hedged with safeguards and performed behind locked doors and curtained windows, because if speculators should gain advance knowledge of the report there might be heavy losses to legitimate traders. Picked guards were posted outside the building. Meals were served to the accountants in the offices during the last day and night before the report was to be released. As an extra precaution, the figures for the estimate were not put into the final report until the last few minutes. The officials in charge of the operation were satisfied that their safety system was airtight—until market movements suddenly soared just at release time, netting fat profits for speculators. This happened on two occasions, leaving little doubt that the crop information had been leaked to Wall Street. But how?

Chief Clerk Moran was assigned to find the answer. Within 3 weeks he submitted his report: A trusted inside accountant was slipping information to a go-between who telegraphed it to the speculators. The method of communication was both novel and simple. The crooked accountant, using a prearranged code, merely raised and lowered a roller window shade in the crop-report office. A confederate on the street below got the coded message, then wired the manipulators. Moran checked the bank accounts of various employees, found one showing heavy increases in deposits made after the two crop-report leaks, and wrung a confession from the wayward accountant who was arrested with his accomplices.

Standing barely 5 feet 6 inches tall, Moran had a certain upward tilt of his jutting chin that gave him the appearance of greater height. He weighed 170 pounds and never had a reducing problem. His shock of brown hair turned snow-white in later years, but never thinned. In contrast to his white hair, white mustache, and fair complexion, his eyes seemed to sharpen from dark brown to penetrating black—one prisoner he questioned came away saying, "When he looked at me I felt like I was being X-rayed!" In dress, Moran was the conservative; in manner, the diplomat. He had a deep bass voice and his words were carefully chosen and uttered.

As Chief, Moran was severe, reasonable, and just. Any agent guilty of an indiscretion was roundly shaken up in a patient, grieved manner that made him ashamed but not embittered, and no man ever left a reprimanding session with the Chief without a firm determination to redeem himself. Many old-timers still in the Service who worked under Moran's direction remember his letters. Whenever one began, "I fail to understand . . ." there was reason for concern.

Moran's instructions were never vague or ambiguous. Once he sent an agent to northern New York State to open a new field office. For more than a week Moran read the agent's daily reports: "Engaged in trying to find a humble abode for my meager belongings."

After 10 days of the same, Moran sent the agent a telegram: "Put those things somewhere and go to work."

Chief Moran believed firmly that the Secret Service should avoid publicity, for in his extensive study of the underworld and its ways he was convinced that public descriptions of the machinery and techniques of crime and crime suppression were major factors in crime increases. The less the Secret Service had to say about its work, the more the criminal element would fear "the unknown quantity."

At all times the Chief took a personal and active interest in the Service. When Woodrow Wilson prepared to go to Paris for the Peace Conference, Moran decided that he himself would supervise arrangements for the President's protection. He sailed for Europe in advance of the President and planned the security precautions with the French police and with American and French troops.

In 1922 Chief Moran was confronted with one of the most unusual cases of his career. A special attorney in the Department of Justice, one Charles B. Brewer, obtained possession of Government bonds bearing duplicate numbers. He took them to Comptroller of the Currency D. R. Crissinger, a close friend of President Harding, and charged that the bonds proved that the Bureau of Engraving and Printing "reeked with corruption and crime" because the Bureau was turning out duplicate bonds to an extent that threatened a financial panic. Brewer repeated his charge to Congressman Louis T. McFadden, Chairman of the Committee on Banking and Finance, and Brewer, McFadden, and Crissinger brought the matter to President Harding. Harding gave Brewer a written order to make an investigation, and it was agreed that not even the Secretary of the Treasury would be told about the "scandal" in his own department.

Within a short time Brewer reported to the President that officers of the Bureau of Engraving and Printing were not only unco-operative, but also belligerent, and he recommended removal of 29 employees, including the Director himself. Harding forthwith fired the Director and 28 workmen, giving as the only reason that the discharges were "for the good of the service."

Sensational newspaper stories charged that a gigantic swindle had been perpetrated on the public by issuance of great numbers of duplicate bonds.

On December 30, 1922 President Harding called a conference at the White House to give Brewer a chance to make an oral report on evidence he claimed to have collected. At this meeting were the Secretary and the Under Secretary of the Treasury, the Attorney General, an

Assistant Secretary of the Treasury, the Commissioner of the Public Debt, Mr. Brewer, and Chief Moran of the Secret Service.

Brewer produced a package of $1,000 bonds saying he had discovered that the numbers on them were not printed at the Bureau, and that experts had assured him that these bonds had been numbered with stencils. Chief Moran asked to see the bonds, which he examined with a magnifying glass.

"These numbers were not applied with stencils," he declared. "They are impressed into the paper and were applied by printing in the customary manner."

President Harding then asked to see the bonds. "I know quite a little about printing," he said. After inspecting them for several moments he turned to Brewer. "You're wrong, Brewer," he said. "These numbers were never put on with any stencil."

A Secret Service investigation revealed that the bonds had been printed with duplicate numbers only because of mechanical errors in the production process, and not as the result of any wrongful intent. In a few cases the bonds with duplicate numbers had been detected and laid aside for destruction, but were stolen by messengers or clerks in the Bureau and later cashed. Other petty thefts in the Bureau had been investigated by the Secret Service from time to time, and over a period of 7 years these thefts represented about $13,000 in cash out of a total of more than 100 billion dollars in money and securities handled by thousands of individual employees. In most of the cases the culprits were identified and punished.

All Mr. Brewer's allegations were contradicted by the Secret Service investigation. The President, deciding that his good faith had been imposed on, instructed Secretary of the Treasury Andrew Mellon to reinstate the discharged Bureau employees. A public apology was made to the former Director, but he declined the Government's offer to restore him to his post.

Another matter of major importance in Chief Moran's administration was the investigation of the Teapot Dome oil scandals, described in Chapter 11.

For several years Chief Moran had advocated a simplification of the design of U.S. paper money as an aid to the suppression of counterfeiting and note-raising (the alteration of a genuine bill of small denomination to one of higher denomination by changing numerals, etc.) In 1925 he served as one of a 15-member committee to study currency changes. As a result of the committee's recommendations, the size and the design of U.S. paper money was simplified and standardized, and the smaller-size bills now in use were placed in circulation in July 1929.

In 1932 Congress passed the so-called Economy Act which, among other things, required payless periods of one month in each year for all Federal employees paid $1,000 or more. Workers were required to remain at work during their payless month and even to put in overtime. In 1933 the incoming administration of President Franklin D. Roosevelt imposed a 15 per cent salary cut without furlough. Annual leave was reduced, as were travel allowances. No salaries could be increased and no vacancies could be filled except by permission of the President.

The crimes of counterfeiting and forgery were mushrooming, and more Secret Service agents were badly needed to cope with the increase. Chief Moran was in a perplexing situation—the law held him accountable for the effective suppression of counterfeiting and forgery, yet he was unable to obtain the money or manpower to discharge his obligation. He asked the Secretary of the Treasury and the Bureau of the Budget for an increase in funds and personnel. His request came back disapproved. He had watched some of his predecessors face the same problem and surrender with a sigh.

As he sat back in his chair, staring out of his office window at the White House across the street, Moran made a bold decision. He picked up his rejected budget papers, strode out of the Treasury, and went directly to the President's office, where he was promptly ushered into Mr. Roosevelt's presence. In a few words he told the President of his dilemma, set out the reasons why he felt he must have more men and more money.

"Chief," Mr. Roosevelt said, "the economy policy is just about as final as the fiat of the Medes and Persians, but you've sold me on your predicament, and by Executive permission I'm going to approve the amount you tell me you must have."

Expressing his thanks, the Chief laid his disapproved budget estimate on the President's desk. "Would you just okay the amount here on this budget justification and initial it?" he asked.

With a lead pencil President Roosevelt scribbled, "O.K., FDR."

Head high, the Chief strolled back to the Treasury Building and to the Treasury's budget committee, handing them the justification sheet. They were both astounded and angry. In Washington no bureau chief ever went over the head of an Assistant Secretary—but Moran had even bypassed the Secretary himself! "You realize, of course, that this constitutes insubordination?" they said.

Stroking his white mustache, Moran answered in his deep bass voice, "Well, gentlemen, what are you going to do about it?"

They restored the cut, but they never forgave the Chief.

Early in the Roosevelt administration Congress passed the Gold Reserve Act of 1934, requiring Federal Reserve Banks to turn over their gold holdings to the Treasury in exchange for credits or a new type of noncirculating gold certificate. Regulations issued by the Treasury prohibited the acquisition or possession of gold bullion, fabricated or scrap gold, gold coin, or gold certificates, except under certain limitations. The Secret Service was designated to investigate all violations of the Gold Reserve Act and regulations and agents completed numerous cases, especially in the Western mining areas.

In one case two Los Angeles men, Louis H. Boyer and William H. Irwin, made a sub rosa deal with an employee of the California Division of Mines to buy gold that had been stolen and hidden in Grass Valley, Nevada. At the time the transaction was made, Boyer and Irwin were already suspected of other dealings in gold and were on the Secret Service suspect list.

Chief Moran assigned a skilled undercover agent to "rope" the pair— that is, to gain their confidence and try to get evidence of their criminal acts. The agent contrived a "casual meeting" and hinted that he knew something about gold and its black market value. Since he had an automobile, and since the suspects needed transportation, they decided to add him to their team to take them to Grass Valley and then to Los Angeles to make a sale.

At Grass Valley they picked up 163 ounces of gold which they took to Los Angeles and sold for $4,629.20. They decided to hire the undercover agent to transport them to various places for other possible deals. Just before they prepared to leave Los Angeles to go "up-country," the agent managed to slip a message to a uniformed guard in the post office, who promptly telephoned it to the Agent in Charge of the Secret Service there. Two agents were sent out immediately to follow the car carrying Boyer, Irwin, and the agent.

On the open highway the crooks suspected that they were being followed. They pushed their speed up to 90 miles per hour over the winding mountain roads. Near Roseville, California, Boyer took two loaded automatic pistols from the dash compartment.

"Let's slow down," he said. "I'm gonna put our friends out of business."

He aimed carefully at the driver of the pursuing car and shot. Although the motion of the car spoiled his aim, his bullet struck the driver in the fleshy part of one arm. Now the Secret Service car sped alongside the other, forcing it to the side of the road, and the two agents leaped out with their guns ready for action. Boyer and Irwin surrendered meekly, and were handcuffed and arrested along with their driver—the undercover agent, whose identity was not yet disclosed.

At the trial the undercover agent's testimony clinched the conviction, and Boyer and Irwin were each sentenced to serve 15 months and to pay a fine of $2,500.

Chief Moran was adamant about the use of firearms by his agents, insisting that no man shoot his gun except in target practice or as a last resort to defend himself. The latter reason was invoked by at least one agent, Edward Tyrrell, who was in charge of the San Antonio District, in a dramatic encounter with a pair of crooks.

One summer evening Tyrrell sat on the porch of his own home with Mrs. Tyrrell. A black automobile drove slowly past the house and parked a few yards away. Two men got out. One went into a grocery store, the other into a drugstore.

From the porch Tyrrell could look through the open doorway of the grocery store, and saw the girl cashier and the man from the car. The girl held a bill up to the light, as though questioning its authenticity. A moment later she shook her head and handed the bill back to the customer, who gave her other money and came out, walking toward the car.

As soon as he saw the girl examining and returning the bill, Tyrrell suspected that it might be counterfeit. Perhaps the customer was an innocent victim, perhaps not. He mentioned the incident to his wife and started out to question the stranger.

"Wait!" Mrs. Tyrrell exclaimed. She rushed into the house, came out with Tyrrell's .38 caliber revolver, which he stuck in the waistband of his trousers.

Near the car Tyrrell accosted the stranger. "Would you mind showing me that bill you tried to spend in the grocery store?" Tyrrell asked.

"Who the hell are you?" the man demanded.

Tyrrell produced his badge. "I'm a Secret Service agent."

In a flash the stranger shoved Tyrrell against the car, whipped out a .45 from a shoulder holster, and opened fire point-blank.

The first shot missed the agent. Before the second could be fired Tyrrell drew his gun and sent a bullet through the stranger's heart, killing him instantly.

With the sound of the shooting, the second stranger dashed out of the drugstore and opened fire. Tyrrell leaped behind a tree and returned the shots. The man jumped into the car and sped away. Tyrrell chose not to shoot again because people were crowding into the street, and he did not want to injure any bystanders.

The dead man was identified as Adrian Senay, master of a counterfeiting ring that had annoyed the Secret Service for months. More than 50 freshly printed counterfeit $20 bills were found in his pocket.

Tyrrell set out to capture Senay's partner, Lloyd H. Anderson, and caught up with him a few days later in a little town in the Texas Panhandle. Anderson attempted to get his weapon, but Tyrrell was faster on the draw. He handcuffed Anderson, brought him to trial, and saw him sentenced to serve 7 years in the penitentiary.

Chief Moran found no fault with Tyrrell's use of his gun in the Senay shooting, and used the episode as an example of the kind of case in which an agent might be expected to shoot to protect himself.

On March 28, 1934 Chief Moran reached the "compulsory" retirement age of 70 years—but President Roosevelt did not choose to let him go. "The public interest," the President said, "requires that Chief Moran be continued in the Secret Service." Thereupon he signed an Executive Order advancing the Chief's retirement date to March 31, 1936; and at that time, once again, the President extended the deadline to January 1, 1937.

After 55 years in the Secret Service—19 years as Chief—William Herman Moran retired at the then maximum prevailing Government retirement pension of $1,200 a year. He had done an important job with dignity, courage, and brilliance, and he wore his honors without ostentation. He was beloved by every agent and clerk throughout the Service, and on the evening of January 16, 1937 a coterie of agents and clerks from various field offices descended on Washington to give their Chief a farewell banquet at the Willard Hotel. Officials of many Government agencies paid tribute to the Chief in glowing letters of praise, and a handsomely bound volume of personal letters from every employee in the Secret Service, led by one from President Roosevelt, was presented to the white-haired crime buster—along with the keys to a new automobile as a token of affection from his men.

William Herman Moran's retirement marked the end of a 72-year policy of Secret Service silence and the beginning of an era of public education in the fight against counterfeiting and forgery.

$$\circ \ 18 \ \circ$$

The New Era

Chief Moran, who knew every man in the Secret Service by his first name, and who was a friend to all of them, wanted to have his successor appointed from the ranks, and recommended several Agents in Charge to Secretary of the Treasury Henry Morgenthau, Jr.

Morgenthau (perhaps remembering how Moran had gone to President Roosevelt to get approval of his rejected budget request) was polite enough to interview some of Moran's choices, but turned them all down, and for a reason which soon became evident. Morgenthau sought to consolidate all the Treasury enforcement agencies (the Secret Service, the Bureau of Narcotics, the Customs Bureau, the Alcohol and Tobacco Tax Division, and the Intelligence Division of the Internal Revenue Service) into one big enforcement group to be headed by someone of his own choosing. He could not make this move, however, without legislation, and although efforts were made along this line, the Secretary and his advisers were unable to convince Congress that the proposed consolidation would be more efficient or more economical than the existing organization.

Mr. Morgenthau then resorted to an alternative that was a close approach to his original idea. He realigned the district boundaries of the various agencies in the field, so that each agency covered the same territory. A supervisor was designated for each district, for each agency, and other offices in the district were subordinate to him. Any special equipment (such as lie detectors) held by one agency was to be made available on request to all, and other resources were to be pooled when necessary—a co-operative plan which admittedly had advantages.

Next the Secretary appointed a "Coordinator" to supervise the activities of all Treasury enforcement agencies, and he also appointed field coordinators to do the same thing on a local level. His first Coordinator was Harold Graves, who was succeeded in September by Elmer L. Irey, Chief of the Intelligence Division of Internal Revenue. Irey had won considerable prestige in the law-enforcement field as the leader of tax-fraud investigators who cracked down successfully on such racketeers as Al Capone, Waxey Gordon, and other big-time hoodlums spawned during prohibition.

In the Secret Service, reporting methods were changed, a uniform filing system was established in all offices, a new "efficiency report" was designed for rating each agent according to his abilities and accomplishments, and all agents were required to meet certain qualifications in the use of revolvers and other weapons under the competent guidance of the U.S. Coast Guard, also a Treasury agency.

As Chief Moran's successor, Secretary Morgenthau appointed Frank J. Wilson, an Agent in Charge of the Intelligence Division of the Internal Revenue Service. Wilson was unknown to most Secret Service personnel except by reputation—it was he who was primarily responsible for digging out the evidence that convicted crime czar Al Capone on tax-evasion charges, and it was Wilson, too, who had insisted on recording all serial numbers of the bills paid to the kidnaper in the Lindbergh case. One of these bills led to the arrest and conviction of Bruno Richard Hauptmann as the criminal.

Frank Wilson became the new Chief on January 1, 1937, feeling somewhat like the heir to an old homestead, who explores its huge rooms, wide halls, subdued lighting, and ancient decorations. One fact was evident. Counterfeiting was at a peak. In 1928 storekeepers and others were victimized by counterfeit passers to the tune of $215,000. In 1936 this loss had mushroomed to more than a million dollars a year. Some authorities believed that the crime of counterfeiting rose and fell with the fluctuating tide of depression and prosperity. Others thought that the repeal of prohibition had driven bootleggers into the bad money racket, and still others attributed the rise to the general increase in crime of all kinds. Frank Wilson, a stickler for figures and facts, decided to analyze the situation.

He had members of his staff and his statistical section make a survey of counterfeiting activity for several years past. The result showed that repeal appeared to have no effect on the incidence of fake money, nor did the business depression. Any changes that might be due to the depression or to repeal were so slight as to be insignificant.

Many old-timers in the Secret Service had other opinions. Since 1931, they believed, counterfeiting had become more and more of a syndicated criminal operation, offering a greater spread of outlets for counterfeit money. Also, they knew from experience in their own districts that the Service was seriously handicapped by a shortage of agents and operating funds, so that counterfeiters faced less opposition than ever before.

If the suppression of counterfeiting had been the only responsibility of the Secret Service, the story might have been different. As it was, however, the Service had to suppress counterfeiting and the forgery of Government checks and bonds, protect the President and his family, investigate thefts of Treasury Department property, investigate the responsibility of bidders on Government contracts, the integrity and character of applicants and employees of the Treasury Department (except the Internal Revenue Service), and had to enforce various Federal laws relating to the Federal Farm Loan Act, the War Finance Corporation Act, the Federal Deposit Insurance Corporation Act, the Gold Reserve Act, the Silver Purchase Act, the Federal Intermediate Credit Banking Act, the Farm Credit Act, and the Government Losses in Shipment Act. In 1936 the number of cases of these types totaled 753. There were then about 246 Secret Service agents available to make investigations of all kinds.

There was a slight drop in counterfeiting soon after Chief Wilson took over, but there were also reasons to believe that it might soon climb again. Wilson was aware that his predecessors had consistently discouraged publicity about counterfeiting, mostly because they did not want to create any lack of public confidence in the currency. Perhaps, he reasoned, this was the wrong approach. If a storekeeper or a cashier were told how to detect a counterfeit bill, surely he would refuse to accept one if it was offered and detected. And if passers got the idea that the Secret Service was teaching money handlers to be experts in detecting phony bills and coins, some might consider counterfeiting as a racket too hot to handle.

Thus Frank Wilson conceived and launched a unique nationwide "Know Your Money" campaign to teach laymen how to detect counterfeits.

Detection of a counterfeit bill is not always easy, not always difficult, depending on the quality of the workmanship. Genuine paper money is engraved on, and printed from, steel plates, whereas most counterfeits are etched with acid on copper or zinc. The skilled engraver maintains perfect control over the cuts he makes by hand in the steel, but the counterfeiter finds it more difficult to control the action of the acid, which generally eats away minute portions of the design and thus creates flaws which will betray his product as an imitation.

The United States issues three kinds of paper money: Federal Reserve notes, bearing green serial numbers and Treasury seal; Silver Certificates, with blue serial numbers and seal, and U.S. notes, with red serial numbers and seal. The Treasury seal is the round medallion with sharp sawtooth points on the face of every bill. These points, incidentally, are always clean and sharp on the genuine, but may be dull or broken on many counterfeits.

The oval portrait in the center of the face of each bill will identify the bill's denomination. This is important in detecting "raised" notes. A raised note is a genuine bill which has been altered to represent a higher denomination. In one New York case a watchmaker actually shaved the Lincoln oval from the faces of many genuine $5 bills without cutting through the paper, thus creating a sort of oval panel. In this panel he pasted a halftone oval picture of a local politician, cut from campaign literature. Using stenciled inserts, he pasted the numeral 20 over the fives in the corners, scraped off the word "FIVE" wherever it appeared, and with pen and ink substituted the word "TWENTY." Several of the bills were passed in stores—and one was actually traced by the Secret Service to the wife of the local politician whose picture was substituted for that of Honest Abe! She had received the bill in cashing a check in a department store, and the fact that she never noticed her husband's photograph typifies the carelessness with which most Americans examine their money.

Note-raisers are perennially active, and it will pay the average person to memorize at least some of the genuine portraits:

George Washington	appears	on	all	$1 bills
Abraham Lincoln	"	"	"	$5 "
Alexander Hamilton	"	"	"	$10 "
Andrew Jackson	"	"	"	$20 "
Ulysses S. Grant	"	"	"	$50 "
Benjamin Franklin	"	"	"	$100 "

It isn't likely that bills of higher denomination will be raised, but for the record:

William McKinley	appears	on	all	$500 bills
Grover Cleveland	"	"	"	$1,000 "
James Madison	"	"	"	$5,000 "
Salmon P. Chase	"	"	"	$10,000 "

The portrait is one feature which is most difficult for the counterfeiter to reproduce flawlessly. On the genuine bill the background of the portrait consists of a crisscross screen of very fine lines, well delineated. On most counterfeits some of these lines are broken, or the tiny squares forming the screen are filled with ink.

In the genuine portrait itself the eyes of the figure are clear, bright, and lifelike, but on most counterfeits there are etching defects which result in a lackluster and lifeless appearance in the face.

The lines of the hair, the shadows on the face, the fabric of clothing, all are created in the genuine by a skillful artistry of tiny lines and dots, and when some of these are missing or defective on counterfeits there are noticeable white areas in the hair, or flecks or blotches on the other features.

The best way to detect a bill suspected of being counterfeit is to compare it with another of the same type and denomination which is known to be good. As in the case of human twins, sometimes it is only when both are together that one can be distinguished from the other.

The Secret Service constantly sees incredible cases in which honest people are deceived by counterfeit passers. For example, a farmer selling potatoes at a roadside stand accepted and made change for what he thought was a folded $10 bill, but which turned out to be a novelty known as "rubber money," made of thin latex rubber and sold in dime stores at three for a nickel.

In several instances careless storekeepers have actually been fooled by counterfeits drawn freehand in ordinary lead pencil or pen and ink —drawings which were decidedly inferior to those which could be produced by a fifth-grade schoolboy.

This was the type of carelessness that Frank Wilson sought to erase by his "Know Your Money" campaign. Advertising agencies were invited to print counterfeit-detection hints on the backs of counter cards used in retail stores, and thousands of these went to retailers all over the country. Magazines, newspapers, and radio stations joined in the unusual campaign to make Americans "counterfeit-conscious." Metro-Goldwyn-Mayer produced a short film called "Know Your Money," which told a dramatic counterfeiting story and also conveyed some educational information to theater audiences.

One of the most valuable factors was a 32-page illustrated "Know Your Money" booklet, designed and produced by the Secret Service, showing differences between genuine and counterfeit bills and coins. Thousands of copies of this publication went to storekeepers and other potential victims of counterfeiters, and the booklet was placed on sale (20 cents) by the Government Printing Office. Although it has been revised several times, it is still considered one of the Government's best sellers and is still in wide demand. A 4-page KYM leaflet is given away free by the Secret Service on request.

Counterfeit-detection articles were published in leading encyclopedias, trade journals, house organs, foreign-language newspapers. Wholesalers of various products, and public utilities companies, co-operated by distributing millions of placards, circulars, and other helpful literature to their customers.

The Secret Service designed a Teacher's Guide to accompany the "Know Your Money" booklet, which was then introduced in numerous high schools as a study unit, and prizes for "Know Your Money" essays were awarded by local banks, Chambers of Commerce, and business firms.

A veteran Secret Service agent, Alonzo H. Rice, of Boston, wrote a script for a Secret Service "Know Your Money" motion picture, and in collaboration with a professional motion-picture cameraman produced an 18-minute film which was shown extensively in schools from coast to coast, and also in some theaters. Actors were Secret Service employees and Washington police officers, and the narration for the film was done by world traveler and newscaster Lowell Thomas.

In later years the Ætna Life Affiliated Companies, Hartford, Connecticut, produced professional films showing how to combat counterfeiters and forgers, and presented prints to the Secret Service for public showings to schools and business groups. The insurance company found the educational movies helpful in its own casualty underwriting.

Displays of actual genuine and counterfeit money, in attractive frames, were furnished to banks and stores so that citizens for the first time might get a close look at the good and bad and see the differences for themselves.

As the "Know Your Money" campaign expanded, counterfeiting losses declined. It cannot be said categorically that this kind of education was solely responsible for the decrease, because World War II was being fought and many counterfeiters or potential counterfeiters were drawn into the Armed Forces, or took high-paying jobs in war industries, or found it difficult or impossible to obtain copper, chemicals, and other materials on the critical list. Also, Secret Service agents were continuing the job they began in 1865—detecting and arresting counterfeiters and sending them to jail. There is no doubt, however, that the educational effort played a tremendous role in driving counterfeiters out of business or into other less hazardous pursuits.

Continuing his fresh, modern approach, Chief Wilson made a thorough inquiry into the value of the polygraph, or lie detector. After observing this instrument in actual use, and after numerous tests, he acquired the device for the Secret Service, and it has since been employed successfully in a great many cases, often being the means of establishing innocence as well as guilt. The Secret Service was probably the first Federal enforcement agency to use this modern tool of crime detection.

Another innovation was a "counterfeit note index," a system of describing each new counterfeit bill on a 5" x 8" index card in such a manner that the cards could be easily filed for quick reference. Whenever a new counterfeit appeared in circulation, a card was prepared and sent to every bank in the United States, with the co-operation of the Board of Governors of the Federal Reserve System.

Frank Wilson's responsibilities as Chief were far greater than those of most of his predecessors. He was charged with protecting the President throughout World War II, and also with the protection of rulers and diplomats of several friendly foreign nations who came to the United States. The threat of big-scale enemy counterfeiting was always of deep concern, and although it never materialized in this country it inflicted considerable damage on the British and would undoubtedly have spread if the war had not ended when it did.

On April 30, 1946, after Elmer Irey retired, Frank Wilson was promoted to the position of Chief Coordinator of all Treasury Enforcement Agencies, serving as such until December 31, 1946, when he also retired. Subsequently he became president of the National Association of Retired Civil Employees, in Washington.

Wilson's successor was his Assistant Chief, James J. Maloney, another career Secret Service man who had stepped into the Number Two spot when Joe Murphy retired in 1943. As a youth Jim Maloney had enlisted in the famed Lafayette Escadrille in 1917, serving overseas for about a year. After his discharge he returned to his native city of Binghamton, New York, where he became captain of the Johnson City Fire Department. Soon, however, he became interested in law enforcement and joined the Binghamton Police Department, at first pounding a beat, later promoted to the Detective Bureau.

Everybody in town knew and liked "Big Jim" Maloney. At 6 feet 3 inches he tipped the scales at 175 pounds. Immaculately dressed, he had an easy, quiet manner and a mild voice that could become stern and sharp when necessary.

After four busy years in Binghamton, Jim accepted an appointment to the New York State Police, later took a Civil Service examination for appointment as a Secret Service agent, and won the appointment on March 9, 1931. In the years that followed he became Agent in Charge of the Buffalo, New York, District, the Newark, New Jersey, District, and the New York District, the latter the most active in the country.

In New York he personally supervised the protection of distinguished visitors including the King and Queen of England, Madame Chiang Kai-shek, Princess Martha of Norway, Queen Wilhelmina of The Netherlands; Sergio Osmena, President of the Philippines, and Prime Minister Winston Churchill. Maloney was also responsible for the protection of members of the Roosevelt family living in his district, and of the Roosevelt estate at Hyde Park, New York.

When Jim Maloney became Chief in 1947 he was promptly hit by an economy wave—the same bugaboo that had discouraged many of his predecessors. The wave was no mere ripple. Congress lopped off a sizable chunk of the Secret Service appropriation, and Maloney was compelled to dismiss 63 agents, 22 clerks, 29 White House Police officers, and 63 uniformed guards serving in the Treasury and the Bureau of Engraving and Printing—a serious blow to the Service and a boon to the underworld.

With the shortage of agents, counterfeiting began to increase. A lively demand for U.S. money had sprung up throughout Europe after the war. Homeless refugees, bound for the United States, sought to convert their foreign currency into dollars, and to get the best rate of exchange they turned to the black market, mostly in France. Here the counterfeiters found easy pickings. Few of the refugees were familiar with the appearance of American money, and the counterfeiters made exchanges at extremely liberal rates. Unfortunately, when the refugees arrived in the United States many of them discovered that their life savings were all counterfeit—worthless.

Chief Maloney dispatched two ace investigators, Forrest V. Sorrels, Agent in Charge at Dallas, Texas, and Albert E. Whitaker, Agent in Charge in New York, to Paris, France, hotbed of the black market counterfeiting activity. Working with the French Sûreté, Sorrels and Whitaker succeeded in locating the masterminds of the counterfeiting ring, finally arrested them, and captured more than 2 million dollars in phony American currency which the crooks were ready to foist off on more homeless people.

On the basis of this haul, and the knowledge that counterfeit U.S. money was being made by other European sources, Chief Maloney won permission from the Secretary of the Treasury to assign an experienced Secret Service agent to Europe to assist foreign authorities in suppressing the counterfeiting of our currency. Agent Guy H. Spaman, a career agent and a first-class investigator, drew the assignment.

Spaman worked with police in England, France, Germany, Austria, Italy, Greece, Egypt, Belgium, Switzerland, and Denmark, and helped to round up scores of counterfeiters and passers. In April 1951, after 3 years of intense enforcement work, European counterfeiting of American money was negligible, and Spaman was brought back to the United States and appointed Agent in Charge of the Los Angeles Secret Service District.

In 1948 Chief Maloney instructed U. E. Baughman, Special Agent in Charge of the New York District, to come to Washington for a conference. Baughman thought that the Chief, among other things, wanted to talk with him about the status of his revision of the Secret Service Manual. A manual of instructions had been issued to agents in the late 1800's in the form of a bound, printed 46-page book about 4 by 6 inches in size, which was revised from time to time. Frank Wilson, finding the manual wholly inadequate and obsolete, had discarded it and issued two new larger manuals—one dealing with investigations, the other with office procedures. Chief Maloney proposed to combine both into one comprehensive work which would undertake to provide agents with clear instructions and descriptive information on every phase of Service activity. To this task he had assigned U. E. Baughman, considered an expert investigator as well as a highly capable administrator.

When Baughman arrived in Washington, he was in for a tremendous surprise. Maloney brought him to the office of Secretary of the Treasury John W. Snyder, without any previous explanation. After introductions the Secretary said: "Mr. Baughman, we're making a few changes around here. I'm promoting Mr. Maloney to be Chief Coordinator of the Treasury Enforcement Agencies—and I want you to take the job as Chief of the Secret Service. How about it?"

Baughman was utterly flabbergasted. As he himself recalls: "My first feeling was one of great bewilderment. The Secretary's statement was completely unexpected. I didn't know what to say—in fact, my throat was so tight I felt as though I couldn't say anything! But I managed to tell him I would be greatly honored, and to thank him for the opportunity. I don't remember just what I did say, but I do recall that my voice sounded as though it were far, far away!"

As the three sat and talked, Baughman recovered from the initial shock long enough to raise an important point. "I'd like to make one condition, Mr. Secretary," he said.

"What would that be?" Mr. Snyder asked.

"I'd like your assurance that every appointment in the Service, and every promotion, will be based strictly on merit, without any political factors."

Secretary Snyder nodded. "I'll agree to that for the Secret Service, one hundred per cent. Now—how soon can you move down here and take over?"

"Within a week, sir."

"Very well. You report a week from today."

On his way back to New York that night the whole span of Baughman's 21 years in the Service flickered through his mind. He began December 27, 1927, as a stenographer in the Philadelphia office, but was so intrigued with investigative work that he won permission from his superior, William H. Houghton, to accompany agents on cases after office hours and on weekends.

He even recalled how one agent, Peter A. Rubano, had taught him to speak a few phrases in Italian and how Baughman had been sent one day to make an inquiry of an Italian woman. He decided to test his knowledge of the language, and when the woman opened the door he showed her his credentials and said in Italian what he thought was, "May I come in?"

The woman stepped back in some alarm. What he had actually said was, "Will you let me out?"

As months passed he helped agents raid counterfeiting plants and made arrests, and then the day came in 1934 when he was commissioned as an agent and could conduct his own investigations and make his own arrests.

Born May 21, 1905, in Camden, New Jersey, Chief Baughman was a "junior," carrying the name of his father, Urbanus Edmund. His close friends, however, and his attractive wife, Ruth (Yessel), call him "UE," a designation which has occasionally resulted in letters being addressed to him as "Hughie" or "Hugh" Baughman. Tall and lanky, he was a good athlete in school, manager of the Ira & Kingsessing Athletic Association in Philadelphia, a first baseman on the baseball team, end on the football squad, center on the basketball team, and a champion swimmer and diver.

Throughout his career "UE" displayed a round-the-clock devotion to duty. Poker-faced, thin-lipped, with a clear and penetrating gaze, he insisted on maintaining the very highest standards in the Secret Service and let it be known that he would not countenance any violations of rules and regulations by any agent, no matter how minor. Yet he has held high the welfare and interests of his men, striving to get them salaries commensurate with their abilities as top investigators, to provide modern equipment for fighting crime, and to make the Secret Service the best-managed, most efficient law-enforcement agency in the Federal Government.

In May 1941 Baughman became assistant to the Agent in Charge in the New York District. Other important posts followed—head of the Newark District, back to New York, to Washington in 1945 as Agent in Charge of the field office, to New York as Agent in Charge in 1947, and finally, on November 29, 1948, he became Chief.

One of his first official acts as top man was to complete the Secret Service Manual. To this task he assigned another career man, Agent Michael W. Torina (now Chief Inspector), who had entered the Service as a clerk-stenographer, been promoted to special agent, and had worked not only on criminal cases in the field but also had served on the White House Detail. Torina's thorough knowledge of all phases of the work was a decided asset in the preparation of the Manual.

It turned out to be a ponderous loose-leaf volume of several hundred pages, well-indexed, with photographic reproductions of all administrative forms and reports, complete instructions for their preparation, and detailed information about investigations in every type of case under Secret Service jurisdiction. It is one of the most complete guides in the entire law-enforcement field.

He established, for the first time, a rigid system of inspection in which picked agents of long experience were appointed inspectors and sent on periodic trips to field offices to make sure that all rules in the Manual were being followed, to interview all agents and clerks and give them an opportunity to air any grievances or to make suggestions for improved procedures, and in general to assure maximum efficiency of operation.

At headquarters Chief Baughman set up a Management Committee, comprised of his top staff members, to make a continuing review of Service activities, to evaluate suggestions from the field, and to act as his advisers in administering the affairs of the organization.

In 1957, reorganizing his central office, he appointed a Deputy Chief (formerly known as Assistant Chief), an Assistant Chief in charge of security (Presidential protection, White House Police, etc.), and a Chief Inspector, responsible for the inspection groups.

Chief Baughman has a keen sense of humor which shows most clearly when he is relaxed and among friends, away from officialdom. At his polished desk in the Treasury Building, however, he wears a shell of austerity which keeps him aloof and which occasionally is hard even for members of his staff to penetrate. It is this very shell that has enabled him to remain coldly impartial toward agents who commit infractions and to mete out whatever punishment seems fair and reasonable, showing no favoritism even to his closer friends. A stubborn streak occasionally sparks arguments which are not easily overcome, yet the same stubbornness, combined with a high degree of perseverance, has helped him to succeed in many of his investigative and administrative achievements.

Officially and personally, U. E. Baughman thinks first and foremost of the Secret Service, to which (as of 1959) he has already devoted some 32 years of his life, and there is little doubt that he has done more to improve the administration of the organization and the welfare of his agents than most of his predecessors.

The biggest enforcement problem during Chief Baughman's administration has been the theft, forging, and fraudulent negotiation of Government checks and bonds. Every year the Secret Service receives some 40,000 forged Government checks for investigation, representing a million-dollar racket that thrives because most retail storekeepers will not insist on thorough identification of strangers who seek to cash checks. . . .

○ **19** ○

The Pen and Ink Pirates

An eager furniture salesman followed a hard-to-get lady customer as she wandered through the floor display of bedroom suites. Finally she stood hesitantly in front of a bureau, tapping one toe on the carpeted floor and cupping her chin in one hand like a female version of Rodin's "The Thinker."

"I like this one," she said.

The salesman extolled the virtues of the pieces and complimented the lady on her wise choice.

"There's only one thing," she said. "I have a Government check for a hundred and twenty dollars. Could I leave a down payment of thirty dollars and get the balance in cash?"

The grinning salesman waved a hand back and forth, flaglike. "No trouble at all," he answered. "You just endorse the check and I'll take care of the rest."

The woman nodded, turned away, and leaned over a table with her back to the salesman. When she straightened up she handed him her Government check. The salesman *never turned it over to see the endorsement,* but gave the lady $90 in change, a receipt, and a retailer's blessing.

Later that day, when the store cashier examined all checks to make sure they were properly endorsed, she was utterly amazed to note that the Government check for $120 had been endorsed in the name of its payee, but that two ink lines had been drawn straight through the written signature, and underneath the endorsement, in ink, were the words: "No good—this check was stolen."

The woman was never caught, and no one knows how the novel confession came to be written. It may be that she had stolen the check in desperation and had panicked when the moment came to endorse it, deciding then to tell all. The point, however, is that the furniture store lost money because an enthusiastic salesman failed to look at both sides of the check, or to ask for any identification.

Identification can be and is often faked. Some check thieves apply for Social Security cards in the names of payees of stolen checks, so that the signature on each card will agree with the endorsement on the corresponding check. The Social Security Board, at the request of the Secret Service, has printed on these cards the inscription: FOR SOCIAL SECURITY PURPOSES—NOT FOR IDENTIFICATION.

Also, by Secret Service request, the Treasury Department prints a warning on the face of every Government check: KNOW YOUR ENDORSER —REQUIRE IDENTIFICATION.

Countless forgers arrested by Secret Service agents boast about the number of stolen checks they have cashed with gullible merchants who fail to ask for identification of any kind. During some such investigations the agents have been told by merchants: "Why should I take the chance of insulting a customer and losing a sale by asking for identification? I'm covered by insurance. I can afford to get stuck." The storekeeper with this attitude fails to realize that he may be helping to further a criminal career, or that he may be setting himself up as a sucker for so many forgers that even his insurance coverage won't protect him as fully as he believes.

Some cases show not only gross carelessness by retailers, but rank stupidity as well. For example, a 12-year-old boy presented a Government check in a liquor store to buy ginger ale. The store manager looked at the check and told the boy to endorse it, which he did, and he got his ginger ale and his cash. On the face of the check was the inscription: "Purpose for which issued—Old Age and Survivors' Insurance"!

One crook, an Army deserter, made two trips across the United States on a pay-as-you-travel basis, cashing checks which he designed. He bought cheap blank forms in a dime store on which he typed the heading, "QUARTERMASTER'S BANK OF THE UNITED STATES ARMY," then made each "check" payable to any name that came to mind and signed it with a flourishing signature. There is no such institution as the "Quartermaster's Bank of the United States Army," which means that this enterprising swindler managed to cheat scores of storekeepers with do-it-yourself checks drawn on a nonexistent bank to the order of fictitious persons, signed by a mythical Army officer. The Secret Service discovered that the forger suffered from a lung infection. Circulars were sent to doctors and a warning was published in a medical journal on the theory that the crook might seek medical advice or treatment. A description of his checks was included. The technique paid off, for he visited the office of a Kansas City doctor who had read the warning, and tried to foist off one of his dime-store checks on the physician, who promptly called the Secret Service.

In one case in New York City the manager of a chain grocery store actually cashed a *negative photostatic copy* of a Treasury check!

Frequently crooks gang up to establish an organized business of stealing, forging, and cashing Government and other checks. Such a crew operated in Georgia in 1957 and 1958, when 17 men and women filched checks worth $10,000 or more from individual mailboxes.

In October 1957 Eddie L. Carter and Walter Johnson stole 4 Government checks which they cashed without difficulty. On December 31—in a single day—they stole 15 more. Fired by this success they recruited more help in the persons of Eddie Hunter and Mary Frances Coleman. When Walter Johnson was arrested by police on a minor charge in January 1958 Eddie Hunter took over leadership of the forgery gang, masterminding their moves without active participation in the thefts.

Hunter "employed" more and more helpers and set up a formal promotion system. All rookies started as thieves, lifting checks from mailboxes. Those who made certain quotas without getting arrested were promoted to the less hazardous task of preparing fake identification. In time they advanced to the forging of endorsements, and ultimately to the pinnacle—cashing the checks.

Rookies made "surveys" of the city to locate areas in which deliveries of Government checks were heavy, especially on the first day of each month, when pension checks and others were due. Once the areas were chosen, the thieves sped from neighborhood to neighborhood in rented automobiles to get to the mailboxes before the legitimate owners could get the checks.

The stolen checks were distributed to the passers, who then drove cars from store to store. Each passer was followed into a store by a "watcher," who observed the negotiation of the check. If a merchant seemed hesitant about handing over the cash because the identification was questionable, the watcher would approach the counter with a show of surprised recognition and would call the passer by whatever name was on the check, thus convincing the storekeeper that the identification was valid.

The identification in most instances consisted of Georgia drivers' licenses. In the State of Georgia application blanks for drivers' licenses may be obtained at many auto-accessory stores and at most gasoline service stations. Regulations require that a person who holds a driver's license and applies for a renewal simply fill out the application blank, on which he places his original license number. The application is supposed to be signed before a notary public or an official of the Department of Public Safety, and is then mailed to the latter department with the necessary fee. A validation stamp is there placed on the application, which is mailed back to the sender and becomes his new driver's license.

The forgery gang managed to steal 2,000 license applications from the Georgia Highway Patrol office in Columbus, Georgia. One application would then be executed for each stolen check, showing the description and alleged signature of the holder—but the name and signature, of course, would represent that of the true payee. Thus if a check passer were asked for identification he would flash his driver's license. Even an observant shopkeeper could see that the person presenting the check was accurately described on the license and that his signature corresponded with the endorsement on the check. Convincing, too, was the "validating" stamp on the license—but the unsuspecting merchant could not know that the official-looking stamp was merely a red tracing of a real stamp!

This Georgia case demonstrated perhaps the ultimate in carelessness on the part of a retail clerk. Each of 4 members of the gang was given 5 checks to cash—a total of 20 Government checks, all in different names. They went to a Columbus liquor store, where each of the four cashed one check in buying whisky. They met with the proceeds at a nearby beer parlor where they all changed hats, then one by one returned to the same liquor store and cashed four more checks payable to four different people. Back at the beer parlor they now swapped shirts and again returned to the same liquor store, where the same clerk cashed four additional checks. By more switching of clothes and by wearing dark glasses, this quartet had no trouble in cashing all 20 checks with the same employee in the same store! When finally they were arrested by the Secret Service, they recalled this episode and laughingly referred to the victim as "the blind bunny."

On one occasion Raymond Howard, Morris Johnson, and Willie Scott, operating "unofficially," stole 4 or 5 checks during their "off time." As Scott looked on, Howard hid the checks in a casket at a funeral home where he was employed as an ambulance driver. Scott later returned to the undertaker's, took the checks from the casket, and brought them to Boss Eddie Hunter, offering them for sale as a bargain, over and above his regular quota. Hunter objected to this spare-time operation, but bought the checks and sent a female member, Lucille W. Buckner, to cash them.

Lucille later returned without checks or cash, explaining that she had been held up and robbed. Hunter, suspicious, made inquiries which revealed that Lucille had cashed all the checks and delivered the proceeds to a boy friend. Angry at the doublecross, Hunter gave Lucille a savage beating. Three days later she died unexpectedly.

At about the same time, Willie Scott became deathly sick and was taken to a hospital, where his stomach was pumped out. He recovered, but as soon as he was discharged he was seized by Raymond Howard and Morris Johnson and severely beaten for stealing the checks from the casket.

One member of the gang cashed a stolen check in a liquor store, but after he departed, the store owner grew suspicious and telephoned his own daughter, who lived across the street from the address of the payee shown on the check. His daughter told him she had seen a stranger take something from the mailbox at the address in question. While the store-keeper was talking on the telephone, the forger returned to the store to retrieve the fake driver's license he had used for identification. On hearing the man's reference to the check on the phone, the crook believed he was talking to the police. The forger rushed to the telephone, tore the instrument from the shopkeeper's grasp, and attempted to grab the man himself.

The merchant, pulling away, ran to the counter, reached beneath it and came up with a revolver. The forger dashed toward his opponent and attempted to seize the gun. The storekeeper fired, and the crook yelled and went down, wounded seriously but not fatally. The police were summoned and took the forger into custody.

When the story unfolded, the police notified the Post Office Inspectors, since the check involved had been stolen from the mails. The Inspectors charged the man with the theft, then notified the Secret Service, as is the co-operative custom in such cases. When questioned by Secret Service agents, the wounded thief named Eddie Hunter as the leader of the gang and implicated other members.

The Secret Service first had to locate and get copies of some of the checks which had been stolen and forged. As soon as this was done, agents arrested two members of the gang and began a search for ring-leader Eddie Hunter. Detective John Chapman of the Columbus Police Department, co-operating with the agents, found and arrested Hunter on June 2, 1958. Hunter was delivered to the Secret Service the next morning and held for trial. He and his two companions refused to make any admissions.

Warnings were promptly sent to local merchants to be on the alert for checks presented by members of the gang using phony drivers' licenses for identification. Within a few days three more members of the gang were taken into custody when they tried to cash a stolen check. They talked in an effort to save themselves, and on the basis of their confessions the agents and detectives of the Columbus Police Department made a clean sweep of the forgery gang with 17 arrests.

In what promised to be a dramatic climax, some of the defendants alleged that Eddie Hunter had fed Willie Scott poisoned whisky in retaliation for Scott's sale of the checks stolen in his "spare time." The poison, they said, was what brought on the illness that resulted in Scott's hospitalization and stomach-pumping.

Even more serious was their charge that Hunter had also given Lucille Buckner some of the poisoned liquor after he had beaten her for giving proceeds of the checks to her boy friend. It was the liquor, they claimed, and not the beating, that had killed the Buckner girl. Acting on this information, a Secret Service agent enlisted the co-operation of the sheriff's office in Columbus. The sheriff obtained a court order for the exhumation of the woman's body, on which an autopsy was performed. According to a subsequent report of the State Crime Laboratory, results were "negative for common poisons, fluoride, and organic chlorides."

According to their own estimates, members of this gang stole, forged, and cashed about 600 checks before they were arrested. Most were Government checks, although they also negotiated several Georgia welfare checks. Victims were generally liquor stores, but a few checks were cashed without difficulty in supermarkets.

All but four of the defendants pleaded guilty. The four stood trial and were convicted. Sentences ranged all the way from probation to 8 years (for Eddie Hunter).

Every year the U.S. Government issues more than 400 million checks for various purposes—salaries, veterans' pensions, Social Security, retirements, income tax refunds, farm payments, Government purchases, and others. Every year thousands of check thieves and forgers are on the prowl to steal and cash these checks. To defeat these crooks, the Secret Service has some sound advice for people who get checks from the Government, and also for those who are asked to cash such checks.

If you RECEIVE checks from the Government:

1. Try to have some member of the family at home when the checks are due to be delivered. The longer the checks remain in your mailbox, the greater the chance that they may be stolen.
2. If you cannot have someone at home to receive the checks when they arrive, at least get a substantial mailbox and keep it locked.
3. Don't endorse your Government check until you are actually in the presence of the storekeeper or banker you will ask to cash it. If you endorse your check and it is then stolen or lost, you will be the ultimate loser.
4. Try to cash your checks in the same place every month to make identification easier. Be prepared to offer full identification.

If you are asked to CASH Government checks:

1. Insist that a person presenting a Government check identify him-

self fully as the person entitled to that check. Remember that every legitimate payee of a check *expects* to be asked for identification.

2. When you are asked to cash a Government check for someone you do not know, ask yourself this question: "If this check is a forgery, can I later find the forger and recover my loss?"

3. Insist that all checks be endorsed in your presence, even though they may already bear an endorsement.

4. Put your initials on all checks you accept, and mark on the back of each check a brief description of the kind of identification offered.

Note to forgers and potential forgers: Persons convicted of forging or altering Government checks face a maximum punishment of 10 years in prison and payment of a $1,000 fine.

Another class of forgers specializes in the stealing and cashing of U.S. Savings Bonds. These criminals are thoroughly aware that a great many people foolishly keep their Savings Bonds in hiding places at home, instead of putting them where they ought to be—in a safe-deposit box in a good bank.

Housewives and others continue to secrete their bonds, and even their cash, in shoeboxes, tin cans, sugar bowls, vases, bureau drawers, and other caches, secure in the mistaken belief that burglars will "never look there." Woe to those who are so naive! Burglars make it a business to know more about home crypts, cubbyholes, and secret storage gimmicks than any law-abiding housewife can conceive—and in recent years many professional burglars have made a specialty of seeking and stealing Savings Bonds.

"Funeral Ben," for example, took nothing but bonds and cash, ignoring silver, jewelry, and other such valuables. "Funeral Ben" read the obituary notices in newspapers in whatever city he happened to visit. He made notes of the times and dates of funerals, and, while the entire family of the deceased mourned in the chapel or at the cemetery, Ben would force an entry to their temporarily vacant home and make a leisurely search for bonds—hence his nickname of "Funeral Ben." He managed to get away with several thousand dollars in bonds before the Secret Service finally caught up with him and sent him to jail.

There is a bright side to the Savings Bonds story for bond owners who are victimized by robbers. No purchaser of a U.S. Savings Bond loses money, even when thieves steal every bond he has. Unlike cash, Savings Bonds that are stolen will be replaced by the Treasury Department, provided, of course, there is no evidence to show that the owners of the bonds conspired in the theft. To facilitate replacements, all bond owners should keep a good record of the serial numbers, denominations, and dates of issue of their bonds, *and should keep this record in a dif-*

ferent place from that in which the bonds themselves are stored. Then, if bonds are lost or stolen, it becomes a simple matter for the owners to give the Treasury definite information about the missing securities. Otherwise it may take weeks or months to locate records to identify the lost bonds.

Whether you buy Savings Bonds, or receive or cash Government checks, or are employed as a cashier or other money handler, you are a *potential* victim of some criminal. As such, you should heed the advice given by Chief Baughman: "The laws designed to protect the citizen cannot be enforced effectively without the citizen's co-operation."

Law enforcement, in other words, needs *you!*

° **20** °

The Secret Service—Then and Now

The Secret Service was organized in 1865 and became the first general investigative agency of the Federal Government. In the intervening years its agents have proved that they rank with the world's finest investigators. In numbers they cannot compare with the king-size enforcement bodies, such as Scotland Yard or the Federal Bureau of Investigation, but in skill, courage, and effective work they cannot be surpassed.

From 1865 to 1951 the Secret Service derived its authority from annual appropriation acts passed by Congress. In other words, every year Congress enacted a law which provided the Secret Service with a stipulated amount of money for operating expenses, and this law also authorized the Service to spend the money to detect and arrest persons violating the counterfeiting laws and other Federal laws relating to the Treasury Department.

In 1950 Congress asked various Federal agencies to seek permanent legislation to replace any "point of order" legislation in appropriation acts. In point of order legislation, whenever the appropriation act was awaiting final action by the Congress, it was possible for a Congressman to voice an objection to the language merely by raising a point of order. Such an objection could result in the deletion of the authorizing language from the bill—and if ever this should happen in the case of the Secret Service it would mean that the organization would have no legal authority to make arrests or investigations or to perform its regular duties. If, however, the powers of the Secret Service were defined in permanent law, then Congress each year need only appropriate certain sums of money for the Service without having to define the purposes for which the money must be expended, and the Secret Service legal authority would not be subject to a point of order.

With this in mind, Chief U. E. Baughman and Assistant Chief Harry E. Neal, working with Mr. Donald Hansen of the office of the General Counsel of the Treasury Department, prepared to draft such permanent legislation. When the time came to present it to the Congress for approval, however, there was opposition from the Department of Justice to a part of the language which authorized the Secret Service to detect and arrest persons committing offenses "against the laws of the United States relating to the Treasury Department and the several branches of the public service under its control."

This language had been set out (exactly as quoted) in annual appropriation acts since 1922, and in very similar form for many years before that, and had never been objected to by any other agency of Government.

The Secret Service considered the language to be essential, since it constituted authority for the Service to conduct investigations of the Gold Reserve Act, the Government Losses in Shipment Act, and to investigate shortages or reported thefts in the Bureau of Engraving and Printing, and the U.S. Mints—duties which the Service had discharged for more than half a century.

The Department of Justice argued that this language authorized the Secret Service to investigate such matters as bribery and corruption in the Treasury Department, which were within the jurisdiction of the Federal Bureau of Investigation, but the Justice lawyers were unable to point to a single instance in which there had been any jurisdictional conflict between the Federal Bureau of Investigation and the Secret Service, or any single case in which the Secret Service had ever made investigations of bribery or corruption since the Federal Bureau of Investigation was established.

At a hearing before a subcommittee of the House Committee on the Judiciary on March 16, 1951, Mr. Allen R. Cozier, representing the Deputy Attorney General, told the Congressmen: "I am here to voice the strongest possible objection to the enactment of that language. For many years appropriations for the activities of the Federal Bureau of Investigation have carried the language, 'for the detection and prosecution of crimes against the United States.' It is thus clear that the Federal Bureau of Investigation has exclusive jurisdiction over all acts involving violations of the criminal laws of the United States *except where the Congress has specifically otherwise assigned such jurisdiction.*"

Mr. Cozier's modification (in italics above) probably represented the policies of the Department of Justice, but was not inherent in the law as he quoted it. In other words, the appropriation act for the Federal Bureau of Investigation gave that Bureau jurisdiction over *all* criminal laws of the United States. Obviously this is not the true case, for Congress has given direct authorization to many other Government agencies to enforce various criminal laws, one example being the Post Office Department, which enforces the postal laws and regulations.

The record shows that Congressman Reed then raised an interesting question: "Who would do the investigating if there was bribery or corruption in the Justice Department?"

Mr. Cozier: "I was anticipating the question and I would not have any answer to that."

Congressman Bryson: "We would have to call the Treasury Department."

Mr. Cozier: "That might be one solution."

Congress had asked that the Secret Service and the Department of Justice get together to work out wording that would be mutually agreeable. Accordingly, the objectionable wording was changed to authorize the Secret Service to "detect and arrest any person violating any laws of the United States directly concerning official matters administered by and under the direct control of the Treasury Department." The Department of Justice said it would offer no objection to the substitute language, and the bill became law when it was signed by President Harry S. Truman on July 16, 1951.

"This should have been done long ago," the President said.

The opposition, however, did not die, for when the new national administration came into power the Department of Justice succeeded in having the Secret Service law amended. The amendment consisted of striking out all the language to which the Justice Department had objected.

The Secret Service pointed out that this would deprive it of some authority, but the Department of Justice assured the Congress that the amendment would not change any of the duties which the Secret Service had traditionally—and legally—performed for so many years.

The next step, however—and unusual it seemed—was the drafting of a "Memorandum of Understanding" between the Justice and Treasury Departments to "supplement" the law which defined the Secret Service powers and duties. The memorandum provided that the Federal Bureau of Investigation would have authority to investigate any Federal offense involving any officer or employee of the Treasury Department or its constituent agencies, or any other person, firm, or corporation acting in concert with any such officer or employee. It also provided that as soon as the Treasury had any suspicion or notice of any offense "in respect of which the Federal Bureau of Investigation has investigative authority, the Treasury Department will notify the Federal Bureau of Investigation and on request turn over to the Federal Bureau of Investigation full information regarding the matter so that the Federal Bureau of Investigation will be enabled to carry the investigation to a conclusion."

Moreover, the agreement said that if the Treasury was in doubt about referring any particular matter to the Federal Bureau of Investigation, the question would be submitted to the Attorney General, "whose decision will be final."

The memorandum also required that the Treasury Department issue instructions accordingly to its officers, "such instructions to be submitted to the Department of Justice for comment prior to their issuance."

The Secret Service suggested to the Secretary of the Treasury that the Treasury also be given an opportunity to see any instructions issued by the Federal Bureau of Investigation to its officers in connection with the memorandum. The suggestion was not adopted—but all Treasury instructions were submitted to the Department of Justice.

The "Memorandum of Agreement" was signed by Attorney General Herbert Brownell, Jr., and George M. Humphrey, Secretary of the Treasury, in February 1955.

Since that time, most if not all of the investigations of thefts and shortages at the Bureau of Engraving and Printing have been made by the Federal Bureau of Investigation, although this duty had been performed effectively by the Secret Service for many years.

The basic authority of the Secret Service is set out in Title 18, U.S. Code, Section 3056 (as amended):

> Subject to the direction of the Secretary of the Treasury, the United States Secret Service, Treasury Department, is authorized to protect the person of the President of the United States and members of his immediate family, the President-elect, and the Vice President at his request; detect and arrest any person committing any offense against the laws of the United States relating to coins, obligations, and securities of the United States and of foreign governments; detect and arrest any person violating any of the provisions of sections 508 and 509 of this title and, insofar as the Federal Deposit Insurance Corporation, Federal land banks, joint-stock land banks and national farm loan associations are concerned, of sections 218, 221, 433, 493, 657, 709, 1006, 1007, 1011, 1013, 1014, 1907, 1909 of this title; execute warrants issued under the authority of the United States; carry firearms; offer and pay rewards for services or information looking toward the apprehension of criminals; and perform such other functions and duties as are authorized by law.

Here are brief descriptions of the Federal offenses covered by the statutes listed by number in Section 3056:

508. Falsely making, forging, altering, or counterfeiting Government transportation requests, or passing or selling such false, forged, altered, or counterfeited transportation requests

509. Making or selling prints, photographs, or impressions in the likeness of Government transportation requests; making or possessing plates in the likeness of plates for printing transportation requests.

The following sections of Title 18 are enforced by the Secret Service only so far as the Federal Deposit Insurance Corporation, Federal land banks, joint-stock land banks and national farm loan associations are concerned:

218. Acceptance of loan or gratuity by farm credit examiner or by examiner of Federal Reserve member banks insured by Federal Deposit Insurance Corporation.

221. Acceptance of unauthorized fees or gifts by Federal land banks, joint-stock land banks or national farm loan associations or by their employees.

433. This section provides that sections 431 and 432, relating to contracts with the Government by members of Congress, shall not apply to contracts under the Federal Farm Loan Act and certain other laws.

493. Falsely making, forging, counterfeiting, or altering obligations of the Federal Deposit Insurance Corporation, land banks, or certain other lending agencies.

657. Embezzlement by employees of the Federal Deposit Insurance Corporation, or certain other credit and insurance agencies.

709. Use of words "Federal Deposit Insurance Corporation" as business name; falsely representing that deposit liabilities are insured by the Federal Deposit Insurance Corporation; falsely representing making Federal farm loans or issuing Federal farm loan bonds; and certain other false advertising to indicate Federal agency.

1006. Employees of Federal Deposit Insurance Corporation, land banks, and certain other agencies making false entries, drawing or issuing credit instruments without authority, and receiving profit or benefit with intent to defraud.

1007. Making false statements or willfully overvaluing securities in connection with Federal Deposit Insurance Corporation transactions.

1011. False statements relating to sale of mortgage by mortgagee to Federal land bank; willful overvaluation by appraiser of land securing such mortgage.

1013. False representations concerning character, security, or terms of farm loan bonds issued by Federal land bank or joint-stock land bank.

1014. Making false statements, or overvaluing property or security, to influence action of Federal land bank, joint-stock land bank, national farm loan association, or certain other credit and insurance agencies in connection with applications, purchases and loans.

1907. Unauthorized disclosure by farm credit examiner of names of borrowers from national farm loan association, Federal land bank, or joint-stock land bank.

1909. National Bank, FDIC, or farm credit examiner performing any other compensated service for any bank or banking or loan association.

In addition, the Acting Secretary of the Treasury, by Treasury Department Order No. 173-1, dated September 14, 1954, empowered the Secret Service to carry out certain responsibilities of the Secretary of the Treasury. The order says:

By virtue of the authority vested in me by Reorganization Plan No. 26 of 1950, there is transferred to the Chief of the United States Secret Service, to be performed through the Secret Service, the function of making any investigation required to carry out the responsibility of any bureau, office, or division which does not regularly make investigations, including investigations required in the administration of the Government Losses in Shipment Act, the Gold Reserve Act, and the Silver Purchase Act, except where the responsibility for performing an investigation has been specifically assigned to some other bureau, office, or division.

The Secret Service has weathered many storms and has made great progress in its first hundred years. In decades past, the Secret Service trained its agents by assigning newcomers to old-timers in action—an "on-the-job" training program. Today the Secret Service and the Treasury Department conduct two of the best training schools in the law-enforcement field.

Years ago, Secret Service agents, writing laboriously in longhand, submitted reports which were terse and even scanty. Today they must prepare detailed typewritten reports in important cases, sometimes accompanied by photographic exhibits, following carefully selected examples set out in Chief Baughman's all-inclusive Manual.

In bygone days many agents in the field offices never saw the Chief or representatives of his office, or at least had contact with them very rarely. Today, with Baughman's inspection system, every agent and every clerical worker has an opportunity to talk privately with a Secret Service Inspector from Washington at least once a year—and every Agent in Charge had better see that his agents' equipment (guns, credentials, notebooks, desks, etc.) are in first-class condition, and that his own office system meets the high standards set for the entire Service.

Although the Secret Service has always been grateful for the help it receives from local police departments, not until recent years has appreciation for this assistance been expressed in person by the Chief or his representatives. Agents in Charge of field offices always maintained cordial relations with police departments in their own districts, but today the Secret Service Inspectors make personal calls on Chiefs of Police, and Chief Baughman himself is a member of the Executive Board of the International Association of Chiefs of Police and an active member of the International Criminal Police Commission (INTERPOL), attending conferences held by both these important police organizations.

Ironically enough, as its history shows, the Secret Service has been penalized more than once for doing its prescribed work effectively and honestly. In numbers of agents it is a small agency, but it has never lost its tremendous prestige among those who know police work—and perhaps the greatest testimonial that could be paid to any enforcement body is the respect in which the underworld holds the Secret Service badge.

The agents who carry the silver star come from all parts of the United States, and each has his personal problems, his fears, his hopes, his happy moments and his sorrows, just as we all do. But each has one thing more—a deep dedication to the silver star and what it stands for, an urge to defeat the lawbreaker, a genuine desire to serve his country and its people. Some of these men have given their lives to uphold the law, some have been seriously injured, some have broken under the strain of long, grueling hours of arduous work.

Scores of these men have died or retired or resigned, and many have never had their names in print. We cannot name all of those who deserve so much more than this small quantity of printer's ink, but merely in token recognition we would like to mention at random the last names of a representative few who have not appeared elsewhere in this book— DiFiore, Connors, Taggart, Merrill, Mazey, Stringfellow, Montgomery, Gallagher, Baber, Haley, Reilly, Grennan, McGinniss, Lyons, Webster, Godby, McGrath, Barker, Slye, Rodney, Horton, Kettl, Prather, Garvey, Hughes, Sullivan, Ellis, Anheier, Grube, Davenport, Albert, Tucker, Straight, Boos, Fisk, Smugai, Cawley, Hutchinson, Shepherd, Moriarty, Gettings, Wasson, Pears, Goddard, Goldman, Osborn, Phillips, Raum, Seckler, Van Fleet. All of these have died or retired. Many others have gone, and many others still "in harness" will one day follow.

To each man, past or present, the five points of his silver star have symbolized and continue to represent Justice, Duty, Courage, Honesty, and Loyalty.

They and those who come after them deserve the thanks and support of the people of the United States.